SCREEN RELATIONS

Library of Technology and Mental Health

Series editor: Jill Savege Scharff, MD

Distance Psychoanalysis: The Theory and Practice of Using Communication Technology in the Clinic
  by Ricardo Carlino, translated by James Nuss

Psychoanalysis Online: Mental Health, Teletherapy and Training
  edited by Jill Savege Scharff

SCREEN RELATIONS

The Limits of Computer-Mediated Psychoanalysis and Psychotherapy

Gillian Isaacs Russell

KARNAC

First published in 2015 by
Karnac Books Ltd
118 Finchley Road, London NW3 5HT

British Library Cataloguing in Publication Data

A C.I.P. for this book is available from the British Library

   ISBN 978 1 78220 144 1

Edited, designed and produced by The Studio Publishing Services Ltd
www.publishingservicesuk.co.uk
e-mail: studio@publishingservicesuk.co.uk

www.karnacbooks.com

CONTENTS

ACKNOWLEDGEMENTS   vii

ABOUT THE AUTHOR   ix

SERIES EDITOR'S PREFACE   xi

FOREWORD by Todd Essig   xiii

INTRODUCTION   xvii

PART I
ON THE FRONTIERS

CHAPTER ONE
The western frontier   3

CHAPTER TWO
Exploring the speculative non-fiction digital frontier   11

CHAPTER THREE
Mapping the digital frontier   43

PART II
IN THE CONSULTING ROOM AND THE
RESEARCH LABORATORY

CHAPTER FOUR
What happens in the consulting room   69

CHAPTER FIVE
From the first laboratory: neuroscience connections   79

CHAPTER SIX
From the second laboratory: technologically   100
mediated communication

PART III
ON THE SCREEN

CHAPTER SEVEN
The mediating device   121

CHAPTER EIGHT
The problem of presence   134

PART IV
MAKING A PLACE FOR SCREEN RELATIONS

CHAPTER NINE
Sometimes it works . . .   153

CHAPTER TEN
The elephant in the room   162

CHAPTER ELEVEN
The toothpaste and the tube   169

CHAPTER TWELVE
To be in the presence of someone   177

REFERENCES   184

INDEX   199

ACKNOWLEDGEMENTS

This book could not have been realised without the ongoing support and invaluable assistance of so many colleagues, friends, and family members on both sides of the pond.

I am very grateful to my UK colleagues, and also my dear friends, Melanie Hart, Carol Topolski, and Gillian Woodman-Smith, for their enduring intellectual challenge and deep friendship. Even across the ocean, with the wonders of technological mediation we continue lively theoretical and clinical debate, as well as sharing personal news over cups of tea and glasses of wine respectively, because of the time difference. While we all agree it is not the same as sitting round each others' kitchen tables, it does help to bridge the gap. Many thanks to Prophecy Coles and Michael Parsons for sharing their extensive experience of authorship and to Annette Byford who patiently read several drafts of this manuscript.

I am profoundly indebted to Joan Raphael-Leff, whose own deeply rooted sense of presence allowed me to find mine.

The editorial team at Karnac, Rod Tweedy, Kate Pearce, and Constance Govindin, have been most helpful in guiding me through the labyrinth of the publishing process. Many thanks to all the team at the Studio Publising Services for their hard work in the production of this book.

In the New World, Starr Kelton-Locke deserves special mention, having faithfully supported my research from its earliest stages and read innumerable revisions of the manuscript with a keen editorial eye. Appreciation is due to Debra Neumann, a fellow pioneer in technologically mediated treatment, who has shared this journey as a colleague and friend.

Todd Essig has been an incredibly generous colleague, including lending me the title for this book. His unstinting encouragement, thoughtful reading, and astute advice on structure have enabled me to shape a much better book than it might otherwise have been. He also taught me not to "bury my lede", and while I cannot guarantee that I will always do that, at least I now know what it means.

A special thank you goes to the clinicians and patients who most enthusiastically gave their time to this project.

My past and present patients, supervisees, and students have given me more than they could ever know, and for this I am truly grateful.

My utmost gratitude goes to my parents, Joyce and Roger Isaacs, for their sustenance over the years. I thank my father, particularly, for teaching me just about everything I know about writing. My children, Adam and Nina Hemmings, have given me immensely loving support, both scholarly and creative, for which I am most thankful.

Finally, this book would never have come to be without the loving and intellectual partnership of my husband, Richard Russell, who never stopped believing in my capacity to see this project through. He read every word of every draft of this book, and though he may now know far more about screen relations then he would have ever wished, was steadfast in his support and encouragement. For this I am immeasurably grateful, far more than words can express.

ABOUT THE AUTHOR

Gillian Isaacs Russell, PhD, is a member of the British Psychoanalytic Council and has been in private practice since 1988. She has been on the Editorial Board and Book Review Editor of the *British Journal of Psychotherapy*. Dr Russell consults, supervises, lectures, and teaches internationally. She currently lives with her family in Boulder, Colorado.

For Richard, with love

It is a great pleasure to include Gillian Russell's *Screen Relations* in the Technology and Mental Health series. Moving with the times, Karnac introduced this series to adapt psychotherapy and psychoanalysis to the realities of life in the twenty-first century. The series already has books which speak to the effectiveness of technology-assisted practice and training in psychoanalysis. These books address the pros and cons of teletherapy, but with extensive clinical illustrations of unconscious communication, including bodily responses, transference, and countertransference analysed in on-screen treatment, they tend towards the view that the results are equivalent to those of in-person treatment. As series editor, I look for all points of view to be represented.

Screen Relations, a beautifully expressive, well-argued book, brings balance to the series by asking the reader to pause and consider more thoroughly the limitations of technology-mediated treatment. Gillian Russell draws on her clinical experience as a therapist who trained in the UK and now lives in the USA, on her understanding of analytic theory from Freud to Winnicott, Klein, Bion, and on to Ogden and Fonagy, and on her research as she examines the use of technology in treatment. She brings together her findings from interviewing therapists and patients about their experience of analysis using Skype, her review of neuroscience research on implicit and explicit memory systems, attention, attunement, and the development of the core self, and her reading of information technology and cyberpsychology.

Russell is committed to the ideal of reliable co-presence as a condition for psychoanalysis. But technical glitches create untimely interruptions that frustrate the patient and analyst who want to respond reliably even though they cannot be co-present physically. She holds that screen relations cannot replace the vivid interaction of two people in the same room exploring thoughts, desires, and feelings. Given that the ego is a body ego, and that problematic behaviours have their origin in the early months of life when interaction was intensely psychosomatic, it seems to her that body-to-body communication is preferable for the development of transference. Providing the holding environment for the patient recalls early parenting, making up for deficit or eliciting the experience of its failures. When the body of the patient and the body of the analyst are in the same room, the patient is more likely to experience trust and the analyst more able to maintain a state of reverie, dreaming along with the patient in a safe holding environment. In contrast to this, the analyst on screen tends to experience a narrowing of focus and distractibility. Russell warns against the degrading of the professional therapeutic relationship conducted under computer-mediated conditions.

Russell describes a land rush towards the use of Skype for psychoanalysis at a distance, sometimes in pursuit of continuity of care, sometimes for economic reasons. She is not against the use of Skype. Indeed, she uses it herself with patients in other continents, but she does not do so blindly. She asks herself what gets through the veil of technology and what gets lost. She asks us all to engage in process and review of what is possible and what is not. *Screen Relations* is a plea for awareness of the difference between in-person and on-screen analysis, and points to the need for more research on the role of technology in psychoanalysis and psychotherapy.

FOREWORD

Psychotherapists wondering about, even struggling with, the dilemmas of screens are not alone. Screens and their dilemmas are everywhere. They have become our world. Have a question? Google it. Never mind what the practice does to one's capacity for sustained attention (Carr, 2011; Jackson, 2008). Need to connect with a loved one? Shoot them a text, or check out their Instagram feed. Forget that easy always-on connections might degrade intimacy and the ability to engage in genuine conversation (Turkle, 2015). And if you are in a position where you actually provide—or receive—psychoanalytic care, then you have some special screen dilemmas arising from the increasingly common practice of providing treatment at a distance via a technologically mediated relationship. Luckily, you are in the right place: this fine book can help you resolve those dilemmas through the way it combines the power of scholarship with the wisdom of clinical expertise.

Screens display some of the thorniest, most complex set of confusing questions I have encountered in a psychoanalytic career that has been connected to technology from the very beginning: when can a screen relation substitute for the experience of being bodies together? When can it not? How are the processes in the two settings the same or different? Do those differences really matter? In addition, most urgently, what will become of our profession as technology continues to develop exponentially if we do not differentiate screen relations from the experience of being bodies together? Will psychoanalytic care even have a future if we believe screens can substitute for physical co-presence?

When I first heard from the author in September 2012, I was immediately struck by the creative curiosity animating her project. Rather than debating whether or not one should provide care at a distance or whether or not it was possible to find evidence of psychoanalytic process in technologically mediated remote treatments, she took a deep dive into the actual experience of such treatments, along with research that could illuminate what she found. I feel privileged to have had many conversations with her while she shaped and developed this book. As someone who is both a psychoanalyst and, well, kind of a nerd, I bring both to my appreciation of this volume. In fact, the ongoing colleagueship that developed ended up being a real tonic for my version of the dystopian funk starting to infect many "early adopters" (Lanier, 2011).

The context for the dystopian funk this book helps to dispel began almost thirty years ago with an early adopter's exuberant techno-optimism. Charging online in the mid-1980s, I was enthralled by the possibilities, even though back then everything was just slow monochrome text. The cutting edge was 300 baud Hayes Smartmodems and BBS systems. Soon, 9600 bps modems appeared. Accessing the Internet from shell accounts using FTP and gopher protocols got easier (remember them?). Along with email (what a wondrous development that was!) we "talked" in "newsgroups" and via IRC (Internet relay chat). Soon, modems hit the screaming fast speed of 14,400 bps—text displayed as fast as it was typed! I took the 14.4 techno-leap while in psychoanalytic training and starting a private practice in downtown New York City.

All this exuberant optimism for the future that online communications were going to bring about led me to launch The Psychoanalytic Connection (psychoanalysis.net) in 1993. I did not want my newfound professional community to miss out on the glorious techno-future I saw rapidly accelerating right in front of our eyes, even though most of my new colleagues saw computers and modems as toys for the socially awkward, a fad best avoided. There were, however, several other analysts talking seriously about technology and the future. There were also a few newsgroups and listservs on which psychoanalytically relevant topics were discussed. But no one had yet plugged in any machines specifically for the use of the psychoanalytic community. So I did, and kept them plugged in until 2009, when my dystopian funk started gathering steam.

I should note what might seem an irony in my increasingly valued colleagueship with the author; all our contacts for exploring, discussing and wondering about what actually happens during technologically mediated treatments, what is gained and what is lost, have themselves been technologically mediated. The fact is that at the time of this writing, we had still not yet met in person. But further reflection shows this fact not to be ironic at all. It is as it should be. The emerging information technologies through which I have come to know the author, just like older, more familiar technologies such as this book you are reading, are wonderful devices for remotely accessing what someone knows and thinks. That is what they do. Both books and screens are wonderful Cartesian devices. They let us know who someone is by sharing their thoughts at a distance.

Yet, is a Cartesian device enough for treatment? That is the question. Perhaps technological mediation is a less suitable conduit for transference and countertransference than it is for a scholarly relationship. Perhaps post-classical psychoanalytic theory has it right in asserting we are more than just what we think. What if who we are includes the full immediate complexity of who we are to each other, a set of indubitable experiences and processes on which we can ground the very state of being itself, something that will always be on the other side of whatever event-horizon technological mediation maps? While there is no irony in a technologically mediated scholarly relationship, perhaps there is irony in taking the relational turn while maintaining the same enthusiasm for screen relations that early adopters experienced using email back in the day of noisy modems displaying text on black-and-white screens.

Or perhaps the apparent incompatibility of theoretical assumptions and accumulated clinical wisdom with the practice of remote treatment is not ironic at all, but a tragedy in the making, which brings me back to my dystopian funk. Seeing so many colleagues flock to remote treatment as the first decade of the twenty-first century came to a close made me fear for our psychoanalytic future. You see, I am still a nerd. I still avidly follow where technology is going while continuing to practise psychoanalysis. What this psychoanalytic nerd saw was a likely path for where remote treatment was headed as information technologies continue the exponential growth of Moore's Law. Remote treatment is likely on an accelerating curve leading to emotionally intelligent programmes running photo-realistic avatars totally indistinguishable from what people encounter on their screens today (for a rudimentary version, just Google "SimSensei and MultiSense"). If physical co-presence can be fully simulated by a screen relation for the purposes of providing psychoanalytic care today, then exponentially developing technology will eventually render obsolete the need for there to be a human therapist controlling the therapist image on the screen; an emotionally intelligent programme will be enough. In other words, psychoanalytic treatment would eventually be automated. A functional equivalence between screen relations and in-person treatments would be a huge step towards a seemingly inevitable automated psychoanalysis.

With those thoughts in mind, you can only imagine what a relief now it is to have this book. It takes the steam out of the dystopian probability of automated psychoanalysis by putting screen relations in their proper place. We can take comfort from the fact that when it comes to clinical work, there is no functional equivalence; screen relations cannot simply substitute for being bodies together. It also provides a framework: every practising psychotherapist needs to decide whether and how to provide treatment at a distance, because some sort of remote treatment is here to stay and we have to make it as useful as we can. Finally, it asks and answers the central question a lively psychoanalytic future requires: what is so special about being bodies together that cannot be simulated with even the best of screens?

Todd Essig
Training and Supervising Psychoanalyst,
William Alanson White Institute
Author, *Managing Mental Wealth* @ Forbes
New York

Introduction

The inspiration for my research, and the book that followed, came from personal experience. My own use of "screen relations" based treatment led me to pose three primary questions.

- Can an optimally effective therapeutic process occur without physical co-presence?
- What happens in screen-bound treatment when, as a patient said, there is no potential to "kiss or kick?"
- How is intimacy affected by radically altering the balance between implicit non-verbal communications and the explicit verbal?

The answers to these questions were only found by venturing beyond psychoanalysis into the fields of neuroscience, communication studies, infant observation, cognitive science. and human–computer interaction.

In the common ground where these fields intersect with psychoanalysis, I discovered that because screen relations eliminate co-present bodies, they limit psychoanalytic process to "states of mind", rather than "states of being". It became impossible to ignore the fact that analytic couples need the traditional experience of presence, and not just technologically simulated presence, to deepen the psychoanalytic process.

This book is divided into four parts. It is no coincidence that we move through it conceptually, as if through the geography of frontiers, consulting rooms, research laboratories and the screen itself. We will discover that our bodies are inextricably connected to, and inform, the abstract concepts we use to think. The metaphor of a journey is linked to our sensorimotor experience: our bodies' positions in space structure our metaphorical conceptualisation.

The embodiment of the mind, in its fullest sense, has a profound impact on the experience of screen relations and this is one of the broad themes that forms a background to this book. Part I begins with an introductory chapter outlining the experiences which brought me to explore and research screen relations. Following this, in Chapter Two, we hear directly from clinicians and patients about their own experiences of using technology for treatment. Chapter Three, in which I give both the history and current thinking about mediated treatments, begins the process of thinking about what happens on the screen.

Part II is a careful examination of clinical theory, and its associated clinical and experimental research. The book then moves back to the screen in Part III, with an enriched appreciation for what does and does not take place there, including an exposition of the key concept of "presence". Finally, in Part IV, there is a discussion of the informed choices clinicians must make in order to decide for themselves what kind of digital-age therapist they want to be.

Psychoanalysis faces a profound irony in the second decade of the twenty-first century. Increasing mobility, the emergence of modern economies, and fast-paced lives are accelerating demand for "screen relations" based treatment. In response, many psychoanalysts are embracing technologically mediated treatment. However, this comes at a time when authorities on how technology shapes relationships are voicing serious concerns about the damage technological mediation does to both intimate connection and reflective solitude. With these concerns in mind, this book initiates a deeper psychoanalytic exploration of what actually does and does not happen in technologically mediated treatment, in an attempt to better weigh the gains and losses of screen relations.

PART I
ON THE FRONTIERS

CHAPTER ONE

The western frontier

I n 2008, I wound down a psychoanalytic practice of over two decades and moved from the UK to the USA. I exchanged flocks of sheep on the South Downs for flocks of wild turkeys in the Black Hills of South Dakota. I left behind a daughter in her final year of school in Hampshire and a lifetime's assemblage of dear friends and colleagues. My son was finishing university in Chicago. Because South Dakota was a temporary home, I did not intend to open a practice. Instead, I wanted to continue work on some pieces of speculative fiction I had begun in the UK.

Speculative fiction begins with the question, "What if . . ." and my what ifs grew from my own grappling with separation from my family, friends, and home territory and my attempts to adjust to a new world and culture. I wondered how it would be if humankind existed spread over remote planets, living in social and cultural isolation, but with advanced technology for instantaneous communication. What if some cultures sanctioned such practices as psychotherapy and others forbade it? What if the concept of the individual and the uniqueness of his/her life story was alien to a culture? What if a society did not recognise the healing potential of human relationships? What if an envoy on a remote planet where psychoanalysis was incomprehensible or prohibited needed help from a therapist on the home planet? My research led me through the history of the Nazi regime to the banning of psychoanalysis as a bourgeois ideology by three generations of Soviet authorities. Then, in one of those serendipitous art–life connections, I came upon an intriguing article about CAPA, the China American Psychoanalytic Alliance. The non-profit organisation was formed to meet the request of Chinese mental health professionals for psychoanalytic psychotherapy training and treatment by providing classes and treatment via Skype, a technological mediation primarily used on computers. They were calling for western psychoanalytic volunteers to supervise, teach, and treat. They wrote about the pleasures and rewards of the work. It was claimed that Skype was incredibly easy to use and secure. "The audio transmission is as good as if we are in the same room. The video also has great clarity" (Kelly & Tabin, 2009). This organisation's working principles for technologically mediated treatment were, first, just as in traditional analysis, the Skype analysis is based on the quality of the relationship between analyst and analysand and the development of the therapeutic process. Second, that Skype analyses were indistinguishable from traditional analyses. Their evidence of this was provided by "blind" presentations of Chinese computer-mediated cases in western seminars where the faculty and students were unable to differentiate between traditional and mediated transcripts of sessions (Fishkin & Fishkin, 2011; Snyder, 2009).

The prospect of being able to teach and treat enthusiastic students of a different culture from my own remote location was highly intriguing. Skype would solve the dilemma of distance and separation, allowing me to transcend space and time. I was not dependent on a physical consulting room or co-present colleagues. The only instruments I needed were myself and my computer.

At the same time, I was contacted by clinicians I had previously supervised in the UK who wanted to continue to work with me, as well as former patients who needed to process the impact of some recent life events. I downloaded the Skype software and began my exploration of technologically mediated communication.

Until that time, although I was experienced in using a computer, I had never worked remotely. I vaguely remembered reading a paper on video-conferencing in Norway when I was on the editorial board of the *British Journal of Psychotherapy* over a decade previously. It was a study of a programme designed to solve the shortage of supervisors in rural areas. At the time, London-centric as I was, it had struck me as very much localised to the particular needs of that country. I commenced conducting computer-mediated supervision and treatment, assured by those more experienced than I who affirmed that it was exactly the same as traditional treatment. As long as you maintain an analytic attitude, the process proceeds identically. The transference happens and is analysed, evenly suspended attention to free association is possible, and unconscious communication occurs.

I also began what finally amounted to three years of meetings with peers who also did technologically mediated treatments in China (and elsewhere). These meetings occurred on screen using Skype and although I have now met two of the participants in person, there is one with whom I have yet to shake hands.

Initially, we were preoccupied with cross-cultural issues, the complexities of which represent an entirely separate field of study. As our meetings progressed, we became increasingly aware of the effects of the technology itself, the impact of which was sometimes brought home to us in our own meetings on Skype. Rather than the audio and video being life-like and crystal clear, mediated communication was riven by poor sound, grainy visuals, and frequent interruptions. We became accustomed to "calling back" several times in sessions in order to get a better connection, and learned to turn off the video to increase the bandwidth by using just audio.

We noticed other anomalies. We had curious lapses. It was easy to forget treatment sessions and the times of our peer group meetings. We were likely to bring a cup of tea or glass of water to a session, something we did not do in co-present sessions. We did more talking with our patients about the comparative times and weather. We did more talking in general, as silences were not so easy. We felt less in touch, less intuitively connected. We missed being bodies together— not just with our patients, but with our peer group as well. Colleagues who had begun remote treatments enthusiastically lost their initial energy. The problematic experience of communication in treatment differed from the more straightforward didactic communication in supervision and teaching.

How could it be that we had just *assumed* that co-present treatment would transport seamlessly into technologically mediated treatment? Perhaps this was partly due to the analytic tradition's propensity to sideline the body and the significance of the immediate environment. Having done that, the therapeutic process takes place between two minds. The distillation of working mind to mind on screens might be familiar and comfortable for those whose tradition does not include attention to the significance of the nuances of embodied relating. I was not someone who concentrated much on the body in the consulting room. Infant research, as well as studies in neuroscience and non-verbal communication, has progressed rapidly since my training in the 1980s. There are rich new investigations into the significance of the mind–body connection and embodiment in the consulting room (Beebe et al., 2005; Boston Change Process Study Group, 2010; Rustin, 2013; Sletvold, 2014).

At the same time, the importance of the human experience of body-to-body communication is being challenged by the use of technology. Intimacy is mediated as we distance ourselves from the unpredictable sloppiness of relationships. Simulation offers an illusion of authentic connection, and we lose the gift of the genuine closeness that takes time and effort (Carr, 2011; Turkle, 2011). "The devaluation of the human body and, by extension, also body-to-body communication cannot be stopped by simply celebrating body-to-body communication. The underlying reality is that our increasingly complex society is weakening the possibility for the modern-day individual to communicate with others" (Fortunati, 2005). It is ironic and disconcerting that psychoanalysts and psychoanalytic psychotherapists are embracing screen relations (Essig, 2012a, 2015) at the very time when their disturbing effects on our relationships are being called to our attention (Carr, 2011; Turkle, 2011).

If we opt to use new tools, we need to know the nature of those tools and how those tools change us. We need to understand the gains and losses and then decide, case by case, if the trade-off is worth it. What happens when we reduce our therapeutic relationships to two dimensions bound by a screen? "You may find talking into a camera difficult at first," writes an analyst about using Skype on his website, "but in a few sessions you get used to it . . ." What does that mean, "get used to it"? Because we are wired to relate, do we unconsciously adjust to a degraded form of communication? What are we settling for? "I fear that we are beginning to design ourselves to suit our digital models of us, and I worry about a leaching of empathy and humanity in that process," says Lanier (2011, p. 39), computer scientist and pioneer in the field of virtual reality, ". . . can you tell how far you've let your sense of personhood degrade in order to make the illusion work for you?" Although it is far beyond the scope of this book to examine, it is hard to deny, in general terms, that we are forgetting on both personal and community levels that mediated modes of communication are generally more limited than co-present communication.

I set out to understand what happens when we practise technologically mediated treatment. I wondered how it works, what were its uses, and what were its limitations. These questions took me into realms where I had not ventured before, such as informatics and communication, human–computer studies, and neuroscience. Determining what happens on the screen made me explore what we think happens in the consulting room. Even this contentious subject is far from settled. I talked to psychoanalysts, psychoanalytic psychotherapists, supervisees, students, and patients in interviews and discussion groups, some transcribed from audio recordings. I learned much from lively and thoughtful exchanges with colleagues. I have let people speak directly in this book, but disguised them to preserve their confidentiality and, where applicable, obtained permission to quote them. In a few instances, people gave me permission to identify them. With regard to the term Skype, many use it as a generic term when they are referring to technologically mediated communication. There are, in fact, other free platforms such as FaceTime and ooVoo, with varying degrees of security. The commercial, paid-for video-conferencing services are more technologically robust, but prohibitively expensive for an independent practitioner.

I use the terms psychoanalysis and psychoanalytic psychotherapy to refer to the therapeutic process "which involves frustration and gratification, insight and relationship, autonomy and dependence, agency and communion, internal and external change, structural and symptom or behavioral change" (Aron, 2009, p. 665). The practitioners of this process, who have had their own intensive trainings and personal analyses, I refer to interchangeably as analysts/therapists or psychoanalysts/psychoanalytic psychotherapists.

By way of clarification, I am not a Luddite. Like most others in the twenty-first century, I use the computer for myriad purposes, including writing this book and talking with my family in various parts of the world. I even conducted part of a courtship relying on technology. I am not saying that technologically mediated treatment should never be used. I have used and do use technology for teaching, supervision, and some treatment. When I refer to computer-mediated communication, I am considering the level of technological development we have available right now.

This book was written because of a dawning understanding that what was happening between me and my patients in mediated treatments was not the same as the co-present process in the consulting room. I wanted to encourage asking questions that were not being asked. In the process, I learnt that we cannot use technological treatments without knowing and acknowledging their limitations, as well as their positive aspects. We need to know the differences they have from co-present treatments and not assume they are identical. I have tried to begin an articulation of the particulars of this difference. When I initiated a dialogue with my colleagues, it was striking that many of us seem to have sleepwalked into the use of technology for treatment. The questions I asked them, as I grappled with them myself, were like a wake-up call. They told me repeatedly that they had not thought through those issues before and were so glad to do so now. As is so often the case, more questions have been raised in the undertaking.

Psychoanalysts are not exempt from the very human desires to abolish distance, avoid separation, bypass frustration, have ease without commitment, and jettison inconvenient bodies with their sensory and physical constraints in search of new modes of existence. The profession is just as prone to respond to the seductions of technology as anyone else, with technological advances creating new human "needs" that then eventually lead to increased consumer demand (Blascovich & Bailenson, 2011).

> As we are still a long way from a complete understanding of the role and social significance of mediated communication, we are often tempted to gloss over the unknowns by singing hymns in praise of technology, or even setting up technology as the last great ideology. (Fortunati, 2005, p. 58)

The apparent solution to dislocation is constant connection. Remaining "always on" not only affects the "tethered" generation of children, who never learn a sense of autonomy, resourcefulness, or privacy, but also the older generation who, plagued by anxiety, are unable to let go and trust that their children will survive. Increased and indiscriminate use of technological mediation leads to impoverished relationships, because it is more limited than bodies being together. We then use technology further "to patch up the rips and holes in the net of our social relations—'a poor substitute is better than nothing'" (Fortunati, 2005, p. 57). We must not lose the sense of what embodied human relating is. An Israeli psychoanalyst, Shmuel Erlich, says that technologically mediated treatment is so routine in China that he met a woman in Beijing "who was astonished that there was some other kind of analysis" (Osnos, 2011). Just as we do not want our children to grow up believing that the convenient substitute of mediated communication is equivalent to embodied communication, so we must not lead our patients to believe that technologically simulated treatment is the equivalent of co-present psychoanalysis.

While I was starting to ask questions about what exactly we are doing when we use technological mediation for treatment, a psychoanalytic land rush towards mediated communication was beginning, fuelled by enchantment with technology, fear of professional obsolescence, and economic anxiety. Psychotherapists are vying to stake a claim in the "new frontier" before it has even been properly explored or mapped. How can we square confining ourselves to two dimensions on a static screen, when it is the essential humanity of the psychoanalytic process that we are offering as an instrument of change? We are not talking heads. Our mental processes emerge from our situation in our bodies and our involvement in a shared environment. It is ironic that some therapists turn to technological mediation as a first choice and without reflection, when what we are there to do is help patients discover what prevents them from feeling fully alive. How could we ever embrace the attitude that "a poor substitute is better than nothing" except in the case of triage or when there is no other choice?

I never finished writing the speculative fiction. Instead, what I encountered was an emerging reality far more fascinating that anything I could imagine. I discovered that we are living and practising in a world of speculative non-fiction. Events in the present-day world have given rise to a series of "What ifs" that need urgent clarification in the here-and-now. My colleagues started to ask questions, patients ask questions, trainees ask questions. Those questions can only begin to be answered if we allow ourselves to engage with fields other than psychoanalysis. If we add technology to the psychoanalytic mix, we need to ask the people who have worked in communication studies, informatics, computer science, and technology long before we entered the mediated scene what impact this addition has on the intense nature of close relationships. These are the questions with which this book is concerned.

CHAPTER TWO

Exploring the speculative non-fiction digital frontier

Conversations with clinicians and patients

I began my conversations with clinicians because I felt in the dark using technology for treatment. I was not in the dark technologically; I could manage the hardware and software. I had been using a computer for many things, including mediated communication, for some years. I was in the dark in the midst of the sessions. Something unexpected and *different* was happening. I felt unable to use my customary analytic skills. This feeling did not happen all at once, it happened very gradually over time as I continued to "see" patients mediated by a computer. I thought that perhaps my colleagues, some of whom had been doing technologically mediated treatment far longer than I had, knew something I did not. Maybe they could teach me what they had learnt about distance treatment. Maybe we could be of some support to each other.

What I discovered consistently was that my colleagues were as eager to talk about their experiences of computer-mediated treatment as I was. They said repeatedly that they felt they had never done so thoroughly before. Like myself, most of them had dived into computer-mediated psychoanalysis or psychoanalytic psychotherapy without knowing anything about the potential gains, losses, or differences in comparison to co-present treatment. Like myself, though venturing into new territory, they approached the sessions as if they were duplicates of those in a shared environment.

Yet, all my colleagues noted differences, some subtle, some glaring, in the experience of computer-mediated sessions. Significantly, most—but not all—noticed changes in their own behaviour, as compared to co-present sessions. Even for those who did not notice any change, it emerged in conversation that behaviour did frequently shift to the uncharacteristic, from sipping a cup of tea during a session to seeing patients from multiple environments, such as home, a home office, the consulting room, and/or a hotel.

Practitioners tell me they see patients using video-conferencing technology for a variety of reasons. Some work with patients who live in a geographical location where there is no available qualified practitioner. They commence a treatment never having met their patients face-to-face. Some continue to meet with patients they had been seeing co-presently after either the therapist or the patient relocated permanently. Others use computer mediation to see patients who could not get to the consulting room because of a chronic or acute illness or disability. Computer mediation is used as an adjunct to co-present treatment during patients' family crises which preclude an office visit and for patients whose work or education requires intermittent travel. One psychoanalyst was affected by a natural disaster that rendered him temporarily homeless and without a consulting room.

Patients, too, are eager to talk about their mediated sessions. Like my colleagues, they are inspired to attempt to define their experience, to put words to the particular distinguishing features of psychoanalysis or psychotherapy at a distance.

It is no coincidence that the themes that emerge during these exploratory conversations, such as those of a safe, holding environment and reverie, recall the fundamental requisites for the therapeutic process. Both practitioners and patients want to explore and clarify how technological mediation impacts on the therapeutic relationship and the unfolding of change in the psychoanalytic and psychotherapeutic process.

Environment: a bed is not a couch and a car is not a consulting room

[Melissa Weinblatt] . . . mixed herself a mojito, added a sprig of mint, put on her sunglasses and headed outside to her friend's pool. Settling into a lounge chair, she tapped the Skype app on her phone. Hundreds of miles away, her face popped up on her therapist's computer monitor; he smiled back on her phone's screen . . . She took a sip of her cocktail. The session began. (Hoffman, 2011, p. ST1)

So begins Jan Hoffman's article "When your therapist is only a click away" on the front page of the Fashion and Style section of *The New York Times*. Ms Weinblatt enthuses,

"I can have a Skype therapy session with my morning coffee or before a night on the town with the girls. I can take a break from shopping for a session. I took my doctor with me through three states this summer!" (Hoffman, 2011, p. ST1)

As extreme as this sounds (at the time it was published, my analytic colleagues were rolling their eyes and groaning in response), it is not so very far from the stories that I have been told by colleagues or the endorsement technologically mediated treatment was given by a senior analyst I know who effusively said to me, "It's wonderful! You can do it anywhere! I do sessions from my hotel room when I am at a conference. Just make sure you have a blank wall behind you."

We know the patient requires the analytic setting to be a secure environment in order to repair early psychic damage. This environment, which is based on the "reliable presence" that the mother offers her baby, enables the patient to achieve the stability to develop towards psychic independence and a whole sense of self (Winnicott, 1955). A good-enough adaptation of the environment to the needs of the patient lies at the heart of the patient's ability *to feel real*. The patient is healed through finding in the analytic setting that which should have been available earlier in life: the facilitating environment which holds and contains. Yet, time after time, a disrupted environment for both the patient and the analyst featured in peer supervisions and discussions and my in conversations with analysts and patients.

It did not occur to most of the analysts I interviewed to discuss with their patients the issue of the safety of the environment and establish a working framework before embarking on computer-mediated treatment. This is despite the fact that all the analysts I have spoken to recognise the importance of this and are scrupulous in providing such a setting in their traditional, shared environment practices. The majority entered into providing a computer-mediated treatment as I did, in blissful digital ignorance. The mere act of establishing contact was their prime aim, whether the patient was in a sitting room, car seat, or a bed, and overshadowed the necessity to create some mutual form of a reliable and predictable setting.

Some analysts *are* particularly sensitive to the necessity of maintaining stability and continuity in their own background environment as visible on the screen. Others try to keep personal information revealed in their surroundings to a minimum in order to preserve a neutral stance, choosing to work with a blank wall behind them, without family photographs or other self-revealing possessions visible. Of course, the blank wall is what the patient sees and the practitioner might have a completely different view of the room in front of her and beyond the scope of the camera, so that both participants are having very divergent perceptions of the therapist's environment. Sometimes, analysts concerned to ensure privacy opt to use headphones and encourage their patients to do so in order not to be overheard.

Because they are affected by such things as the availability of an Internet connection, the timing requirements of the session (especially if they are working across time zones, so that an analyst might have to meet with a patient very early in the morning or very late at night), and the psychoanalyst's commuting and travel requirements, analysts often have to choose an environment other than the office/consulting room where they would normally meet with patients. Dividing work time between a home office, a consulting room, or possibly another room in the home, such as a living room, is not uncommon because of time constraints or for convenience, and, as I mentioned above, it is not unheard of to work from a hotel room.

There seems to be a general tendency for many analysts not to note or address changes in their own environment in the session. In the co-present consulting room, the response of the patient to even minute changes in the setting is noted and explored for its personal meaning. There is no need to narrow the focus in an effort to maintain connection when bodies share a physical space and are at leisure to observe it together. Physical communication is a given, leaving space to concentrate on other forms of communication. (When we cannot hear a co-present patient because they are speaking inaudibly, this is grist to the mill—not an external imposition.) The capriciousness of the computer connection diverts the attention of both participants. Often other issues, such as the significance of the state of both environments, are sidelined by the relief when the technological connection goes relatively well. Yet, in screen-to-screen treatment, even small changes in the analyst's environment are noticed by the patient: "I saw the corner of a picture hanging on the wall. It hadn't been there before. I could only see a little corner of the frame. I wondered what I *couldn't* see, what I was missing that patients in the consulting room could see easily."

Large changes, such as moving the consulting room site also have repercussions: "When I changed offices I explored this thoroughly with all my local patients", says Peter, a psychoanalyst who moved his consulting room from an office building to his home. "It brought up intense feelings for all of them: everything from loss and anger to excitement in being allowed in my home." "However," he continues, "for some reason I did not anticipate that this would make an impact on my Skype patient. Somehow, I perceived her as portable, as not residing *in*, or even a party *to*, my space. I was taken aback when she was as negatively affected by my move as some of the patients I see face-to-face."

Peter is talking about a permanent move and his view of his patient "as portable", as if she were a ghost in the machine. The fact that many otherwise traditional analysts with a respect for the necessity of boundaries and maintaining a secure base find it acceptable routinely to shift their environments between different sites speaks to a sharply different conception of what happens in the mediated space. The "tool" is changing the users, both the patient who mixes a mojito and the analyst who works from a hotel room.

When therapists do not work from their consulting rooms, they have increased difficulty in keeping their own space private and free from intrusion. This includes such things as telephones ringing and family members making noise or mistakenly entering the room. "I could be interrupted more easily in a way that I couldn't be in my office," says a Colorado therapist. "In the time after the floods when we were evacuated, I was sharing a small space with other people and it was much harder not to be interrupted . . . or the phone would ring sometimes. . . . And now when I work from my home office, I do have other work and correspondence on my desk: that can be distracting."

Patients, too, use a variety of environments from which to work. Melissa Weinblatt's poolside "couch" is not so far-fetched. Psychoanalysts tell me that their patients work from their bedrooms, living rooms, work offices, home offices, and even from a car in a work car park. Patients sometimes choose to see the therapist at the beginning and end of the session via camera and then turn off the camera for the session itself, equating the loss of vision with the use of the couch— although the patient might not actually use a couch and opt to sit on a chair. An astonishing number of patients actually lie on their beds, many under the bedclothes, and their analysts accept this as correspondent to the use of the couch.

Normally, the psychoanalyst provides the setting (cf. Winnicott, 1955) including a room, possibly a waiting room, a toilet, chairs or the couch, a blanket, tissues, or water. Obviously, in a technologically mediated session, the analyst can provide none of the above.

Four analysts from disparate parts of the USA discuss the differences between co-present and technologically mediated sessions in an evening Skype meeting. Their pictures make a quartet of squares on the screen, like an American high school yearbook. "I was thinking about [the patient]: sometimes she would cover herself with her own blanket. I wondered, if she were in my office, would she use my blanket . . ." muses Nancy. She has never met her patient in person, as she lives a great distance away in another country. "Because the analysand was never in my office in person, I never saw her in an environment that she associated with me. It is hard to get to grips with the transference dimension of all that." Stephen says, "I think of how my patient chooses and arranges the pillows and maybe gets the blanket . . . it's just not there for us to think about [in a technologically mediated session] . . ."

Because there is a time lag in transmission, Catherine waits a moment to make sure she is not interrupting Stephen and adds, "One of my patients normally rides his bicycle to my office, rain or shine. When it is rainy, he leaves a huge wet spot on my couch—obviously this is important 'acting in' material to think about. This sort of thing is unavailable when he and I work on Skype." "Yes, that sounds so familiar to me," Lynn nods vigorously, "one of my patients often spends a long time in the bathroom after a session. I have no idea what she does after a Skype session. Nothing like this is there to explore."

All the analysts I interviewed comment on the difficulty of their patients' keeping their spaces safe and free from intrusion. "Usually it is the therapist's role to maintain that [holding] environment . . . and [with Skype] it has to be the patient's . . . You can provide certain elements of safety: being there on time, ending the session . . ."

The choice to protect the environment becomes the patient's responsibility and varies from patient to patient. "My patient worked from four different environments, all bedrooms. The patient made a conscious decision not to sit on the bed in order 'to preserve the formality'. She said she needed 'to keep in tune with the reality of the situation'." Colleagues may intrude if the patient has a session from work, babies may be sleeping in the same room or on the patient's lap. "Patients are interrupted by the phone, knocking on the door, dogs; you get introduced to family members, children come in . . ." Most analysts find this kind of interruption disruptive: as one described, "One moment when [the patient's] mother called her from outside her room . . . alerted me that there was a potential for intrusion . . . that she [the patient] was not so clued up about . . . we have to rely on them [the patients] to keep that environment protected for themselves."

The necessity for the patient to do the lion's share of maintaining secure boundaries and providing for his/her own environmental needs represents a serious shift from the co-present to the mediated setting. Implicit in the analytic foundation of a facilitating environment is the patient's opportunity to regress, to be provided with a safe holding setting to foster the possibility of psychic change. Indeed, many patients come into therapy precisely because they have been precociously "holding themselves" since infancy, and to continue to do so in a mediated relationship would create an interminable analysis, possibly with an illusion of change. Winnicott connected the formation of a compliant false self to the patient whose environment failed in such a way as to not protect him/her from gross impingement that interrupted the patient's infant self from the sense of "going on being"(Winnicott, 1965).

Bella, a psychoanalyst whose patient is an English-speaking doctor in a remote country where there are no English-speaking therapists, tells me this story:

My patient's computer broke. It was going to take a long time to get it fixed. She had to borrow a computer from a friend who lived quite a long distance away. When we began the session, she sat in a chair in the friend's living room. She was actually very upset and very much in need of this session. As we progressed, I noticed someone walking in behind her and commented on it. It was the friend's husband, who was not aware of the situation. She was at a loss as to what to do. She did not feel comfortable asking him to leave a room in his own house. I asked her if she would feel more comfortable ending the session and rescheduling. She was unhappy about this, as she felt an urgent need to talk with me. Finally, she got up and moved outside on to the patio, where, a bit later, more family members appeared. There was a very small broom cupboard off of the patio. She got up and shut herself in it. She managed the rest of the session in that tiny, sweltering space, surrounded by mops and brooms and buckets.

The nature of working in dual environments means that Bella is powerless to provide a secure setting for her patient. She cannot protect the patient from gross impingement into her session. While it might be argued that Bella can interpret the patient's repetition of her experience of an unsafe environment and her solution of relegating herself to a tiny and uncomfortable space, it seems unreasonable to expect the patient to provide for herself the very thing which she might be unable to imagine. Bella is unable to give her patient the experience of security and freedom from intrusion in which she can be held safely enough to be free to do the psychic work necessary for change. This provision needs to be a fact, not just a concept discussed cognitively.

There is also the issue of the analyst being privy to the patient's personal world. This is not part of traditional analytic practice, where the analytic process is contained in strict privacy within the consulting room. Claire, an analyst from Oxford, is distracted by her window into the patient's environment and finds it a difficult adjustment to her usual way of working: ". . . one of the ways I had to adjust was to not be curious about that [the patient's different space] so that I could just concentrate on what she was telling me . . ."

Yet, some analysts consider the opportunity to make a "house call" as positive. "I learnt a lot by using it [Skype]. You know, you're in people's houses: it's like a family visit . . . I saw aspects of the patient I wouldn't have otherwise." These analysts talk about how they feel that what they observe is vital information (i.e., a patient's artistic creations, choice of personal decor). "I can see where they live, whether they have a dog or how a mother might deal with her child." They perceive that they are obtaining important information about the patient that they would not have known any other way, information that is key to the treatment. It has been suggested that

> people who are doing these treatments have to compensate for the lack of richness, repleteness. It is a compensation on an immediate surface level because you never have an actual shared experience: it compensates for having only a degraded shared experience in the physical world by giving you the illusion that you are having the experience of experiencing their physical world . . . Information can squeeze through the wires much better than relationship can. (Essig, personal communication, 2012)

What is it about this experience of "information" that is so compelling? "You get a lot of *information* on Skype," declares an analyst. There is confusion as to what this information is and its value in the therapeutic process. As Lakoff (1995) said about the Internet, "It will be different information, not more information".

The possibilities that Skype opens up for more apparent information could work unconsciously in the minds of practitioners who are finding it difficult, because of the demands of screen relations, to maintain an analytic state of mind. The visual "clues" might seem to speed up and deepen understanding, and could genuinely add to the practitioner's concrete knowledge of the patient in some powerful external ways. But perhaps seeing a patient's physical world is not the invaluable key to the analyst's knowledge of the patient's internal world and way of processing unconscious experience that these analysts might think. Indeed, it could make it all the harder to focus on the unconscious and implicit aspects of the analytic work, and for the analyst to have a clear field for the use of his/her countertransference, one of the fundamental sources of analytic information. Seeing into the patient's personal environment is a simulacrum of the granted wish to see truly and truly be seen as a whole person. Bella tells me, "I think there is something important about seeing a patient out of, or unattached to, his or her home environment. An essential aspect of the work between patient and therapist is trying to articulate a home space together. Therefore, the therapist's seeing the actual home on the screen stamps all over this joint creation."

Patients, too, remark on the distinction between a shared co-present environment and dual environments in technologically mediated sessions. Lucy, a nineteen-year-old university student, tells me, "When I drink my analyst's water, it is more intimate. When I use his tissues, it is like he is helping me to get clean. In my own space I have to see to more of my own needs."

If the tool is changing the user, it is also changing the practice, and in ways that are unsettling. The analytic setting and relationship is highly unusual and different from all others. Indeed, many patients spend a considerable amount of time in the beginning of their therapy implicitly and explicitly learning just that. We have determined that a particular set of conditions is required to foster a particular process, and we say as much to patients: "You may find therapy odd/ different/unlike any other relationship." Patients might spend time testing or avoiding testing the boundaries, depending on their characters. "I don't want to leave, I want to stay with you all the time"; "I don't want to be a patient, I want to be your friend/lover/ daughter"; and, ruefully, "*I know the rules, but . . .*" That particular combination of intimacy and limitation is the crucible in which transference–countertransference can take place and transformation can occur. With intimate connection come tests of separation: outside *vs.* inside, the external world *vs.* a profoundly close shared space. The question is whether these conditions can be fulfilled in dual external worlds, when they are so very particular to begin with. A bed is not a couch and a car is not a consulting room. The analytic setting's parameters, which provide safety and continuity, space for reverie, and time-limited intensity, are precisely what is *not* "out there". As a patient, I mourned that I could not be with my analyst all the time and she replied, "Maybe I am not like this all time." There is a good reason why sessions come in fifty-minute chunks: neither the analyst nor the patient can sustain for long such an intense and controlled setting in the service of the freedom and creativity required to rebuild a damaged self. As Winnicott said, in the analytic situation the analyst is much more reliable than people are in ordinary life.

Peter regarded his patient as "portable", but his patient thought differently. The senior analyst rejoiced that she could work from *anywhere*, even a hotel room. Melissa Weinblatt, who had originally had a co-present therapy and transferred to technological mediation when her therapist moved, celebrates taking her doctor with her through three states on her summer vacation.

We were in training analysis before we became practitioners. We grappled with the frustration of separation. We learnt the importance of continuity and the significance of maintaining a holding environment for our patients when we were patients ourselves. Later, we find it is often very hard work to attend to these things. It takes effort and some sacrifice to provide the safe, facilitating, holding environment that Winnicott describes, to plan and preserve continuity in the physical layout of the consulting room, to project many months ahead for breaks, to bear the anger and anguish that patients feel when we are away. I think there is excitement for the therapist (and the patient) when these requirements for a safe setting are jettisoned. With technologically mediated treatment, no longer is the therapist solely responsible for providing that environment. No longer must the therapist *be there in that environment* as a reliable presence. Therapists can consider themselves and their patients portable, intoxicatingly freed from the constraints of time and space. We are freed from the hard work we were taught was necessary. We—and our patients—do not have to undergo the sometimes restrictive requirements for commitment and stability that we did as patients and trainees. Our parent–therapists were wrong. The therapeutic couple become like "brains in the vat", with "safety" provided by the inherent screen separation, but, because we are not brains in a vat, and because, as Damasio (2005) reminds us, Descartes made an error, we must revert to our bodies and our need for being bodies in the world *with* another. Thus, we make mistakes when disembodied in cyberspace that we would not make in the shared consulting room.

Reverie

"I'm not saying that you can't have evenly suspended attention while using a computer," says London analyst Anna, "but you have to be aware of the associations to the automatic kind of thinking you do when you use one. That is what we unconsciously anticipate when we sit down at our screens."

Yet, the prerequisite for the therapeutic process is "a state of calm receptiveness" (Bion, 1962). Freud asked that the analyst "simply listen, and not bother about whether he is keeping anything in mind" (Freud, 1912e, p. 112), and Ogden (1996) described the necessity of the shared process of reverie between analyst and patient facilitating the unconscious interplay of their overlapping unconscious intersubjective experience.

"I think that when I am using Skype, the fact that I might be doing something else occurs to me. I found myself wondering what my email was. I think the nature of the device encourages multi-tasking." For more analysts than one would expect, wondering about email immediately precedes actually checking it surreptitiously. Patients, too, leave programme windows open and can monitor emails as they come in. Phones are left on desks, set on "silent", but available for a glance as texts and messages come through.

The absence of shared presence in the same space can weaken the impetus to behave with full attention and inclusion of the other. "In the office together, you know the other person is in the room and you know you are both doing the same thing. My house is my own private house and not a shared domain. This is my house and I can do what I want," says Sara, a psychologist who is doing an analytic training, speaking to me on Skype. "I think the boundaries [of the screen] are more like walls between my therapist and myself. I could be nibbling on something or fiddling with my keyboard , but he wouldn't necessarily know that. All he knows is what I choose to tell him or let him see, what he can read in my voice and words. If I have a cup of coffee with me: that's what I do at home, it's not what I do when I am sitting with a patient . . . it's not a shared environment any more so that makes it OK. It's not like you and I are together and I'm having coffee and you're not. I feel I am alone having coffee and talking to my therapist on the computer. This is *my* familiar territory." "And you are not taking me into that?" I ask her. "No, no way. I'm not reaching out to you in that way either. I don't need to say, 'You don't mind if I put my feet up, do you?' It doesn't matter. It's not as relevant. The other things that are going on are not as relevant. So our interaction is in some ways more focused, but in some ways more limited and colder."

In an effort to compensate for this distraction, analysts find themselves "glued to the screen". "My concentration had to be intense [rather than free-floating] . . . concentrating on a small screen—are you concentrating on more signals? Because of limitations, are you concentrating harder?" Being "glued to a screen" is not conducive to "that state of mind which is open to the reception of any 'objects' from the loved object . . ." (Bion, 1962, p. 36). It is a *narrowing* of focus, rather than a broadening, casting a wide perceptual net. "I found myself more intensely watching her than I bother to do when I am with somebody [in the consulting room] . . . when you are with somebody *you can move in and out* . . . but it's harder when it's on the screen." Analysts describe the intensity of attention required by technology as the opposite of the type of attention required in an analytic session. Patients experience this effort of attention, too: "On Skype I find it much harder to be silent," Ajia tells me. "There is so much interference that if I am quiet you might think I have dropped off the edge of the universe. I have to focus more keenly and listen more keenly and that is not conducive to a stream of thought." This intense concentration may be the result of an effort to compensate for the degraded sensory experience inherent in screen-to-screen communication. The image of mentally "moving in and out" implies an availability of a consistent and rich range of multi-sensory information implicitly apprehended, accessible to be used when necessary. The mind is free to move in an unconstrained fashion, internally and externally, when the analyst is assured of this implicit information remaining "at hand". "I wasn't able to feel at ease and be so relaxedly just listening, just observing. I was sitting in an upright chair *peering at the screen* . . ." Using today's technology, without focused attention, sense of presence cannot be maintained, and it takes intense concentration to attend to the screen (Essig, 2012a). Without the freedom to move in and out, the analyst's mind is shackled to the screen, unable to alternate between form and content, internal and external. Even if the analyst has turned off the visual, his/her narrowly intense dependence on the mediating device as the conduit of all information is nothing like the free-ranging somato-sensory experience in the co-present consulting room. Speculating about his experience of the difference between sharing a space and working screen-to-screen, one analyst suggested, "I don't think that it was something 'filtered out' and that if we had worked harder, we'd have found a way of filtering it back in. I think it simply isn't possible to find that quality of unconscious engagement [on Skype]."

If the analyst is not free to "dream the patient", he/she cannot safely maintain a reverie (Ogden, 2004). When Ogden writes about dreaming the patient, he emphasises the jointness of this experience. The analyst and patient participate together in a reciprocal experience that allows the patient to come into being as the analyst begins truly to know the patient (and the patient comes to know the analyst) with a unique recognition. The ability to move away and reconnect under-lies a mutual sense of presence, the feeling of "going on being", which releases both the analyst and the patient into the possibility of reverie.

> Mine [reverie] was definitely interfered with: . . . physically there was a lot more effort going into the mechanics of being with her . . . but then maybe I could have changed that . . . got a bigger screen, rearranged the room, that sort of thing. But I think that would have been an attempt to create something rather duplicitous, you know, I might have fooled myself into thinking that because she was bigger and I was more comfortable, something was happening that actually wasn't. I'm imagining that that attempt to improve the materials' conditions . . . might have a compensatory aspect to it . . . but not necessarily achieving what you were hoping to achieve—which is a place in which free associative listening is possible . . . when you're with somebody . . . those clues get picked up like one has little microscopic hairs on one's antennae, but it's harder when it's on a screen.

The analyst quoted above is speaking of the danger of confusing enhanced technology with the potential broadening and deepening of the patient's and analyst's joint capacity for reverie and communica-tion, both explicit and implicit. The sense of presence evolved to allow us to distinguish self from other and our internal world (what is happening in my head) from the external world. The smooth free cycling in and out of attention with a human being that is required for secure mother–infant relations is the same kind of fluid attention required for creativity between therapist and patient (Maclaren, 2008). That smooth cycling is necessary both jointly and within each indi-vidual. The participants must feel free to turn their attention inward to consult with themselves, while knowing that that the "other" remains available to "dream" together. When presence is compro-mised, both analyst and patient lose touch not only with an inherent neuropsychological process on which we depend for survival, but also with a secure base which allows us both to refer back to and venture forth in creative exploration.

Communication: "It's like trying to see someone better by shouting"

Analysts speaking of their technologically mediated experience refer to a different quality of communication to that in the shared consulting room. "It's absolutely different . . . there are smells . . . you are much more aware of their body [for example] if they're relaxed on the couch . . ." They compare their sensitivity and perceptions when bodies are together to when a screen separates them. "In the consulting room . . . you can experience the body language better, more of a gaze, with the patient more solid . . . smells . . . you can see if they're tearing up a bit: I can see that on Skype to some degree, but more easily live, in person, so you're a little more tuned in to the affect live than on Skype . . ."

Anna began a co-present treatment with an American diplomat in London. When he was transferred to another country, Anna continued to see him via computer until he made the transition to another analyst. "The major difference [was that] I didn't feel that I was with him in the same way. I felt . . . that if we hadn't already established a deep contact, I don't know that we would have been able to on Skype." Stephen also describes the communication changes when he began to see on screen a formerly co-present patient who had moved to another part of the country. He feels it is impossible to anticipate a repeated important affective shift in the patient: "I could tell in person when she was building up to a contemptuous attack: she sort of puffed up: it was very subtle. I could feel the tension in person: I couldn't feel it coming unless we were in the room together."

Although many are not conversant in the specifics of embodied relations or the terminology related to implicit communication, nevertheless analysts notice and describe just these things: "I wasn't able to pick up, you know, the cues I was used to on a subliminal level, I suppose. [Be]cause I was with the same person and their body language was the same . . . but there was just something missing for me . . . I felt deprived of something: something important." They are aware that there is an impact on their normal implicit modes of perception and communication. "I do think the presence of a whole body in the room with your whole body is different from Skype. There is a way in which, I think, we connect physically with one another without much awareness of it, which is not the same on Skype." Anna elaborates, "Even if you *did* see the whole body, the feelings we're talking about don't get represented in, for example, specific jerks of the left foot. *They're not necessarily things you can see.* They're creations of an expressive atmosphere." Even without the technical words to describe their altered experience of their non-verbal, implicit communication, therapists depict it vividly. An analyst speaks of a three-year, five-sessions-per-week treatment: "Those vibes . . . psychic energy . . . you know what I'm talking about, like we're beaming each other . . . when we're in the same room. I don't think I have ever had that experience on Skype."

Interesting sensory metaphors come up in conversation about screen-to-screen communication: ". . . I could try and pick up subtle nuances from her way of communicating—but I found, I must say, it's very muffled compared to being in the same space"; "It's like you're trying to get closer to someone using the wrong tools . . . It's like trying to see someone better by shouting."

Working screen-to-screen, rather than as bodies together, brings up the subject of two dimensions rather than three dimensions. Metaphors of thin as opposed to thick appear repeatedly in therapists and patients' comparative descriptions of working on the screen and co-presently. Louis, a psychoanalyst in Los Angeles, observes, "When you are doing Skype, even though there is a person back there, it's a flat screen, so it's almost like reading a comic book *vs.* reading a novel. So, there's a thinner experience on Skype." He is describing the sensation of perceiving the other on a two-dimensional screen as having a shallower, comic-book quality, whereas being co-present feels like the "full-bodied" imaginative experience of reading a novel.

Reality is equated to three dimensions: "After meeting the patient in person, she was a much more three-dimensional person to me . . ." says an analyst of a first-time co-present session with a patient he had previously seen only on screen. Conversely, when an analyst transfers from working in the consulting room to working on-screen, she observes, ". . . it's curious, in some ways she became less real to me because she wasn't with me, because the texture wasn't there. Although I knew and cared for her, she just wasn't as real mediated through the machine . . ." A lower sense of presence connects with a weaker sense of reality, requiring more effort to communicate: "We were both doing our best to communicate with something that was definitely *thinner*. It had a thinner quality, but because we both knew and trusted each other and there was affection there, it was good enough . . ."

One therapist feels this diluted connection works as a convenient defence: "Sometimes I am filled with profound countertransference reactions, like terror or grief. It's easier with Skype: they [the patients] can hurt you less—and they're probably saying the same thing!" Whatever you might make of that particular use of the screen, it is significant that this therapist feels that a technologically mediated connection is less immediate and vivid than his experience co-presently in the room. Another analyst says, "I call it 'Relationship Lite'."

Celia, an analyst in London, describes to me a patient who ostensibly opted to move temporarily from co-present sessions to computer-mediated sessions because of heavy work commitments. "She was ill from exhaustion, travelling to several different work sites, and found fitting in her sessions very difficult. However, she was highly motivated to continue therapy and at the time I felt that her short-term technological solution would give us some breathing space to think about her difficulties putting limits on her punishing schedule." The patient never resumed co-present sessions, although Celia did her best to explore what her reluctance to come to the consulting room meant. She terminated, apparently having done the work she wanted, but without ever meeting Celia face-to-face again. "There was something about this patient opting to use Skype to diminish my significance. I think that I and the therapy became less important. I really liked her and empathised with her, but maybe she and I started to fade for each other. There was certainly a lot of regulation of distance. It was protective. I do wonder how her therapy would have played out had she not had the option to Skype, which weakened our connection."

Patients, too, speak of the contrast between relating in two and three dimensions. Tanya, a graphic designer in her early twenties, perceptively links the concepts of presence and the distinction between self and other:

> Because I am deprived of the potential for physical action, I feel more pressure on my words to do the job. My words are inadequate—

words alone. We are disembodied heads. In the same room, the pressure is taken off and my words are more grounded in reality. On Skype the "three-D ness" gets stripped away. Things that aren't three-D I can control. I can control YouTube, Facebook, Netflix, and television. Three-D you can't turn on and off or control. I have more confidence in something that is three-D. It emphasises that they are different from me: they are another person. The more control I have (like Facebook) the more that you [*sic*] are under the illusion that it is you. For me, Skype re-enacts omnipotence.

Tanya is illustrating her anxiety that the diminished feeling of presence in screen relations causes her to lose the sense of differentiation between self and other and the reminder that the "other" is a separate intentional being. She explains that when using technological mediation, she feels that her explicit communications have to carry the full weight of the relational transaction, whereas, when co-present, her words are grounded both in her body and in the shared environment with the therapist's separate body as a complete communication, both explicit and implicit.

When Tanya says, "In the same room, the pressure is taken off and my words are more grounded in reality . . . I have more confidence in something that is three-D. It emphasises that they are different from me: they are another person", she is referring to properties crucial to the depth of the process of change set in motion by the therapeutic facilitating environment, including the therapeutic relationship. She and the analysts speaking above struggle with the limitations of screen relations, experiencing something "thinner" which they hope is adequately transmitted when supported by familiarity, trust, and affection.

Something very precious

Maria Celano is a clinical psychologist who trained at the New School for Social Research in New York. She is a candidate doing a psychoanalytic training at the William Alanson White Institute. Throughout her analytic training, she has participated in both phone and co-present sessions as a therapist and as a patient, which have inspired her to think and write about technologically mediated psychoanalysis. Maria is totally blind. For her, use of the telephone and use of technological mediation is relatively the same, though she does like to be hands-free, and prefers the freedom of speakers to headphones. We speak on the telephone and she tells me, "I have begun to wonder about the effects of phone sessions on my relationship with my analyst . . . Despite the fact that I am unable to see my analyst even during live sessions, I feel a loss when we are not together. I was very interested to realise that, no, it's not just being able to 'see' the person. There's something about being in the room with them. There's something not visual, and not necessarily auditory."

Maria describes a conversation she had with a blind Skype friend whom she has never met in person. "There's a big difference between being in the same room with someone or having them on your cell phone, speaker, or whatever. One of the things we came up with was the possibility of being able to touch someone. This is very interesting because even though I wouldn't necessarily touch my therapist—I am pretty big on boundaries—the fact that I am in the room with her, that she is touchable [is important]. A person is more accessible if they're live and in person." She adds that sharing the same environment when "we're both in the same room with the same furniture, we're both in the same office building" heightens her sense of presence. "You know the other person is in the room and you know you're both doing the same thing."

Maria is keenly aware of the intrusion of the technology into her reverie both as a patient and a therapist. "The last time we had a phone session . . . at one point in the conversation I was silent for a long time. Now, if I'm silent for a long time in the room at least she [the analyst] knows that I'm still there. I found myself thinking, 'Oh, I've got to say something so that she knows I'm still here.' Maybe she is at the other end thinking we got disconnected. I felt that I had to be quiet for that moment, but also intruding upon my need to be quiet is the need to take care of my therapist and reassure her that I'm present. That affects the spontaneity and the holding environment." I ask Maria what it feels like with her patients. She is silent, considering. As we have been talking about the need for silence, I am particularly sensitive to not intruding on her thoughts. The silence extends. "Hello?" I say. No answer. We have lost the telephone connection.

I redial and when she answers she says ruefully, "Well, you know, *that's* another thing . . ." Taking up the thread, Maria tells me that when she is talking remotely with her patients "there is a sense of being a little bit forced. I am thinking 'well, this is going fine. We are still getting information across,' but you don't have to do that when someone is there. If we were together, I wouldn't have had the sense, 'well, this is working anyway.' There is a self-consciousness about it. You can't relax. If you share something of our world in the office, there is more of an overlap of worlds. If I'm talking to you here and you are there, neither of us is experiencing as much as if we were in the same room. When one is on the couch talking about things, reliving things, it is sharing an inner world, but it is physical presence as well. Maybe that physical presence makes what is imagined or relived in the transference more real than if you were on phone. It does take you out of your head. Right now as we talk I am not imagining that you are here with me, I am imagining that you are on the phone. When people say that when talking on the phone the transference is a less contaminated and more pure process because it may be more exclusive of real things, it is also not as connected with real life."

Maria brings up an intriguing idea. Quoting Winnicott, she says, "You can't be alone in the presence of another. Because there is an effort in concentration, a narrowing of focus, that experience just to 'be' is reduced to a little box. It is more concentration on the verbal, and it becomes less rich." Maria is referring to Winnicott's paradoxical concept of the development of the infant's capacity to be alone when someone else is present. It is the ability safely to become unintegrated, simply to be, without acting or reacting to external impingement. This state of experiencing being alone can only take place when the infant is secure in the presence of the mother. It leads to the experience of feeling real. In adults, it would correspond to the feeling of relaxing and is also a necessary development during the psychoanalytic treatment (Winnicott, 1958). Maria suggests that the effort and self-consciousness she experiences using technology, combined with a diminished sense of presence, precludes the secure state of relaxation required for reverie and free association.

I ask Maria to comment on the many references made in papers and discussions on technological mediation by analysts who claim that the absence or reduction of visual and other sensory communication causes them to become more attuned to other sensory cues in a heightened way, like a blind person (e.g., Carlino, 2011; Hanly & Scharff, 2010; Scharff, 2012)). She responds,

No, I disagree. The things that would be more salient to a blind person are not present over the phone or with Skype. My attention is more narrowly focused on what we're saying. I am not comfortable with that statement 'like a blind person'. I would say that I don't get as much from a voice over the phone or on Skype. I have to try harder. I have to strain. When I am together with someone I am able to perceive the richness of everything else around me, but if it is filtered through technology I am labouring within the limits of less rich communication. What makes it less rich is my knowing you are not present, not feeling your presence . . . Maybe your voice isn't as meaningful as when we are together. It is just a voice. I don't know that I pick up any more on the phone or on Skype because I am blind.

I wonder with her if the analysts who put forward that idea, which she finds rather reductionist, are confusing the intensified focus and concentration required when using technology for psychotherapy with a heightened sensitivity of perception using alternative senses. There is a difference between being in a shared environment and attending to things in a free-ranging way and trying hard to pick up signals narrowly filtered by technology.

"I am an ardent fan of 'live performances' and the need to 'keep it real'," Maria tells me. "I know that using mediation is definitely different and I know that I prefer to be in person. I am interested in the quality of that difference. It is important to know what presence means, because it is something very precious."

Moving through space: "turning off the computer is not a journey"

Motility, movement in space, is a key feature of presence and the experiencing of a sense of self. It contributes to differentiating the internal and external world. Maxine Sheets-Johnstone (2011), philosopher and dance scholar, suggests that we discover ourselves and the external world through the "primacy of movement". Our embodied experiences of ourselves comes from our existing and acting in space with the capacity to move, constantly changing our perceptive and proprioceptive encounters with the world (Meissner, 1998a; Riva et al., 2006). Yet, movement in space, both in the intentional journey to and from the consulting room, and within the shared environment itself, does not happen within the connection between screens. Yes, there are movements in individual spheres, for example, the grasping and manipulating of the computer mouse (which has been likened by psychologist Anne Curtis (2007) to the use of autistic sensation objects which are auto-generated and self-soothing); however, there are no movements that involve the self in what Giuseppe Riva (2008), psychologist and researcher on the impact of mediated technologies, would call "presence-as-feeling", which comprises enacting with an Other within a shared external world.

"You have to move in space to get places. It's confusing to just turn on Skype, because that's not how you get places. The effort to connect is taken away: it makes you think you don't have to make an effort," says the graphic designer, Tanya, of her computer-mediated sessions. In a separate conversation, Lucy echoes this thought, "Turning off the computer is not a journey . . . there is no destination . . ."

This lack of destination, this deprivation of the potential to move in space, eliminates the experience of acting with intention with external objects in a shared framework in space and time. We shall see that many investigators in human–computer interaction, cognitive and neuroscience, infant research, and psychoanalysis agree that emerging selfhood depends upon this process. Lucy explains how it feels to her as a patient:

> It is harder to retain things that happen in a Skype session because there is no journey. I find the journey to and away from the consulting room an important aid to retaining, internalising the session . . . Skype cuts your therapy short. You are deprived of the journey time. Putting aside time to think doesn't work, because it is in your hands. I like the fact that there isn't a choice: that you have to go away from your therapist, moving. You may not like the journey or you may feel relieved, but you have to do it . . . If you try to make one for yourself by making time, going for a walk or drive, it is not absolutely necessary to do that. It becomes false, a simulation . . . it is an important learning curve to accept the journey away and that it isn't in your control. I don't like it that after a Skype session if you want the journey, you have to construct it yourself. There is no destination. You are fooling yourself. After a real session, when you are going home, you know the consulting room is not your home. [Leaving a Skype session] is like having a Caesarean instead of a natural birth.

Therapeutic work is not only done in the confines of the session. The moments leading up to the session and following it are important spaces, too. Both analysts and patients agree that there is an inherent difference in the feelings of anticipation, reflection, digestion, and consolidation between a computer session and a session requiring a journey. "My patient told me she prefers to come in person to sessions because of the 'transition', the time getting there and especially the time leaving," says Catherine. "She tries to walk afterwards and think about things."

The ease of computer use, "when your therapist is only a click away", presents a paradoxical dilemma. The speed and convenience of connection fails to reproduce something meaningful and useful that the effort of moving in space provides. "You are summoned by the click of a mouse and turned off in the same way," says Stephen. "He called me and he was there. You know, the Skype phone rings and you answer it and there is this instantaneous vision of a person there . . ."

"Bodies matter," says Todd Essig (personal communication). He cites Marissa Mayer, the young CEO of Yahoo!, who banned telecommuting because she felt having all her employees physically together under one roof would increase communication, collaboration, and quality of work. "The inconvenience of the getting to the office matters. Yes, it's going to drive some people away, but that inconvenience increases the experience of commitment and connection. Making it easier doesn't make it better: it just makes it easier."

Moving intentionally in space has an impact on the internal work one does on either side of the consulting room. The richer our embodied experience of acting and moving in space, the more profoundly it affects our perceptions and consciousness. Movement, intrinsic to our feeling present in the world, is not only fundamentally connected to our embodied concepts and representations: it could be said that movement anchors thought (Hannaford, 2007, p. 109). It is integral to learning, thinking, and mental processing.

Not only do patients move to and from the consulting room, but also within it, and their choices of where to be are highly significant. Analyses where patients are free to use the consulting room space as they wish are highly fruitful. Where patients position themselves and how they move in the consulting room has great significance to the progression of the therapeutic relationship and the process of change in the therapy. I well remember my analyst moving to a new consulting room. It was far larger than her previous one, and had in it a couch, a loveseat, a *chaise longue*, and several chairs. I stood in the doorway, bemused, trying to figure out where I should go. Turning to her with that question, she replied with a wave around the room, "Anywhere you like." The possibility of such freedom made a huge impact on me and I began to experiment with the novel (to me) concept of positioning myself according to my needs and wishes. In a screen analysis there is no possibility to move in a shared space, and no opportunity for the analyst to observe how the patient chooses to use that space from moment to moment. "In a shared consulting room space there could be the possibility of exploring and discovering its safety," says Anna. "It limits the exploratory possibilities hugely, including, of course, the move from chair to a couch, or sitting in a different place: the movement through space."

Analysts discuss the difference in quality and significance between angry patients storming out of a shared environment session or simply disconnecting from a Skype session. "The ease of exit is really problematic: exiting from a session by the flick of a switch," says Charles, a Boston psychoanalyst. "It takes courage to enter a room and walk out of a room." Some mentioned that because Skype connections can be unreliable, some patients could disconnect "accidentally on purpose". Celia speculates about her disappearing patient, "Maybe it was just that turning a switch on and turning a switch off is different than a journey to somebody." One analyst tells me of a long-term intensive analysis where the patient lived in a country thousands of miles from her. After a particularly difficult period, the patient terminated with a click of the mouse, followed up with an email stating he was finished, and then refusing to make any further contact. The analyst feels doubtful that such acting out would happen this way in a shared environment.

Making a journey implies the potential for separation. Turkle points out the challenges for the technologically "tethered" generation to separate from parents and make the transition to adult independence in a culture where everyone is "always on" (2011, p. 173). Winnicott describes the early beginnings of the separate self as the achievement of "unit status", where the infant can recognise him/herself as a whole person engaging in a continuous interchange between inner and outer reality. This is equally applicable to the patient and he posits that through the mother/therapist's empathy with the infant/patient, the infant/patient is able to internalise and feel safe in the movement from dependence to autonomy (Winnicott, 1971a). Inherent within that growth is frustration and separation. Winnicott describes the good-enough mother starting off with almost complete adaptation to her infant's needs, gradually lessening the active adaptation according to the infant's ability to tolerate frustration and separation. "Incomplete adaptation to need makes objects real" (Winnicott, 1975a, p. 238). It is the finding of self, the experience of presence that roots us in reality and that selfhood and sense of reality is what analysts are there to help their patients discover.

Winnicott wrote about communication: "There comes about a change in the purpose and in the means of communicating *as the object changes over* from being subjective to being objectively perceived, in so far as the child gradually leaves the area of omnipotence as a living experience" (Winnicott, 1965, p. 181). The "flick of the switch", instead of the journey through space, decreases the sense of reality, of real connection. If our sense of presence and our embodied experience of our selves depends upon our moving and acting in space with intentionality, then the instantaneous nature of technological connection challenges that evolutionary sense.

Here we move toward what might be viewed as a floating world of signification, that is, a world in which the relationship of language to the ongoing practical activity is ambiguous if not irrelevant. It is this new floating world that is facilitated by the expansion of absent presence. (Gergen, 2002, p. 235)

If the lack of physical journey increases a sense of unreality, a breaking down of the separation between the "me" and the "not-me", so, too, does that "anywhere, anytime" aspect of technologically mediated communication that facilitates patients talking to analysts from their cars and analysts taking their patients, figuratively, to their hotel rooms on conferences.

We may be free to work from anywhere, but we are also prone to being lonely everywhere. In a surprising twist, relentless connection leads to a new solitude. We turn to new technology to fill the void, but as the technology ramps up, our emotional lives ramp down. (Turkle, 2011, www.alonetogether.com)

While there is certainly a gain to be considered in being able to maintain continuity in a treatment when it may be potentially interrupted by various uncontrollable circumstances, there is also a gain in the weathering of separation and the exploration of those feelings post-separation. Patients and analysts do get ill or are unavoidably called away for personal reasons, just as mothers might have to make their babies wait for a time before they can respond to their cries of hunger. This is part of the comings and goings of the object that becomes internalised creating a sense of inner connectedness and resilience. It is often the most valuable part of a treatment.

Patients who never get an opportunity to test those gaps, Grotstein's "baptism of space", never initiate the process of separation and true relatedness. As Lucy says, "I like the fact that there isn't a choice: that you have to go away from your therapist, moving. It is an important learning curve to accept the journey away . . . you may not like the journey, or you may feel relieved, but you have to do it." The illusion of being always connected is just that, an illusion. It is only with separation that we come to experience the affective missing of the object. With the feeling of missing, eventually comes the acknowledgement of the value and connectedness to that which is missed. A thread of continuity is internally established, which co-exists with a sense of presence, of going-on-being.

The theme of moving in space has connections to the previous theme of use of the environment, and also, as we shall see, links to the next theme of potentiality.

Potentiality: kissing or kicking

Winnicott writes in one of his final papers, "The use of an object", of the need for opposition in the apprehension of the reality of the object (1969). He distinguishes between what he calls "object relating", meaning relating to objects as "subjective objects" ("a bundle of projections"), and "object-usage". He says, "The object, if it is to be used, must necessarily be real in the sense of being part of shared reality" (1969, p. 711). He stresses that this capacity is not inborn, and neither can it be taken for granted. The development of the capacity to use an object is part of the maturation of the individual in a good-enough facilitating environment. He describes the failure of the developmental achievement of object-use as the most irksome of all the early failures that come in [to the consult-ing room] for mending. The thing that is in between relating and use is the subject's placing of the object outside of the area of the subject's omnipotent control, that is, the subject's perception of the object as an external phenomenon, not as a projective entity, in fact recognition of it as an entity in its own right. (p. 712)

Winnicott states that the subject experiences the reality of the object, when the object is perceived as *outside of the subject's omnipotent control*. This happens through the subject's experience of destroying the object and the object *surviving* the destruction. He elaborates on his word destruction, as it is applied to an infant, as "eagerness" (there-fore, nothing to do with anger, it is the combined love–strife drive), as he is aware of how difficult it is for the idea of destructiveness to be accepted (Winnicott, 1989). He elaborates, "In this vitally important early stage the 'destructive' aliveness of the individual is simply a symptom of being alive" (p. 239). ". . . after 'subject relates to the object' comes 'subject destroys object' (as it becomes external) . . ." (Winnicott, 1969, p. 712). It is the subject's recognition that the mother/ therapist, outside the subject's omnipotent control, can survive the destructive attack (unconscious and in fantasy), and because of the object's survival it is perceived as whole, separate and external.

At the point of development that is under survey the subject is creat-ing the object in the *sense of finding externality itself*, and it has to be added that this experience depends on the object's capacity to survive. (It is important that this means "not retaliate".) If it is in an analysis that these matters are taking place, then the analyst, the analytic tech-nique, and the analytic setting all come in as surviving or not surviv-ing the patient's destructive attacks. This destructive activity is the patient's attempt to place the analyst outside the area of omnipotent control, that is, out in the world. Without the experience of maximum destructiveness (object not protected) the subject never places the analyst outside and therefore, can never do more than experience a kind of self-analysis, using the analyst as a projection of a part of the self (1969, p. 714, my italics).

In "screen relations", the patient can never truly test the analyst's capacity to survive. The extent to which the patient can "imagine" the destruction of the analyst (by zealous love or hate) is bounded by the barrier of the screen. Whatever moments of "functional equivalence" the screen offers are inevitably grounded in the awareness of simulation, which automatically confines potentiality. Therefore, the use of the object is foreclosed by the limitations of the medium.

Patrick, an analyst in Sydney, Australia, tells me this story about a patient he started to see via computer mediation after Patrick relocated:

> The patient had difficulty expressing anger on Skype . . . It's a shame because if he had been able to keep going in person the analysis would have really developed. [It was] something about my being able to see through every angry episode in person that affected both of us. When he blew [up] I needed to be very thoughtful and patient with him and it took him a long time to calm down and think about what his contempt and rage was about. It felt like there was something about being on Skype that made it just not possible.

Patrick speculates that the patient needed him there in the room both to witness and survive his attacks, and keep thinking. Screen-to-screen communication meant that there was no way the patient could truly test that his rage did not destroy the analyst or make him go mad. The inherent "protection" of the screen dissipated the potential impact of the patient on the therapist. Patrick helped the patient to transfer to an analyst with whom he could be in person.

Certainly, there is a vital aspect of trust and testing between the analyst and patient, especially for patients who have experienced breaches of trust in their past. Ellie's first analysis ended disastrously when her analyst tried to kiss her. She tells me that her co-present sessions "revealed my analyst's weakness and my strength in ways that the non-physical experience of Skype could never have permitted." Risk is not just a fantasy in co-presence and the potential to touch in the consulting room has very real meaning and consequences. The patient misses the crucial experience of authentic safety in the analyst's presence. Ellie reminds us of the consequences of being separated by a screen: "Skype actually obscures the *therapist's* potential for professional fallibility, while it may heighten the potential for his fantasy unchecked by reality," she tells me. "You might think, ah, well, that's a good thing surely. But not so fast. The good therapist *chooses* to be professional in drawing physical boundaries. But Skype *forces* the therapist to draw physical boundaries. Therefore, the patient can never observe the therapist's *choice* to create a safe environment and not to act on impulse." Analytic restraint is not possible on the screen. The act of not kissing on the screen is not the same as the act of not kissing in person.

Anna, the analyst from London, considers the use by some patients of the bed instead of the couch in technologically mediated sessions:

> They're not lying down *literally in the presence of their analyst*. That to me seems almost perverse ... because the quality of the trust is precisely because there is another person there who can touch you, who could get up and do something ... and there's no vulnerability. You're not risking that physical vulnerability of coming in and lying down, which for some people might take a while to be able to risk. That risk is never faced, never felt. They're in control all the time and the illusion that you can recreate that [risk and vulnerability] by having a camera behind your head: that's absolutely crazy.

However, I would place the element of risk *within* the area of potentiality. What Winnicott is describing is an even deeper and more crucial experience: that of the capacity to perceive an object with its own autonomy and life, able to survive its ongoing destruction in the subject's unconscious fantasy resulting in the achievement of "unit status".

Will is a geologist in the oil industry who periodically spends some time working in the field. He is nearing the end of a five-year analysis in which he uses technological mediation when he is working away from his home base. "I always felt that if anyone knew me as I really am, they would be really shocked and probably abandon me. It has been crucial that I saw my analyst in person in order to work that out. Being on a screen was just not the same. I needed to see that he didn't flinch, wasn't afraid of me, or disgusted with me *in person* ... that he didn't need the protection of Skype to be with me ... and stay with me."

Loving, as well as destructive, fantasies also have no potential to be enacted. Speaking about a foreign patient she had never met in person, an analyst said, "[The patient] would talk about wanting to hug me and never let me go ... she would also talk about not being able to smell me and what perfume I wore."

"When you share a physical space, even if you don't act it out, there is always the potential to touch, whether that means kicking or kissing," points out Tanya, the young graphic designer. "When not in a shared space all physical potential is taken away, but the important thing is to have *the potential*, not necessarily the acting out." We can relate Tanya's thoughts about physical potential in a shared space to Winnicott's idea about the developmental necessity of the subject's placing the object *outside* of the area of omnipotent control, to be recognised as an entity in its own right. We will see that this concept also links with researchers' in human–computer interaction description of the experience of social-presence-as feeling, the non-mediated perception of an enacting other within the external world. I do not see that "unit status", the capacity to perceive an object as a separate autonomous entity, can develop without physical, intentional bodies interacting on all levels, both implicit and explicit. A patient says, "For me, play has a physical element: you can't play properly on Skype: that potential is taken away." It is important to note Winnicott's (1969) caveat that the subject who can never place the analyst outside the self experiences a sort of "self-analysis". Rather than truly using the analyst for nurture, the patient engages in a sort of pseudo-analysis "feed[ing] only on the self" (p. 713). The patient might even enjoy the experience of analysis, but will not essentially change.

It has been suggested that the concept of virtual space can be regarded as "transitional space", a realm that lies somewhere between the inner world and external reality, following Winnicott's ideas of transitional phenomena (Allison et al., 2006; Carlino, 2011; Suler, 2006). I think we need to be very careful before assigning that role to "cyberspace", however initially poetically apt it may seem. Winnicott (1975a) sees the stage of using transitional objects as an intermediate stage during which the baby is helped by the good-enough mother to separate internal and external worlds. This comes from using the transitional space as an area of creativity and play, but the negotiation of this space depends on a gradual process of disillusion. The baby discovers that he/she is not omnipotent and that the mother is an "other", that there is a me and a not-me. The transitional object is used as a bridge between subjective reality and a shared external reality. Having said this, there has to be an experience of an internal reality *and* shared external reality in order to dwell in what Winnicott refers to as the third area, the place of creativity and symbolism. The task of accepting reality is always ongoing in a person's life and no one is ever free from the tension of relating inner and external reality. Winnicott sees psychoanalysis as a highly specialised form of playing in the service of communication with oneself and others (1971b, p. 41). The importance of the consulting play-room is that it is a *shared* space, *both* real and imagined, where the patient can begin to distinguish what belongs to the inner world and what belongs to external reality.

The patients above, from Patrick's patient who needed him to be present to survive his rage, to Tanya, who speaks of the need of the potential to kick or kiss, illustrate vividly that you can never test reality if you cannot ever leave the realm of the intermediate, much less the area of omnipotent subjective reality. Tanya poignantly longs for a sense of the reality of the other, and is anxious about the omnipotence she feels when she is not genuinely grounded in the reality of her therapist's presence in the consulting room.

"You hit a wall," says Hannah. She is a training and supervising psychoanalyst, a writer, and a professor. She has treated three patients using technological mediation. One of them, who lived abroad, she never met. The analysis lasted for more than five years. "You move along in the analysis and most of it feels familiar. There is the transference and the countertransference. There are moments of intensity, moments of boredom, moments of insight. And then something happens. You just hit a wall and you can't go any deeper. You can't go any further. I found myself wanting to meet with my patients more in the flesh, the ones who lived in this country, but further away. The patient I never met . . . well. He finished his analysis and he felt he had been helped. But something was just missing. Some spark of real connection. You hit a wall. I had high hopes for Skype therapy. I felt we might be able to reach out to people who were not easy to reach. I wouldn't feel comfortable doing it again."

Freud writes, "For when all is said and done, it is impossible to destroy anyone *in absentia* or *in effigie*" (1912b, p. 108). He is talking about the reality of lived experience and the immediacy of the moment in the consulting room. We make ourselves available to our patients to work through their internal damage and discord *in vivo*. Can true and lasting change take place *in absentia* when the therapeutic couple appear *in effigie* to one another? When both participants must more than momentarily forget the screen that is proof of their not being there? When the analyst is not truly present to survive, to keep thinking without a protective veil, to exist embodied in three dimensions as a separate intentional subject? Our capacity to live in the world, to make choices, to have an impact on others and our environment is not an abstract theoretical experience. It is a practical embodied reality we experience in living.

What does it mean to be engaged in a process whose very aim is to establish a sense of true self, a sense of presence, a sense of reality, yet transmitted by a vehicle that creates a simulation? Turkle (2011, p. 287) says, "Simulation is often justified as practice for real-life skills—to become a better pilot, sailor, or race-car driver. But when it comes to human relations, simulations get us into trouble". While it does seem possible temporarily to "suspend disbelief", to muster enough "imagination, desire, and attention" to engage in some form of therapeutic work mediated by technology, the underlying awareness of the simulation of presence, the foreclosure of potentiality, puts inescapable bounds on the quality of emotional interaction and the true possibility for deep psychic change (Essig, 2012a).

CHAPTER THREE

Mapping the digital frontier

P sychoanalysts have been grappling with the appropriate use of developing communication technologies since Saul wrote his cautious, "A note on the use of the telephone as a technical aid" in 1951. It was not until fifty years later that Aronson edited the major collection of papers on this subject, *Use of the Telephone in Psychotherapy*, in which she observed,

> ... serious consideration of the therapeutic implications of telephone contact between patients and therapists had lagged behind the actual practice ... The paucity of literature on the subject, the absence of open discussion among colleagues, the lack of information available in graduate and postgraduate training programs led me to bring together the chapters in this book. I hoped that the effort would leave professionals feeling less hazy in their understanding of the practical, theoretical, and technical implications of the increasing use of the telephone in psychotherapy. (Aronson, 2000, p. xxv)

At the same time, around the turn of the twenty-first century, "video telephony" was becoming available through free Internet services such as Skype. Webcams were being integrated into both laptop and desktop computers and later into mobile phones, making audio-visual computer-mediated communication available to anyone with an Internet connection. There is a fashionable unproved meme that "digital natives", growing up in the age of digital technology, think and process differently to "digital immigrants", easily incorporating rapid shifts and advancements in technology into their daily repertoire (Carr, 2011; Prensky, 2001). Inevitably, these technological advances have been brought into the consulting room, both as material discussed by patients and media used by both patients and practitioners. As Hill predicted in 2000, before the advent of Skype, ". . . like death, taxes, and managed care, computer-mediated therapy is coming our way and is a discussion we need to begin".

While originally aimed at the user in the workplace, technologically mediated communication has been rapidly adopted by the home user, with four principal trends influencing the alteration of the home communications landscape: communication styles, communication infrastructures, communication possibilities, and communication cost models (Kirk et al., 2010). The convergence of communication devices has resulted in users seeing their home computer or mobile device as a means for multiple forms of communication. Immense investment in telecommunication infrastructures has made Internet access achievable for large sections of the international population. Video communication (cameras and microphones) has been integrated into computers as standard, and low cost or free models of data exchange have become affordable for the personal user (Kirk et al., 2010). All these technological and economic shifts have made audio-visual computer communication, once considered part of an imagined speculative fiction future, widely integrated into our everyday lives.

Just as Aronson (2000) cited the lag between the practice of telephone use in treatment and serious consideration of its therapeutic implications, so it is with the use of technologically mediated audio-visual psychoanalysis and psychotherapy. Computer-mediated sessions have become frequently used as adjuncts to a treatment, and increasingly, as the primary or sole method of communication in treatment (Carlino, 2011; Fishkin et al., 2011; Neumann, 2012; Saporta, 2008; Scharff, 2012). Patient–therapist mobility, work requirements, illness, family commitments, remote locations, unavailability of qualified professionals, and, perhaps most problematically, patients' and analysts' financial considerations (in the case of the analyst, psychoanalyst Ricardo Carlino (2011) refers to this as "clinical survival methods") have motivated both members of the therapeutic couple to initiate the use of audio-visual communication in place of face-to-face sessions.

> Analysts in considerable numbers are showing greater tolerance for leaving classic moulds. They understand that a considerable number of people, due to existential and/or work conditions, either temporarily or permanently, require analysis carried out through the technological resources of communication. (Carlino, 2011, p. 9)

In a less restrained style, the TeleMental Health Institute (http://telehealth.org) offers online "professional training" for psychological practitioners to establish computer-mediated practices, trumpeting, "Bring your practice online for more clients and patients, more convenience, more profits" (Maheu, 2012). There is a call for analysts to respond to globalisation and a "socio-cultural metamorphosis" that engenders a "new psychoanalytic culture" (Berenstein & Grenfeld, 2009, cited in Carlino, 2011, p. 28).

Psychoanalysts and psychotherapists offer Skype sessions as a treatment option on their online websites, and the American Psychoanalytic Association has approved long-distance psychoanalysis conducted over Skype in some cases. Moreover, in 2009, the International Psychoanalytic Association issued a new policy approving "supplementary" analysis via telephone or Skype for candidates in exceptional circumstances (Hanly & Scharff, 2010). For example, Chinese candidates may use technological mediation if the first 100 hours of a training analysis are done in person (Neumann, personal communication, February, 2013). Plans to amend this requirement are in process as I write, so that child and adult psychoanalytic training analyses might soon be conducted, in some instances, entirely via technological mediation. Non-psychoanalytic websites offering exclusively online treatment have sprung up on the Internet, as well as organisations dedicated to teaching and discussing "telehealth" and "telemental health". Insurance companies in the USA and the UK are accepting billing codes for telemedicine. Liability, licensing, reimbursement, and confidentiality are all hotly debated by individuals and by state and registering bodies (Hanly & Scharff, 2010).

A decade ago Zalusky (2003) wrote of telephone analysis: "What makes telephone analysis so controversial is that it almost always represents a therapeutic compromise, and because of this, it is inherently conflictual. It is never the treatment of choice" (p. 14). In 2014, not only is telephone analysis/therapy sometimes "the treatment of choice", but also technologically mediated treatment is being embraced enthusiastically by expanding numbers of practitioners.

The increased use of technologically mediated communication has elicited a wide spectrum of responses from the analytic community. Reactions range from an assertion that computer-mediated sessions are indistinguishable from shared environment sessions (Fishkin & Fishkin, 2011; Fishkin et al., 2011; Scharff, 2012; Snyder, 2009) to the opinion that technologically mediated sessions are not psychoanalysis (Argentieri & Amati Mehler, 2003).

Essig (2013c, 2015), psychoanalyst and writer for Forbes.com, has pointed out that in order to properly assess the potential gains and losses in technologically mediated sessions, one must accept that they are profoundly different from co-present psychotherapy. He cautions that when we simply import our clinical technique and theory of traditional shared environment treatment, we are in danger of idealising technology, perceiving only positive gains and enhancements. This same warning was put forth fifty years ago when Heidegger (1966) wrote that the impending "tide of a technological revolution" might "so captivate, bewitch, dazzle, and beguile man that calculative thinking may someday become to be accepted and practiced as the only way of thinking" (p. 56). Our capacity for "meditative thinking", in which he saw the heart of our humanity, might be sacrificed in the name of impetuous progress.

In contrast, those uncomfortable with the pace of technological change might anxiously distance themselves from the gains that technology has to offer. The potential gains in the use of technologically mediated communication for treatment are clearly seen as the world becomes increasingly globalised with advances in transportation and telecommunication. Business people in Australia may have a videoconference with their colleagues in France, grandparents in New York may "Skype" with their grandchildren in Japan, and students in Brazil may meet with their tutors in the UK. I, myself, keep touch with my son in London, my daughter in New York, and my friends, colleagues, students, and supervisees all over the USA, UK, and China.

Patients and therapists are naturally embedded in larger society with its changes and technological advances. They are more mobile than ever before, and that mobility can threaten the continuity of a therapy. Analysts and patients have opted to use Skype, following an increased use of the telephone, in order to continue a therapy that would otherwise be interrupted by work-related travel requirements or family re-locations (Carlino, 2011; Scharff, 2012). In addition, Skype has been used when illness has prevented a patient attending a session, when a university student travels either home or to university (depending on where the treatment is located), or when a patient resides in a geographical area where there are no available practitioners (Carlino, 2011; Essig, 2012a; Neumann, 2012; Scharff, 2012).

It has been suggested that the use of technological mediation can be clinically beneficial because the unusual circumstances of the communicative device and dual settings potentially promote more vivid transference–countertransference experiences. Issues and fantasies that might not come up in a shared environment may be more easily accessed via technologically mediated communication (Richards, 2001; Suler, 2001; Scharff, 2012). The safety of distance allows certain affective states which may previously have been withheld or dissociated to emerge. This has been attributed to "continuity [which] fosters intensity and distance [which] protects from impulsive action" (Scharff, 2013a):

> [Neville] Symington, whose analysand had to travel after years of in-person psychoanalysis, found that the dislocation of being away from home and having to connect with him on the telephone revealed a transference delusion previously not brought into the consulting room. (Anderson et al., 2009, cited in Scharff, 2013a, p. 65)

Other advantages specific to the properties of technological mediation have been proposed. Analysts describe their ability to observe the analysand's choice of setting as usefully revealing elements of early emotional experience. They also suggest that the illusion of the analyst's voice being delivered directly to the analysand's mind with the use of headsets makes it easier for the patient to internalise the image of the analyst (Hanly & Scharff, 2010).

Mental health professionals envisage a range of potential uses of technologically mediated communication, from bridging a temporary gap in treatment, eliciting otherwise inaccessible psychic material, to offering treatment in remote areas where there is the possibility that the therapeutic couple will never meet "in the flesh" (Fishkin et al., 2011; Hanly & Scharff, 2010; Neumann, 2012; Snyder, 2009).

What happens on the screen: the story so far

There is now a substantial literature on psychoanalysis and psychoanalytic psychotherapy conducted on the telephone (Aronson, 2000; Argentieri & Amati Mehler, 2003; Brainsky, 2003; Leffert, 2003; Richards, 2001, 2003; Rodriguez de la Sierra, 2003; Sachs, 2003; Saul, 1951; Scharff, 2010, 2012; Yamin Habib, 2003, Zalusky, 2003). These discussions enumerate the reasons why the telephone was chosen to continue a treatment, including geographical moves, illness, business travel, crisis intervention, and fear of intimacy. They consider the transference–countertransference motivations for the choice of using the telephone, the positive aspects of continuing an otherwise potentially interrupted connection, and the issues that might be brought up via telephone that would not arise in the room. Some say that the sensorial deprivation increases intimacy (i.e., the voice directly to the ear) (Scharff, 2012) and some say it decreases all non-verbal aspects of the transaction, disabling both analyst and patient (Argentieri & Amati Mehler, 2003).

In fact, in their descriptions, some of the papers elide telephone use with audio-visual technological communication, as if one is simply an extension of the other, with the addition of the visual element to the aural (Scharff, 2012). While these papers have many useful things to say in their general assessment of how working on a technological device in separate environments might affect a treatment, they do not examine the unique features and intrinsic differences in the two media. Although they may be analogous, it would be simplistic to regard audio-visual communication as identical to telephone communication.

Carlino (2011), a psychoanalyst from Buenos Aires, has written the first book on technologically mediated treatment, *Distance Psychoanalysis: The Theory and Practice of Using Communication Technology in the Clinic*, in which he comprehensively covers all aspects of "distance communication". In this groundbreaking work, Carlino argues that in this rapidly technologically evolving world, psychoanalysts are already using technology for communication in treatment and that it is necessary for them to assimilate these changes and develop a framework in which to practise, keeping pace with the impact of global mobility and technology. He covers a range of synchronous and asynchronous technological communication potentially used in treatment, including the telephone, written chat, email, and audio-visual media. Having assumed the inevitability of this form of treatment, he is thorough in covering the skills necessary to use technology in the consulting room and proposes a theory of the technique of distance analysis. He discusses issues of privacy and confidentiality, specific legal issues that might arise when practising across state or national boundaries, tax obligations, and the potential criminal use of technological mediation.

Carlino's stance on the concept of presence is that it is no longer linked to physical proximity. He proposes that this actually encourages those who are geographically distant to feel closer to those "who are in easy reach of communication". He suggests,

> The experiential dimension that can be achieved between participants in the analysis is directly related to the psychoanalytic quality of the dialogue. When one achieves a certain or honest feeling of proximity in the "contact" and closeness in the "encounter," it is the result of the psychoanalytic depth that operates by minimizing or decoupling the significance and importance of the possible effect of geographical distance. (2011, p. 103)

Carlino argues that the psychoanalytic method can continue to be applied to a new technologically mediated setting because, in his view, the analytic process remains unaltered.

> In the distance framework, the idea of *presence* is separated from the need to be in front of the other person. It acquires an abstract and symbolic conception. The *presence*, when separating it from the need of a direct physical meeting, is bound to the idea of *contact* and *encounter* between analyst and patient. (2011, p. 64)

He suggests that the reality of the pre-arranged times of sessions, the devotion of the analyst, the maintenance of an ethical stance, the charging of fees, and the reaching of expected goals by the analytic couple are enough to contribute to a sense of presence, although he also states that "distance analysis, as a method itself, has greater need of contact and a deep transferential encounter . . . which significantly contributes to the sensation of presence" (pp. 104–105).

As the various elements suggested by Carlino are the normal foundations of the analytic framework, it is unclear as to what would meet the requirement of distance analysis's "greater need of contact". He seems to invoke a mutual collaboration in a suspension of disbelief for the therapeutic couple, a sort of "consensual hallucination" in cyberspace (Gibson, 1984, cited in Sand, 2007, p. 84).

> Given all the considerations expressed regarding distance and instantaneous communication, as well as the degree of reality involved in analytic dialogue, the idea of *presence* is clearly detached from the absolute need for a mutual physical presence of both participants in the dialogue. It acquires a more abstract and symbolic conception . . . (Carlino, 2011, p. 105)

Carlino focuses on the concept of "communicative presence" and the potential for emotional encounter, attunement, and lack of attunement as they occur in all psychoanalytic settings. He considers this "abstract and symbolic conception" of a meeting of minds importable into technologically mediated sessions and sufficient for deep psychic change. In contrast, Essig compares the experiences of a co-present treatment and a mediated treatment: "The context for the immediate, phenomenological moment in one setting is another person. In the other it is a device through which one simulates encountering another via an audio-visual or audio representation" (personal communication, 2012). What happens when the immediacy of the body is lost in technological mediation, if it proves that the body and the non-verbal dimension is *integral* to basic communication and the feeling of presence?

Freud was an astute observer of the nuances of non-verbal embodied behaviour in his patients. His detailed descriptions of Dora and her reticule and his comment, "He that has the eyes to see and the ears to hear may convince himself that no mortal can keep a secret. If his lips are silent, he chatters with his finger-tips; betrayal oozes out of him at every pore" (1905e, pp. 77–78) is an illustration of this. But Freud did not go on to develop this aspect of his theory, and concentrated instead on dreams and symbolism in the fantasies of the verbal communication of his patients, despite the fact that he was "not at all inclined to leave the psychology hanging in the air without an organic basis". He confessed to Fliess,

I do not know how to go on, neither theoretically nor therapeutically and therefore must behave as if only the psychological were under consideration. Why I can not fit it together [the organic and the psychological] I have not even begun to fathom. (Masson, 1985, p. 326)

Shapiro (1996) explores how the cultural process of "civilising", that is, controlling the body and sensual experience, caused clinical psychoanalysis to develop in such a disembodied way in "The embodied analyst in the Victorian consulting room".

I want to focus here on the impact of the civilizing process and the Cartesian worldview on the form and procedure of psychoanalysis . . . Psychoanalysis is the talking cure. Patients talk, we listen. We sit quietly in our chairs, seeking to remove our body from the patient's objective experience. The patient may fantasize about our bodily state, but as much as possible our bodily state remains opaque. (p. 308)

The resulting diversion from the integration of the non-verbal and the physical into psychoanalytic theory has continued to have an impact on psychoanalytic trainings to this day. Theodore Jacobs (1994; in Beebe et al., 2005) points out that while non-verbal aspects of the therapeutic relationship are of prime importance, instruction in this area remains minimal or absent from current trainings. Many experienced senior analysts have little practice in attending to and interpreting embodied non-verbal communications. As a result, nuanced non-verbal communications are overlooked in training analyses and supervisions, while training analysts and supervisors remain in the comfort zone of more familiar verbal material.

The result, all too often, is that in his clinical work the candidate uses his ears to the virtual exclusion of his eyes, focuses single-mindedly on the verbal material, and sooner or later develops a scotoma for material expressed in bodily language or through other nonverbal means. In this way a significant deficiency in analytic technique is transmitted from one generation of analysts to the next. (Beebe et al., 2005, p. 185)

Analysts who use technologically mediated tools for treatment speak to me of their own psychoanalytic trainings, which were traditionally orientated with an emphasis on the explicit verbal aspects of communication. "I was not working in any conscious way at all with bodily material, nor was my analyst . . . it was not part of

my original training: my original training was very word-orientated."
When using technologically mediated communication, it is the verbal
aspects that they expect to give them clues to unconscious process, but
many are not prepared for the much larger implicit communication of
which they are deprived. Only lately, as recent research and writing
has been published on the implicit and embodied aspects of relating,
have they begun to think about that mode of communication. "My
training didn't prepare me to think about physicality, but my *analytic
experience* did"; "My first analyst didn't pay any attention that I was
aware of to any physical manifestations . . ."

Psychoanalysts who are accustomed to working chiefly in the
"reflective–verbal" domain might find using technologically mediated
communication ego-syntonic. If you do not fully attend to body language and other non-verbal communication, or recognise the importance of implicit communication, then the limited visual input on the
screen might seem sufficient, a novelty, or even something to be
avoided. While the limited visual access might feel enough, the comprehensive sensory limitations might not be appreciated. This is illus-
trated by the way some analysts and patients opt to turn off the visual
input during the session, *as if* that equated with the patient using the
couch. The analysts who do that do not fully appreciate the many
other modes of sensory communication available (including peripheral vision) when an analyst and patient are inhabiting the same space
during the entirety of the session, regardless of a temporary limitation
of direct visual contact when the patient is using the couch.

"One reason I loved my analytic training," says Michael, an
analyst from Washington, DC, "is that I discovered all I had to do was
use my listening mind to tune in on the patient's mind. My body was
incidental, and so was the patient's body. Both of us were quite still.
That suited me as I had never been comfortable with my body—and,
no, I didn't explore that in my training analysis. I had to wait until my
second analysis to do that."

To emphasise the symbolic and the abstract at the expense of
"being there" recalls the problematic issue of Cartesian dualism and
the belief "I think, therefore I am". Historically, the explicit and symbolic aspects of the therapeutic relationship have been the focus of
attention for over a century. However, we are coming to understand
that our communication also contains a significant implicit component
and that both the explicit and implicit domains of human experience

are embodied. Indeed, the American Psychological Association Presidential Task Force on Evidence-Based Practice (2006) defines interpersonal clinical expertise as the capacity to form a therapeutic relationship, to encode and decode verbal and *non-verbal* responses, and to respond empathically to the patient's explicit and *implicit* experiences and concerns.

In the coming chapters, when we examine the requirements for both the therapeutic process and the experience of a sense of presence, as well as recent studies of embodied cognition, questions will arise as to the proposition that the experience of presence can be funnelled into "an abstract and symbolic conception". Non-verbal, instantaneous, implicit communication is a large part of all relationships, including the psychoanalytic relationship. It is *not* rooted in abstract and symbolic thought. Further, the concept of presence, as defined by information and communication technology researchers, depends on the location of the self in a shared external space in which he/she can interact with others. They underline the necessity to link the experience of presence with physical experience.

> At its core, presence is the feeling we get from attending perceptually to the present world (in both time and space) outside ourselves. Mediated presence is primarily the perceptual illusion of being in an external, sharable world. It is not an internal, imaginary "thought experiment". (Waterworth & Waterworth, 2003a)

The psychoanalytic model of the development of the self towards ego autonomy depends on locating the self in space, and, through relational interaction, realising separateness between self and other. If it is necessary to have an embodied experience of presence in order to feel a whole self, then it is difficult to imagine the therapeutic efficacy of solely depending on the quality of an explicit analytic dialogue, much less a dialogue conducted screen-to-screen from separate environments. As we shall see, rather than being confined to the abstract, symbolic, or verbal realms, the experience of presence is rooted in the body and in shared perceptual and reciprocal experience.

Early pioneers on the technology frontier

John Suler, a psychologist, is a pioneer in thinking about the psychology of "cyberspace". As early as 1999, he posted an online multimedia

hypertext book on the subject with a section devoted to "psychotherapy and clinical work in cyberspace" (Suler, 2006). In this ebook,
which he has continuously updated, he considers various sorts of
computer-mediated psychotherapy, both text and audio/video based,
asynchronous and synchronous, assessment of a patient's suitability
for online psychotherapy, and the possible future of online clinical
work. Noting the unusual intensity of affect that may occur when
using technology, including behaviours that range from acts of great
kindness to "flaming" and bullying, Suler originated the concept of
"online disinhibition effect". Online disinhibition arises because of
lack of cues normally occurring in shared environment interaction,
and can lead to both useful and toxic behaviour in computer-mediated
situations (Suler, 2004).

Daniel Hill (2000) is another early creative thinker about computer-
mediated psychotherapy, particularly video-conferencing (Skype was
not released until 2003). Citing Marshall McLuhan's theories about
media, he wonders what the effect of the computer medium will be
on both patient and therapist. He asks specifically, "Is physical presence necessary as a condition for creating a therapeutic process?" and
questions whether computer-mediated therapy can provide a holding
environment sufficient for therapeutic progress. Mediated relational
experiences might not have the same therapeutic value as in-person
treatment because "There is simply more at stake in in-person encounters and those stakes are bound up with the presence of the body"
(2000). Hill questions whether one can care sufficiently about someone
whom "we've never laid eyes on". If direct perception of a physical
object is more real than mediated perception, does the need to
suspend disbelief and imagine interfere with the capacity to care? He
presciently cautions,

> If we do not understand the online media we risk simply transporting
> to cyberspace the techniques of in-person treatment—some of which
> may not travel well. We also risk missing the opportunity to develop
> new techniques that computer-mediated-communication makes possi-
> ble. (Hill, 2000).

Thirteen years later, he writes to me, "Since writing that article I've
become interested in affect regulation and have considerable doubts
about the effectiveness of computer-mediated-therapy for any kind of
'in depth' work . . . I am convinced that computer-mediated-therapy

can never match the impact of face-to-face treatment with the current technology . . ." (personal communication, 21 February, 2013).

Psychoanalysts active with the China American Psychoanalytic Alliance (CAPA) are some of the first to use computer-mediated treatment (Fishkin & Fishkin 2011; Fishkin et al., 2011; Neumann, 2012; Rosen, 2010; Snyder, 2009). This non-profit organisation incorporated in 2006 is responding to a nationwide Chinese mental health initiative. Mental health professionals in China have approached western psychoanalysts requesting to be trained in psychoanalytically orientated psychotherapy, as there are very few psychoanalytically trained analysts or psychotherapists in China. The organisation comprises psychoanalysts throughout the West, including the USA, Europe, South America, and Israel, who teach in four-year psychoanalytic psychotherapy trainings. The courses, a two-year foundation course and a two-year advanced course, are organised around clinical and theoretical classes and supervision, all conducted via audio-visual computer-mediated channels. As with all trainings of this type, a personal psychoanalysis or psychoanalytic psychotherapy is recommended for the trainees, and these, too, are conducted via video-conferencing. The use of computer-mediated communication meets a training requirement that could not otherwise have been fulfilled (for a history, see Osnos, 2011).

The challenges of this project are great as the treatments are conducted in English, the patients do not meet their analysts prior to commencing treatment, and the cultural differences are significant. It has been made clear by the organisation that its goal is to enable the Chinese psychoanalytic psychotherapists to take over their own training initiative once there are enough trained professionals able to do so. As the first Chinese Internet analysis was commenced in 2005 (Fishkin & Fishkin, 2011), the analytic members of CAPA are in the vanguard of practitioners who conduct technologically mediated treatment. CAPA members have to think equally about issues of language and culture and issues of computer-mediated treatment, and it is sometimes difficult to disentangle the two. Practitioners have commented on the inevitable disruptions in Internet connections, which at times are extremely intrusive to treatment (Fishkin & Fishkin, 2011; Neumann, 2012; Rosen, 2010). Using clinical vignettes, several authors (Fishkin & Fishkin, 2011; Rosen, 2010) describe the unfolding of the transference and the process of the treatment as indistinguishable from same-environment sessions (Fishkin & Fishkin, 2011; Snyder, 2009).

Neumann (2012) wrote a comprehensive paper, including a historic literature review, on factors that must be considered in establishing and maintaining a psychoanalytic frame when doing a computer-mediated treatment. She addresses precedents for the use of technology in psychoanalysis. She confirms the frequently expressed view (Carlino, 2011; Scharff, 2012) that psychoanalysis must keep pace with global cultural, sociological, and technological advances. Her conclusions stress the importance of recognising the impact that computer-mediated treatment makes on the transference–countertransference, defences, and unconscious material of the patient, as well as the analyst's capacity to foster a therapeutic alliance.

Scharff is another analyst active at the forefront of thinking about the integration of technology into treatment. In 2012, she wrote a thorough review of literature on telephone analysis, conflating it with video technology. She comments, echoing Carlino (2011, pp. 36, 108–109), that when one route of sensory communication is blocked, other routes compensate because of cross-modal channels of sensory communication. As I discussed with Maria Celano, this hypothesis, as applied to the practice of technologically mediated treatment, has frequently been put forward, citing as an example the heightened sensitivity of the functioning senses of blind or deaf persons (Hanly & Scharff, 2010). It is unclear whether subjects with fully functioning senses, using a mode which artificially deprives them of the use of one or more at comparatively brief intervals in their lives, would be able to develop a heightened use of the functioning senses in the same way that permanently impaired persons develop a neural plasticity to channel sensory input. Scharff suggests that if the loss of sensory data is acknowledged, then the analyst and patient are "free to develop a heightened appreciation for unconscious communication via the transmission of sound" (2013a, p. 72).

In writing about the differences and similarities of "tele- and traditional analysis", she contends that the analyst and patient are able to conceive and maintain representations of each other in fantasy, thereby creating a new form of psychoanalytic process (2013b, p. 498). As with the CAPA psychoanalysts, she, too, has presented process notes to colleagues who were unable to distinguish a technologically mediated session from a co-present session (2013b, p. 497).

In 2013, Scharff edited a collection of papers by psychoanalysts and psychotherapists on the uses of communication technology in treatment and training. *Psychoanalysis Online: Mental Health, Teletherapy, and Training* supports the use of technological mediation in treatment, suggesting that in the future it might not be only a convenient adjunct to co-present treatment, but preferable in specific therapeutic circumstances.

Essig (2011, 2012a,b,c, 2015) is an innovative thinker and writer about the impact of technologically mediated communication on culture and society. The fact that he is also a psychoanalyst makes his work particularly pertinent. He has written several leading edge papers on what he terms "screen relations" in which he considers both the technologically mediated relations that patients bring as clinical material into sessions and the actual use of technology in treatment. Essig designates the word "simulation" to describe mediated relations (2012a, 2015).

I spoke with Essig quite early in my exploration, interviewing analysts about their experiences of technologically mediated treatment.

> The process of being with an other when you're in the same consulting room is a direct unmediated experience that evolution has primed us to be able to do, including affect attunement systems, mirror neurons, olfaction, and body sensation. These whole series of things that are present in the consulting room are not present when we are trying to connect via technology. (Personal communication)

He points out that evolution prepared us to be embodied beings sharing the same space, and that all screen relations are simulations of that experience. He goes to some lengths to clarify that this word does not imply a value judgement, but that it is a signification of *difference.* "I think there has to be a recognition that what you're doing [when using technology] is fundamentally different to what one does face-to-face" (personal communication). In addition to the requirements that technology be interactive, reliable, and available, Essig proposes that maintaining an "emotional illusion" of telepresence requires imagination, desire, and attention (2012a, pp. 13–14). He describes the highly demanding emotional contribution necessary to maintain a suspension of disbelief, an affective connection, and analytic attention (for both analyst and patient) in a mediated situation.

"When someone having these three human qualities, attention, imagination and desire, is in the presence of a technology that is available and interactive, they are able to have an experience of functional equivalence." Essig tells me,

> Not for a second do I question the experience my colleagues are having in CMC [computer-mediated communication] treatment. They are experiencing those moments of functional equivalence. What they're not experiencing, because they're not paying attention to it, are the moments when functional equivalence breaks down ... [They are assuming] if I've had this *experience* of functional equivalence, then it must *be* functionally equivalent.

Even if technologically mediated communication goes well, Essig suggests that it is important to keep in mind the differences between sharing an environment and relating screen-to-screen. He defines three differences that persist in those experiences. The first difference he calls *risk*, pointing out that "safety in the presence of risk is different to the absence of risk" (2012a, p. 14). There is a difference between experiencing intense feelings in the bodily presence of an other and having those feelings in the presence of a technologically mediated representation of the other, as the patient, Ellie, reminded us earlier. Essig says, "I've had several patients over the years say to me things like, 'No matter how seductive I was, it was really important that you never touched me.' That factor [the real risk of being touched] is technologically impossible."

The second difference is *repleteness*. This richness of experience he refers to is a quality, not a quantity, as in the measure of the bandwidth or information. He warns that the user of technology must be equally aware that mediation could limit or efface important aspects of relational experience (sensory, expressive, non-verbal) or create new possibilities that we are not yet prepared to understand or even notice.

The third difference is *relational embodiment*. "Being bodies together is different than imagining being bodies together" (2012a), p. 15). He cautions against confusing the "rapid cognitive inference made from interactive, reliable, and available information" divided into discrete channels and reproduced at a distant location with the direct embodied experience of the other (2012a, p. 15).

Simulation avoidance: nothing has changed

Essig has created two descriptive concepts that he calls *simulation avoidance* and *simulation entrapment*. These terms depict two states of reduced self-awareness when using technologically mediated communication. While he uses these terms clinically to describe his patients' personal interactions in "screen relations", he also finds them useful to describe states of perceptual limitation that can affect practitioners doing technologically mediated treatments (2012a, p. 15; 2015).

"Simulation avoidance" occurs when practitioners are in denial about the immense technological changes that are affecting our culture. It is characterised by an anxious distancing from the issues that arise from the use of new technologies and an inability to think in a balanced way about the implications. Essig tells the wonderfully germane story of presenting a paper at a psychoanalytic meeting about a purely cybersex affair via voice, text, and video, in which the participants had never met physically or had traditional "embodied" sex. In his presentation, he discussed the implications of this significant and powerful relationship for his patient. One of the discussants emphatically disallowed that there was anything new and different about these cybersex encounters. He cited George Bernard Shaw, a century earlier, saying, "The perfect love affair is one conducted entirely by post". Hearing this, the audience heaved a collective sigh of relieved agreement. Essig comments, "It was as though a wide experiential gulf did not exist separating letters . . . from high-definition, fully interactive video where each did the other's bidding while receiving immediate visual feedback as to the results" (2015). This mass denial recalls various papers about telephone psychoanalytic sessions, as well as audio-visual communication, which cite Freud's use of letters in Little Hans' analysis, or even the couch itself, as mediating devices precedent and comparable to present-day technology. Essig says that to deny the fundamental differences blinds the users to both the gains and losses of the medium.

Simulation entrapment: protecting the simulation

"Simulation entrapment" occurs when practitioners become so caught up in a simulation's power that the participant forgets that "it is not the actuality that it is replicating and extending . . . Under the sway of simulation entrapment one acts inside the simulation, and expects consequences for one's actions that are *exactly the same* as the traditional actuality" (Essig, 2015, my italics). Essig tells me,

> They [practitioners] are entrapped [when] they have experienced the simulation working and taken that to mean that there is not a point at which it stops working . . . I think people who would keenly do Skype treatments are like people who are in a flight simulator and instead of taking it to be an educational experience, an experience that replicates what the experience of flying is like, actually expect to get some place.

Analysts who are experiencing "simulation entrapment", not paying attention to the limitations inherent in "technologically mediated intimacies", have an unconscious tendency to push mediated sessions away from regressive states, because those states can neither be properly sensed nor managed at a distance: "they protect the simulation" (Essig, personal communication, April, 2013). Thus, the analyst can be blinded to various moments, those times when the patient retreats but the analyst cannot gauge it, or when something pivotal is happening, but the medium allows the analyst to "coast in the countertransference" (Hirsch, 2008).

> They don't push the treatment into areas where you *would* call the functional equivalence into question. If either of those three qualities, desire, attention and imagination, disappears then the experience of functional equivalence disappears. Take, for example, really regressed schizoid states that happen in my office with sometimes alarming frequency. If that were to happen via a Skype session, that would eliminate the capacity for imagination necessary for the patient to be experiencing a moment of functional equivalence. They would no longer be in a transitional space. They would no longer be in contact. They would be alone in the *absence* of the other, as opposed to what happens in our office, which is being alone in the presence of the other. Because of that there is an inclination among analysts to push the treatment done on Skype away from regressive states. It happens unconsciously and you aren't aware of it.

Essig suggests that it is possible that some of the glowing reports of technologically mediated analyses as indistinguishable from co-present analyses come from within simulation entrapment (e.g., Fishkin & Fishkin, 2011; Snyder, 2009).

Good examples of this are particularly highlighted in technologically mediated analyses where the participants, who have never met, finally do meet. Fishkin and Fishkin (2011) report the subsequent meeting in person of Chinese patients whom they had treated initially on Skype. In one case, the co-present session proceeded as if there had been no change in the environment. The shift from screen-to-screen sessions to a session in a Chinese teahouse was unremarkable. The patient felt relaxed and treated the session as if it were familiar and routine. The analyst writes, "I finished my tea and we concluded our session. Upon my return from China, two weeks later, we resumed our Skype sessions uneventfully" (Fishkin & Fishkin, 2011, p. 103). This is interpreted as demonstrating that the use of computer-mediated communication and the vast geographical distance between them did not make any difference to the analytic relationship (Smolen, 2011, p. 138). Yet, there are immense differences between working in two dimensions over a gulf of thousands of miles (not to mention very different cultures) and working in three dimensions sharing the same room and a pot of tea. Those differences were not explored at the time of the session or subsequently, although the patient might have brought them up obliquely later in the analysis, an analysis in which, the analyst reports, the patient highly idealised her analyst.

> During the course of the analysis, Ms. A has explored her transferential relationship to a mentor who was initially idealized, subsequently devalued, and more recently has become a more reality-based figure, important and helpful to the patient's professional development, but clearly with limitations and deficiencies. (Fishkin & Fishkin, 2011, p. 103)

What is not directly explored is how it feels to come into embodied contact with your analyst for the first time, an analyst who, in reality, has limitations and deficiencies. Neither are the limitations and deficiencies of the technology explored. Certainly, the joy in finally meeting a beloved therapist (and a cared-for patient) may temporarily eclipse the possibility of exploring the differences in the shared environment experience and the subsequent losses in returning to computer-mediated sessions. But the opportunity to acknowledge the impact of the co-present meeting on the analysis, the subsequent change back to two dimensions, and the separation of tremendous distance is not taken up.

> Recently there have been hints of the negative transference toward me, amid the glowingly positive "grandmother" transference that has been constant. There were a number of canceled sessions, initiated by each of us, due to conferences, illnesses, and vacations. Ms. A admitted, with great difficulty, that she was surprised to notice that she felt relief when we canceled, as she was running out of "problems" to bring to the analysis . . . I suggested that the treatment was becoming less important, as many conflicts had been resolved. (Fishkin & Fishkin, 2011, p. 104)

Just as hints of the negative transference manifest, the relationship becomes looser and less intense, with increased cancellations on both sides. The patient begins running out of problems to report.

There seems no doubt that the patient's relationships in the external world have clearly improved. Many of her concrete problems have been resolved. But there is no mention of the relationship with the analyst, mostly distant, with one brief "shock of the real" being tackled and explored. The impact of the mediating device is not brought into the conversation. In fact, it seems to have been elaborately avoided.

A second patient conducted his first in-person session as if it was a social meeting. The analyst described it as cordial and unproductive. This patient was rather reserved and distant during his technologically mediated sessions, with an anxiety about informality and intimacy. The patient reacted to the news that his analyst was coming to China with caution and uneasiness: "Would it interfere with the analysis, and what would we accomplish?" (Fishkin & Fishkin, 2011, p. 106). He did attend the arranged session in the analyst's hotel room on time, but was extremely awkward. Unable to make eye contact, he said he did not feel that they could have a regular session in such an exceptional circumstance. While the analyst did try to engage him in how they observed differences in their screen and co-present appearances, the patient was not able talk about them. The rest of the session consisted of superficial pleasantries. The analyst wrote, "When I returned to the US, and we resumed our scheduled appointments, we fell back into our regular routine" (Fishkin & Fishkin, 2011, p. 107).

The analyst speculates about whether, contrary to the recommendations of the IPA, which requires a period of co-present analysis before beginning a technologically mediated analysis, in some cases actually meeting co-presently would be negatively disruptive to the treatment. Akhtar suggested to the analyst the relevance of the "waking screen" concept as an explanation of what occurred between them. The waking screen is described as the background of one's earliest perceptual experience that sets up expectations that play an active role in the way one perceives all new experiences throughout life. The analyst understood this to mean that the computer screen was the waking screen, the background of perceptual experience, through which the analytic couple related to each other. The removal of this background experience caused the analyst and patient to assume defensive postures. However, it was emphasised that this disruption to the analytic process was only temporary and that the analysis easily resumed their analytic work when they returned to the (actual) screen (Fishkin & Fishkin, 2011).

The concept of the waking screen refers to ones' *earliest* perceptual experiences, laid down in the first two to three months of life (Pacella, 1980). It is, perhaps, a bit of an imaginative stretch to extend this concept to two adults using twenty-first century screen technology who already have established their individual sensory systems. It is the same sort of stretch that analysts make when they say that their remaining senses are sharpened like a blind person's senses when they experience diminished sensory input while using technology.

In this case, it seems that the computer-mediated sessions afforded the patient an opportunity to engage in a simulation of an analytic encounter, protected by the barrier of the screen. The face-to-face meeting sent the patient into a position of defence and retreat, while the analyst protected the patient by maintaining a cordial social atmosphere. It is not reported whether this experience was thoroughly explored, but the implication was that the familiar mediated analytic pattern was simply resumed without comment.

"When I made an extended trip to China," Joanna, an analyst who teaches and treats patients for CAPA tells me, "some of my students travelled a thousand miles to meet me in person. My patient, on the other hand, refused point-blank to meet me when he was offered this rare opportunity. He declared that there was absolutely no possibility that he would travel any distance to have an in-person session. My patient used his computer extensively for interactive porn, as well as analysis with me. I think that meeting would have challenged a fantasy he was maintaining. Unfortunately, without the reality of a meeting, the fantasy can be continued, untested."

To have an embodied meeting is to break out of the entrapment, to stop protecting the *simulation*, and become aware of the differences and limitations of working screen-to-screen. This can be frightening and painful, and both therapist and patient may be unwilling even to think about comparing and contrasting their mediated and co-present experiences.

When Essig speaks professionally at workshops on technology and psychoanalysis, he suggests that an initial discussion with patients about the gains *and* losses of technologically mediated sessions should be considered an ethical requirement. He frequently encounters resistance from clinicians who are reluctant to initiate a discussion with their new patients about these issues. In addition, Essig experiences disinclination from workshop attendees when he suggests that they are also obligated to tell their patients that technology-based treatments are experimental procedures for which there is little or no available data or experience. To cite decades of psychoanalytic research and experience as evidence of efficacy, as Essig says someone inevitably suggests, is to operate within simulation entrapment, in denial that there is no difference between technologically mediated interaction and the shared environment experience. He is not saying that computer-mediated treatments are not helpful, but that they are profoundly different and cannot be regarded as simply a duplication of a shared embodied experience.

> Clinicians must focus on the differences between screen relations-based treatment and what happens with traditional physical co-presence. The basic questions are what is gained and what is lost. Only by asking these questions can clinicians and patients together make informed decisions about how best to proceed together.

He adds, "I think it is possible to be both in and out of the simulation, to experience moments of functional equivalence without becoming entrapped. In fact, that dual focus is what I think is the optimal listening stance" (personal communication, 2013). Essig defines his use of the term functional equivalence as that which has "the same (perceived effect) *for a particular purpose*—but not really the same process" (personal communication, April, 2013). The subtlety of distinguishing technologically mediated treatment as having the same *perceived* effect for a particular purpose as shared environment treatment—but a different process—is key. If it is a different *process*, then technologically mediated treatment may not sufficiently allow the realisation of the ultimate aim of psychoanalysis: for the patient to become most fully him/herself.

Extending the map

Communication requires not just a voice, not just the face, but the whole body. That whole body communicates not only with words, but paralinguistically through an array of non-verbal language, including gestures, movement, facial expression, posture, and all those meta-communications that are "between the lines". The therapeutic process requires both explicit and implicit action to be effective. While technologically mediated treatment might be able to convey explicit, language-based interventions, there are compelling questions as to whether it can support the implicit non-verbal aspects of the therapeutic relationship. The diminished sense of presence and the limited conveyance of implicit embodied communication might impinge on the efficacy of communication in screen-to-screen treatment.

Despite how various clinical pioneers have been thinking about these issues, there is scant psychoanalytic data on technologically mediated treatment as I write. The small number of published papers to date, consisting of some speculation and case reports, do not make use of current cross-disciplinary research in the fields of neuroscience, cognitive science, and human–computer behavioural science (sometimes called communication studies or informatics). For example, significant new neuroscientific thinking about embodied cognition includes the realisation that our vision of ourselves is embedded in our body, that action and perception are linked, that our sense of self and experience of existing is dependent upon intentionality. In view of the radically different experience of embodiment on the screen, this theory of cognition can be valuably incorporated into any investigation of mediated forms of communication in psychoanalytic treatment (Clark, 1998, 1999a; Damasio, 1999, 2005; Gallagher, 2005; Gallese,

2006; Lakoff, 1995; Pally, 1998; Riva, 2006, 2008, 2009; Schore, 2005; Waterworth & Waterworth, 2003b).

I discovered the digital frontier to be a place where minds and bodies, and thinking about minds and bodies, intertwine in new unexpected ways. "I come from Cyberspace, the new home of the mind", says Barlow (1996) in his Declaration of the Independence of Cyberspace. "Cyberspace consists of transactions, relationships, and thought itself, arrayed like a standing wave in the web of our communications. Ours is a world that is both everywhere and nowhere, but it is not where bodies live." What do we make of this dramatic statement, especially as applied to clinical work? After all, from the beginning of life, physical presence mediates our implicit and explicit transactions. The development of a sense of self, whether defined by psychoanalysis, neuroscience, cognitive science, or communication and computer science, requires a specific sense of physical presence. If it transpires that the sense of physical presence is experienced quite differently when mediated by technology (sometimes referred to as "telepresence"), it will be essential to assess just what those differences are. When bodies are not in the same environment, inevitably something is changed. So, we need to ask whether and how those changes are clinically important. How does the experience of being co-present bodies in psychoanalytic communication differ from the experience of engaging in a screen-to-screen therapeutic relationship? If, indeed, "the medium is the message", and these new technologies are already being accepted and utilised, it becomes imperative to understand the effects of computer-mediated communication on the therapeutic couple. An answer to these questions will not be found just on the digital frontier where practice pushes ahead of understanding. Instead, to find our answers, we have to move back to clinical consulting rooms and research laboratories across various disciplines.

PART II

IN THE CONSULTING ROOM AND THE RESEARCH LABORATORY

CHAPTER FOUR

What happens in the consulting room

Elements of therapeutic effectiveness

S ome years ago a general practitioner spoke to me of her mysti-
fication about what happens in psychotherapy. She said, with
rather vehement frustration, "I tried to find out about it when I
was training, but whenever I asked to observe what happened in the
consulting room they just wouldn't let me sit in!" It was interesting to
think about her rather circular problem, because without knowing
what happens in therapy, it is difficult for a non-therapist to imagine
why the process would not lend itself to a third party observer. Of
course, like the old joke, if you got three therapists together to try to
explain it to her, each explanation would differ.

Yet, determining just what happens in the consulting room is
important when we want to consider the relationship between the
therapeutic processes in single-environment sessions and technologically mediated sessions. What elements specifically constitute therapeutic action and are required for therapeutic effectiveness? The
answer to this question is perhaps much less straightforward than it
appears, as assessment of what is precisely therapeutic about psychoanalysis has changed over the years and still is a matter of fierce

debate. Recent developments in the analysis of what constitutes therapeutic action have expanded from Freud's original concept of the exclusive use of transference interpretation to create insight, and "transform what is unconscious into what is conscious" (Freud, 1916–1917, p. 294).

Freud developed the concept of the fundamental rule of free association in which the patient is required to verbalise whatever thoughts or feelings come to mind, without censorship or editing, in order to enable the emergence of a form of communication which makes the unconscious material more accessible:

> Say whatever goes through your mind. Act as though, for instance, you were a traveller sitting next to the window of a railway carriage and describing to someone inside the carriage the changing views which you see outside. (Freud, 1913c, p. 135)

The emphasis here is on a verbal transaction between the patient and analyst to which the analyst can respond with articulated interpretations of unconscious content to enable insight. For Freud, interpretation was the main mutative technique in psychoanalysis.

The Hungarian psychoanalyst Sandor Ferenczi, whose association with Freud would end in rupture, was one of the first to draw attention to the transformative impact of the reciprocal relationship of analyst and patient at both conscious and unconscious levels. He stressed the positive aspects of the relationship as central to the therapeutic process, rather than to be regarded as a failure of analytic neutrality. Bass (2003) points out,

> From the beginning of the talking cure, there was a strong tendency within classical circles to exclude action, in fact and theory, from a process that was regarded as verbal to the core. The distinction between talk and action, word and deed, was at the heart of Freud's theory of the mind and his development of analytic technique. (p. 659)

This tension between word and deed is a hallmark of the debate between the classical and relational schools of thought that has continued to the present day, particularly in the USA (Wallerstein, 1988).

In 1960, Loewald foreshadowed the broadening view of what effects psychic change in psychoanalysis by noting that change "is set in motion not simply by the technical skill of the analyst, but by the fact that the analyst makes himself available for the development of a new 'object-relationship' between the patient and the analyst" (Loewald, 1960, p. 17). British object relations theorists such as Donald Winnicott emphasised the analyst's establishment of a safe "holding" or facilitating environment in which the patient was able to internalise a new affective relationship between self and object (Winnicott, 1965). As a result of this groundwork, multiple modes of therapeutic action are now taken into account, so that there is no longer such a sharp demarcation between interpretative and relational aspects of thera-peutic elements in psychoanalysis. Gabbard and Westen (2003) suggest,

> Insight into aspects of the relationship itself that are corrective may foster further change, and the content of interpretive comments may at times be less important than the often unconscious meanings, including relational meanings, transmitted in the course of the inter-pretation. (p. 824)

The expansion of the definition of therapeutic action in the "talk-ing cure" to something more than verbal is significant in considering the elements that must be included in technologically mediated treat-ment for it to be considered feasible. If the curative properties of psychoanalysis continued to be considered purely verbal, then com-munication via computer, or telephone, for that matter, would not raise any questions for exploration. However,

> . . . contemporary analysts have come to appreciate the degree to which the transformative power of the psychoanalytic relationship is largely between the lines. While theorists of all persuasions strive to articulate the source of therapeutic action and change, daily clinical experience often reflects the powerful effect of what can be located in inchoate experience, the often preconscious resonance we have come to regard as enacted in the transference–countertransference. (Bass, 2003, p. 658)

Contemporary literature on the elements necessary to forward the therapeutic process therefore includes requirements comprising both the explicit interpretative action of the analyst and the more implicit aspects of the analytic relationship. We need to establish some historic clinical and theoretical ground from which to extend our considera-tion of the recent practice of technologically mediated psychoanalysis and psychoanalytic psychotherapy. If we can attempt to develop a framework to understand what actually happens in the consulting room, we can then begin to apply that to the practice of screen-to-screen treatment.

A safe, facilitating environment

Winnicott based his understanding of the establishment of what he called a "holding" environment in the analytic relationship on his observations of the mother–baby relationship. He described the "holding" or "environment" mother as a carer who provides continuity, stability, and a sense of "going on being". She offers her "reliable presence" and, in continuing to be herself, to be empathic, and to receive the infant's spontaneous gesture, she allows the infant to achieve the stability to develop towards independence (Winnicott, 1965, pp. 76–77). This maternal holding environment is carried over into the analytic setting. The setting promotes a "good-enough" environment enabling the patient to heal early psychic damage. In his 1955 paper, "Metapsychological and clinical aspects of regression within the psycho-analytical set-up", Winnicott began to separate aspects of interpretation and setting. He outlined "the material presented by the patient to be understood and to be interpreted", as well as, ". . . the setting in which this work is carried through" (p. 20). He listed twelve requirements for a safe setting in which to do analytic work, which he believed were Freud's intuitive choices for the original psychoanalytic setting:

1. At a stated time daily . . . [the analyst] puts himself . . . at the service of the patient. (This time was arranged to suit the convenience of both the analyst and the patient.)

2. The analyst would be reliably there, in time, alive, breathing.

3. For a limited period of time prearranged (about an hour) the analyst would keep awake and become preoccupied with the patient.

4. The analyst expressed love by the positive interest taken, and hate in the strict start and finish and in the matter of fees. Love and hate were honestly expressed, that is to say not denied by the analyst.

5. The aim of the analysis would be to get in touch with the process of the patient, to understand the material presented, to communicate this understanding in words. Resistance implied suffering and could be allayed by interpretation.

6. The analyst's method was of objective interpretation.

7. This work was to be done in a room, not a passage, a room that was quiet and not liable to sudden unpredictable sounds, yet not dead quiet and not free from ordinary house noises. The room would be lit properly, not by a light staring in the face, and not by a variable light. The room would certainly not be dark and it would be comfortably warm. The patient would be lying on a couch, that is to say comfortable if able to be comfortable, and probably a rug and some water would be available.

8. The analyst (as is well known) keeps moral judgment out of the relationship, has no wish to intrude with details of the analyst's personal life and ideas, and the analyst does not wish to take sides in the persecutory systems even when these appear in the form of real shared situations, local, political, etc. Naturally if there were a war or an earthquake or the king dies the analyst is not unaware.

9. In the analytic situation the analyst is much more reliable than people are in ordinary life; on the whole punctual, free from temper tantrums, free from compulsive falling in love, etc.

10. There is a very clear distinction in the analysis between fact and fantasy, so that the analyst is not hurt by an aggressive dream.

11. An absence of talion reaction can be counted on.

12. The analyst survives. (Winnicott, 1955, p. 21)

While Winnicott stressed the analyst's behaviour is central to this environment, none the less, he included the physical environment, specifically describing its characteristics, as part of the provision the analyst made for the patient. He called it, "The provision of a setting that gives confidence" (1955, p. 22).

Providing a safe holding environment to foster the possibility of psychic change has become part of the psychoanalytic clinical tradition (Balint, 1979; Langs, 1979; Milner, 1969; Modell, 1976). This concept is comparable to the "secure base" in Bowlby's attachment theory. In the therapeutic treatment, the therapist establishes an environment informed by consistency, responsiveness, and attunement. This does not only consist of the therapist him/herself, but also the therapist's frame, including consistency of time, place, room, and technique. ". . . there has to be a safe space, both literally in the therapist's room and also an 'internal' space in his or her mind" (Holmes, 2010, p. 90).

When considering the application of the concept of a safe holding environment to technologically mediated treatment, we hit an immediate snag. A safe holding environment cannot be established in the traditional way in the screen-to-screen relationship. Many analysts I interviewed, such as Bella, whose patient had to withdraw to a broom cupboard, expressed great frustration over their inability to provide a safe space for their patients. The patients I interviewed, such as Lucy, who missed having some of her basic needs met by her previously co-present analyst, felt the impact of having to provide for themselves in the analytic relationship. When the patient is in a separate setting no longer provided and managed by the practitioner, we have seen that there are serious challenges to the safety of the holding environment. Indeed, the requirement that the patient provide his/her own space could ultimately limit the therapeutic experience, just as the foreclosure of potentiality does. The patient is never allowed to have the experience of truly depending on the analyst in a place where he/she can "simply be" without impingement.

Evenly suspended attention and reverie

While Freud recommended that patients be encouraged to follow the fundamental rule of free association (Freud, 1913c), he suggested that the analyst adopt a complementary attitude of "evenly suspended attention" in which he

> could . . . surrender himself to his own unconscious mental activity . . . to avoid so far as possible reflection and the construction of conscious expectations, not to try to fix anything that he heard particularly in his memory, and by these means to catch the drift of the patient's unconscious with his own unconscious. (Freud, 1923a, p. 239)

Bion extended this concept of analytic listening, using the term "reverie". Like Winnicott, he based his observations on mother–infant behaviour: ". . . [the] state of mind which is open to the reception of any 'objects' from the loved object . . . therefore capable of reception of the infant's projective identifications whether they are felt by the infant to be good or bad" (Bion, 1962, p. 36). This state of readiness to contain the infant's intolerable emotions and return them detoxified, he termed "maternal reverie". Likewise, he encouraged the analyst to be open (as container) to holding the patient's projections, working in the present moment "without memory or desire" (Bion, 1967). This echoes Freud's injunction that the analyst "should simply listen, and not bother about whether he is keeping anything in mind" (Freud, 1912e, p. 112).

Ogden (1996) reconsidered and elaborated upon the necessity for reverie by describing it as a shared process between analyst and patient in which the unconscious interplay of both their states of mind creates an overlapping intersubjective experience. He emphasised the need for a shared space in which both the analyst and the analysand have the freedom and privacy each to turn their unconscious "like a receptive organ towards the transmitting unconscious" (Freud, 1912e, p. 115) of the other.

We have heard from both analysts and patients that this kind of free thinking, which is key to the analytic process, is a challenge to maintain in technologically mediated treatment. The limitations of the technology and the absence of the implicit cues normally available in co-present sessions tend to create a focused attention that hinders reverie. It is difficult to surrender oneself to the privacy of one's own unconscious when not assured of the presence of the other.

Provision of a new relational experience

As early as 1934, James Strachey theorised that patients internalised their analysts' neutrality in a way that softened a harsh superego (Strachey, 1934). Loewald, in his groundbreaking paper, "On the therapeutic action of psycho-analysis" (1960), spoke of structural changes in the patient's psyche that cause a resumption of stalled ego development dependent on a relationship with a new object, the analyst.

> I say new discovery of objects, and not discovery of new objects, because the essence of such new object relationships is the opportunity they offer for rediscovery of early paths of the development of

object relations, leading to a new way of relating to objects as well as of being and relating to oneself. (Loewald, 1960, p. 18)

This echoes Winnicott's extensive work based on his paediatric experience with infants. The patient is enabled to use the analyst as a separate object, if the analyst is able to provide a facilitating environment (the "good-enough" analyst) in which the patient can begin to experience the analyst as a resilient, non-retaliating object (Winnicott, 1965, 1969).

The therapeutic relationship offers a different experience of relating in which the patient internalises various functions and attitudes of the analyst.

> [Interpretations] combine with the material setting provided by the analyst to form the analyst's affective contribution to the formation of a trial relationship, within which the patient can recapture the ability to make contact and communication with external objects. (Rycroft, 1956, p. 472, my italics)

The patient is enabled "to find himself in the therapist's mind and integrate this image as part of a sense of himself" (Fonagy & Target, 2000, p. 870).

Of particular significance in the consideration of the therapeutic relationship as a conduit of therapeutic action are the non-verbal effects of the analyst's presence and the reciprocal perception of analyst and patient's non-verbal cues, which can operate relatively independently of both language and consciousness. The subject of non-verbal communication has become particularly pertinent for psychoanalysis, especially in view of recent research in cognitive neuroscience, which I will discuss later. It has been said that 60% of communication is non-verbal (Burgoon et al., 1989), and the analysis of that body-to-body exchange must be relevant both in the consulting room and in screen relations.

Interpretation and insight

Interpretation, which is aimed at promoting insight, is also fundamental to analytic activity. It is an explicit intervention by the analyst whereby he/she expresses an understanding of the patient's inner world, Freud's (1916–1917) method of bringing the unconscious into consciousness. Interpretations may be based on the patient's descriptions of memories, fears, wishes, fantasies, expectations, and other expressions of psychic conflict formerly unconscious or only partially known to the patient.

These observations may include extra-transferential material not directly exhibited in the therapeutic relationship or transference interpretations that involve "here and now" explanations of repetition and distortions in the therapeutic relationship that the patient replicates from past experiential patterns (Moore & Fine, 1990). A well-timed interpretation, in which the analyst is able to meet the patient at a point of readiness to hear and internalise the observation, can lead the patient, through understanding his or her internal world, to make a shift in feelings and behaviour.

Interpretations are explicit communications that certainly can be transmitted via technological mediation. Questions will arise, however, when we explore the genesis of the well-timed interpretation. If the verbal message is rooted in an embodied implicit experience of the other, how well can we participate in this joint implicit process screen-to screen?

Other types of intervention

Several subsidiary methods of intervention can contribute to significant psychic change. Many kinds of challenge contain implicit or explicit suggestions for change. Although the analyst attempts to refrain from being directive, simply pointing out a patient's patterns of behaviour can imply areas that are unresolved and require exploration. Related to this is direct confrontation that might be required to overcome an analytic impasse and the exploration of impaired, distorted, or irrational beliefs, with the implication that the analyst may have a differing point of view (Stewart, 1990). Handled sensitively, this strategy can be a useful method of helping the patient to begin to see the potential for two separate minds operating in the same space. Mutual problem solving, involving the therapist and patient thinking together about new conscious ways of decision making, can also redirect the trajectory of a patient's growth (Gabbard & Westen, 2003).

A therapist's circumspect self-exposure for damaged patients with impaired capacity for mentalization, both explicit and implicit affirmation, and finally "facilitative strategies", which include those forms of social and communicational processes that serve to enable a satisfactory working alliance, all have their places in a psychoanalytic treatment (Castonguay & Beutler, 2006; Gabbard & Westen, 2003, p. 836). These auxiliary practices, which are cognitive and largely language-based, and the primary elements such as the centrality of the therapeutic relationship outlined above, are also highlighted by the Task Force of Division 12 of the American Psychological Association and the North American Society for Psychotherapy Research as principles of therapeutic change in their comprehensive review, *Principles of Therapeutic Change that Work* (Castonguay & Butler, 2006).

Having outlined what psychoanalysts propose happens in the consulting room to promote therapeutic action and change and begun to consider whether or not this might be realised through technological mediation, we will now turn to the recent contributions that neuroscience has made to widen and deepen our understanding of communication between therapist and patient.

CHAPTER FIVE

From the first laboratory: neuroscience connections

N o enquiry into the nature of the mechanisms of communication in the consulting room, much less the forms it might take when mediated through a technological device, can ignore the recent attention that psychoanalysts are giving to the non-verbal aspects of practice and the underlying neuroscientific hypotheses and research. There is a body of neuroscience and cognitive science that is of great interest to psychoanalysts wishing to find some sort of explicative bridge between daily clinical experience and theoretical inheritance. While there are a number of competing explanatory models in neuropsychoanalysis, they share many commonalities that are useful for thinking about possible communicative processes.

Freud said that "the ego is first and foremost a bodily ego" (1923b, p. 26). Winnicott wrote that if a baby reaches a state in which it has a sense of wholeness, then it is "living in the body" (Winnicott, 1975b, p. 264). Yet, as Jacobs (1994) points out, although Freud was historically a perspicacious observer of his patients' non-verbal behaviour, he did not develop this area of his analytic work, and his theories advanced more in relation to verbal communication. As psychoanalysts have become increasingly interested in non-verbal communication, what Grotstein (2005) calls "body rhetoric", they have begun to study and synthesise information across various fields of study, including infant observation, cognitive psychology, and neuroscience (e.g., Bucci, 1994, 2000, 2002; Lyons-Ruth, 1998; Nahum, 2002; Olds, 2006; Pally, 1998; Schore, 2010, 2011; Stern et al., 1998; Westen & Gabbard, 2002a,b).

Neuroscience, itself, has had a paradigm shift in the last two decades. No longer is Cartesian mind–body dualism regarded as a model, with the body considered as peripheral to the understanding of the nature of the mind. Rather than the mind being considered an independent entity, it is dependent upon emotions emanating from the body, as well as movements and actions (Clark, 1998, 1999b; Damasio, 2005; Lakoff, 1995; Sheets-Johnstone, 1998).

> Certain implications for our vision of ourselves are clear. We must abandon the image of ourselves as essentially disembodied reasoning engines, and we must do so not simply by insisting that the mental is fully determined by the physical, but by accepting that we are beings whose neural profiles are profoundly geared so as to press maximal benefit from the opportunities afforded by bodily structure, action, and environmental surroundings. Biological brains are, at root, controllers of embodied action. Our cognitive profile is essentially the profile of an embodied and situated organism. (Clark, 1999b, p. 14)

The nature of the human mind is determined by the form of the human body, and properties of cognition, emotion, and consciousness are shaped by properties of the body. This view has been called "embodied cognition" (Wilson & Foglia, 2011, para.1).

Lakoff, in his innovative co-authored book *Metaphors We Live By* (Lakoff & Johnson, 2003), suggests that rather than being a purely linguistic construction, metaphor is conceptual, embodied, and central to the development of thought. "Our ordinary conceptual system, in terms of which we both think and act, is fundamentally metaphorical in nature" (p. 3). He claims,

> We are neural beings. Our brains take their input from the rest of our bodies. What our bodies are like and how they function in the world thus structures the very concepts we can use to think. We cannot just think anything—only what our embodied brains permit. (Brockman, 1999)

For example, we speak metaphorically using human spatial concepts: "The stock market is *up*"; "Prices are going *down*". Lakoff and Johnson argue that our proprioceptive experience, our bodily position in space, informs the construction of language via metaphor. The metaphorical process moves from a more concrete concept rooted in the physical and interactive body to the target of a more abstract concept. In the metaphor that "life is a journey," for instance, the conceptualisation of life involves our assumptions about the concrete experience of journeys: we are embodied beings who move through the world intentionally. Life is the corresponding abstract concept being elucidated by our physical experience of journeying. Metaphors are linked to our sensorimotor experience. The regularity with which different languages use the same metaphors has led to theories that they are computed neurally via circuitry connecting the sensorimotor system with higher cortical areas of the brain (Lakoff & Johnson, 2003, pp. 254–259). The body is the source of meaning and the development of thought. "The mind is embodied, in the full sense of the term, not just embrained" (Damasio, 2005, p. 118).

An emerging trend within the field of embodied cognition is the recognition that action and perception are linked. As will be discussed below, with reference to the philosophers Merleau-Ponty and Heidegger, perception requires an active organism. To quote Gallagher from *How the Body Shapes the Mind*:

> Conscious experience is normally of an intermodally seamless spatial system . . . One of the important functions of the body in the context of perception and action is to provide the basis for an egocentric [body-centered] spatial frame of reference. Indeed, this egocentric framework is required for the very possibility of action, and for the general structure of perceptual experience. The fact that perception and action are perspectivally spatial (for example, the book appears to my right or to my left, or in the center of my perceptual field) is a fact that depends precisely on the spatiality of the perceiving and acting body. (Gallagher, 2005, p. 59)

Perception, and the sense of "being-in-the-world" (Dreyfus, 1991) depends on interaction between the subject and the environment, and also relates to our body position and functions: *"the awareness of the environment derives from how it reacts to our movements"* (Riva et al., 2006).

In *Descartes' Error*, neuroscientist Antonio Damasio (2005) argues that emotions themselves are embedded in the body and have a direct connection and influence on everyday reasoning and conscious decision-making. They arise in the body before one experiences a conscious feeling. He proposes that emotions such as pain and pleasure form the basis for an organism's rationality, which are body-based and survival orientated.

Recent cognitive models variously termed subsymbolic (Bucci, 1997), connectionist (Westen & Gabbard, 2002a,b) and parallel distributed processing (Rumelhart et al., 1986, cited in Westen & Gabbard, 2002a) emphasise the fact that most information processing takes place simultaneously in multiple parallel channels, largely outside conscious awareness. This implicit domain does not have the form of verbal language, and in addition to visual images, it includes images and perceptions in other senses. It is related to experiences such as intuition, empathy, and emotional communication between individuals (Bucci, 2002; Westen & Gabbard, 2002a).

While an in-depth exploration of contemporary cognitive models is beyond the scope of this book, I feel it is crucial to stress the significance of the conclusion of this ongoing research as it applies both to psychoanalysis and, particularly, to the conducting of psychoanalysis via technology. Much of cognition is unconscious. Emotions are communicated via facial movement and bodily movement, in nuanced ways that might require bodies actually being together to perform. Intersubjective relating involves an embodied interaction, that which the French philosopher Merleau-Ponty would call "intercorporeity", communication between two bodies: "it is precisely my body which perceives the body of another, and discovers in that other body a miraculous prolongation of my own intentions, a familiar way of dealing with the world" (Merleau-Ponty, 1962, p. 354; see also, Gallagher & Roy, 2011).

Vittorio Gallese (2006), a professor of neurophysiology and social neuroscience at the University of Parma, borrows the word "intercorporeity" from Merleau-Ponty to describe his theory of embodied simulation, which is automatic, non-conscious, and prelinguistic.

Mirror neurons and embodied simulation

In the early 1990s, a new class of premotor neurons was discovered in the macaque monkey brain. It was found that the neuron fired both when the animal acted and when it observed the same action performed by others (for a full explication of this research, see Gallese et al., 1996; Rizzolatti et al., 1996). Neurons with similar properties were later identified in humans (Gallese et al., 2007), where the mere observation of an object-related hand action caused an automatic activation in the observer of the same neural network that was active in the person performing the action.

The discovery of these neurons caused great excitement in both the cognitive neuroscientific and psychoanalytic communities. Experimental research by Marco Iacoboni at the UCLA Brain Mapping Center suggested that the observations of actions embedded in contexts yielded a significant signal increase, indicating not just action recognition, but an understanding of the "why" of the action: action intention (Gallese et al., 2007). For example, mirror neurons could indicate, by means of the area of the brain they fired in, whether a person observed picking up a cup from a table was intending to drink from it or clear it away. This led them to hypothesise that mirror neurons might be the basis for helping the human to understand the actions and intentions of other people, including the human capacity of empathy. Iacoboni explained in an interview,

> When you see me perform an action—such as picking up a baseball—you automatically simulate the action in your own brain . . . When you see me pull my arm back, as if to throw the ball, you also have in your brain a copy of what I am doing, and it helps you understand my goal. Because of mirror neurons, you can read my intentions. You know what I am going to do next . . . and if you see me choke up, in emotional distress . . . mirror neurons in your brain simulate my distress. You automatically have empathy for me. You know how I feel because you literally feel what I am feeling. (Blakeslee, 2006, p. C3)

Gallese and colleagues (2007) use the term "embodied simulation" to describe

> a mandatory, nonconscious, and prereflexive mechanism that is not the result of deliberate and conscious effort aimed at interpreting the intentions hidden at the overt behavior of others . . . It uses the outcome of simulated actions, emotions, or sensations to attribute this outcome to another organism as a real goal-state it is trying to bring about, or as a real emotion or sensation it is experiencing. (p. 143)

Note that Gallese and co-authors have included emotion and sensation in their description and suggest that this is not achieved by "analogy" (the *conscious* generating of the imagined or predicted mental states of the other, their desires, feelings, and beliefs), but by a direct *non-conscious* experience consisting of a shared body state.

> According to this hypothesis, when we confront the intentional behaviour of others, embodied simulation, a specific mechanism by means of which our brain–body system models its interactions with the world, generates a specific phenomenal state of "intentional attunement" . . . by means of embodied simulation we do not just "see" an action, and emotion, or a sensation. Side by side with the sensory description of the observed social stimuli, internal representations of the body states associated with these actions, emotions, and sensations are evoked in the observer "as if" he or she were doing a similar action or experiencing a similar emotion or sensation. (Gallese et al., 2007, p. 144)

Gallese and colleagues (2007, p. 145) use Meltzoff and Moore's (1977) studies of newborns merely hours old who were capable of imitating adult mouth and tongue movements, not in a reflexive way, but in a responsive way that matches the observed behaviour of an other. The newborn was able to translate visual information into motor information in a process Meltzoff called "active intermodal mapping", which is not limited to any one form of interaction, visual, auditory, or motor. Gallese and colleagues (2007) relate this capacity to the existence of shared neural sensorimotor networks which form the basis of intersubjective processes similar to Winnicott's (1971a) "apperception" (the mirror-role of the mother) and Stern's (1985) concept of "affective attunement". Infant researchers such as Meltzoff and Stern describe, respectively, presymbolic and early symbolic forms of intersubjectivity that predate the theory of mirror neurons. Their observations suggest that the infant recognises correspondences between his/her action and that of an other. Mirror neurons may be seen as an underlying biological counterpart to their theories of infant perception (Beebe et al., 2005).

There are varying responses to the research on mirror neurons. Some researchers hail their discovery as the key to our humanity, including our powers of empathy, language, and culture. Others are far more cautious, reminding us that we are in the very early stages of mirror neuron research and suggesting that they are embedded in a complex network of brain activity (Jarrett, 2013; Kliner & Lemon, 2013). James Kliner and Roger Lemon (2013), neuroscientists at University College, London write in a balanced review of research thus far,

> For us, the discovery of mirror neurons was exciting because it has lead to a new way of thinking about how we generate our own actions and how we monitor and interpret the actions of others. This discovery prompted the notion that, from a functional viewpoint, action execution and observation are closely-related processes, and indeed our ability to interpret the actions of others requires the involvement of our own motor system. (p. 1057)

What is important here is the concept that our ability to understand the intentions and actions of others is at least in part an implicit embodied experience.

Naturally, these findings have significance and implications for psychoanalysis, where the unconscious dialogue between the analyst and patient is pivotal to the therapeutic action. Gallese and co-authors propose that based on the findings related to mirror neurons and embodied simulation, virtually any interpersonal interaction would create an unconscious "induction" in each participant of what the other is feeling (p. 148). While this implicit resonance is not therapeutic in itself, it could certainly contribute to an empathic understanding between therapist and patient, leading to the therapist's "metabolising" of the patient's affective expression (Bion, 1970). The findings might have implications for transference–countertransference processes, as well as such mechanisms as projective identification. Finally, Gallese and colleagues point out that while the mirror system and embodied simulation may be hardwired into the body, there are a wide range of individual differences in the ways that those capacities are realised, in both mother–infant and patient–therapist relationships. If the relationship is "good-enough", then the underlying neural system enables the mother/therapist, like Winnicott's mirroring mother, to respond to the baby/patient with empathic understanding, which helps the patient to establish an authentic sense of self.

Memory systems

Along with the shift of perspectives on cognitive processing, there has been a re-examination and new definition of memory. Two kinds of memory, explicit and implicit, with very different features and neural substrates have been described (Westen & Gabbard, 2002a). Explicit memory consists of episodic memory, including the autobiographical recollections, memories of life experience, and generic memory, which is all conscious memory that is not autobiographical, including semantic memory, learnt information, and theory.

Implicit memory is observable in behaviour (for example, typing on a keyboard or playing the piano), but not consciously brought to mind. There are two kinds of implicit memory: procedural, the type of memory that allows people to remember how to ride a bicycle or tie their shoes without consciously thinking about the process, and associative memory. Associative memory, to which we do not have conscious access, consists of the ability to learn and remember implicitly the relationship between unrelated items.

While the action of explicit memory in the consulting room may be familiar (both members of the therapeutic couple remember details of the patient's life, dreams, past sessions, etc.), both forms of implicit memory have equal significance to therapeutic practice. It could be suggested that the transference, itself, is an unconscious enactment of procedural memory (Clyman, 1991). Freud wrote, in "Remembering, repeating, and working-through",

> . . . the patient does not *remember* anything of what he has forgotten and repressed but *acts* it out. He reproduces it not as a memory but as an action; he *repeats* it, without, of course, knowing that he is repeating it . . . the patient does not say that he remembers that he used to be defiant and critical towards his parents' authority; instead, he behaves in that way to the doctor. (1914g, p. 150)

It has been suggested by the Boston Change Process Study Group (2010) that forms of procedural memory are connected with the implicit knowledge of relating. Procedural or implicit memory is embodied, non-verbal, and emotional. They describe an implicit procedural knowledge that specifically involves knowing about interpersonal and intersubjective interaction, in addition to implicit procedural memory of performing actions such as riding a bicycle. Associative memory gives us the unconscious means to find connections in patients' narrative material. Again, both forms of implicit memory are unconscious and instantaneous processes. Memory has implications for the experience of the thread of continuity in psychoanalytic treatment, the possibility for relational connection, and the holding of the other in mind.

The theme of memory as it relates to the use of technology first came up for me in a curious way. In conversation with peers who were using computers for treatment, we noticed that technologically mediated sessions were easy to forget. Highly experienced practitioners who rarely, if ever, had forgotten a co-present session found it difficult to remember a scheduled screen session: "I was working in my office and checked my emails. Only then, when I saw his [the patient's] email asking where I was did I realise I had completely forgotten his session. This has never happened to me before. I felt terrible about it," says one colleague. "If I had not had the computer on and heard the Skype ring tone, I would have missed the session," adds another.

We wondered why so many of us had these completely uncharacteristic lapses. We can speculate about the impact of a co-present experience *vs.* a screen experience on the memory. Is there something about being present in a shared environment, with a rich exchange of multi-sensory communication, which is more memorable than two-dimensional images on screens? Certainly, remote workers have encountered the "out of sight, out of mind" phenomenon, even when they have experimented with leaving a screen open in the office all the time, so that the absent person can be referred to or chatted with "as if" they were really present. Scott Hanselman, a remote worker with Microsoft, went so far as to design a mobile "embodied social proxy", which he also calls a "crazy webcam remote cart thing" (Hanselman, 2010). He explains,

> . . . the idea is that you want a physical stand-in for yourself. Sure, people can call me and contact me in any of a dozen ways, and honestly, it's one click at Microsoft. I'm on the address list, I'm on chat, and I've even got a 5-digit phone extension. I've done all this and more to integrate into headquarters. However, out of sight, out of mind is really true. *People subconsciously or not like to associate something physical with you.* (2010, my italics)

Hanselman's embodied social proxy increased his fellow workers' attention and rapport with him. The fact of its physical presence improved their interpersonal relationships: he was no longer so completely "out of sight, out of mind". But it was not just the physical presence that was important. After all, he had previously appeared on a stationary screen that was always on and made him constantly available for chat and consultation. What was different was the mobility of this contraption, in which he was "embodied". He could control his proxy's physical movements in three-dimensional space within the remote location, and that made a more abiding impression on his colleagues.

The embodied experience of acting and moving in space is connected to learning, mental processing, and memory. Movement and the three-dimensional qualities of physical co-presence may make a greater and more lasting impact on our memories. Researchers have found that the experience of more complex movement, such as handwriting as opposed to typing, not only improves cognitive abilities, but also affects memory. "There is something really important about manually manipulating and drawing out two-dimensional things we see all the time", says Karin Harman James, Assistant Professor of Psychology at Indiana University, who led an MRI study on the affect of handwriting on learning and memory (Bounds, 2010). Significantly for clinicians doing screen-to-screen treatment, she is referring specifically to transforming that which we experience in two dimensions to a physical experience in three dimensions and how it affects our brains.

Other research points to the hand's particular relationship with the brain when it comes to constructing thoughts and ideas. Dr Virginia Berninger, a professor of educational psychology at the University of Washington, notes that the hand and finger movements involved in writing activate vast regions of the brain involved in thinking, language, and memory. In contrast, typing, the pressing of identical-looking keys, does not affect the brain in this complex way (Bounds, 2010). The richer our embodied experience of acting and moving in space, the more profoundly it affects our perceptions, consciousness, and memory.

Is our experience of two-dimensional screen relations attenuated in such a way as to make less of an impact on our memories?

For some analysts, remembering a screen-to-screen session itself presents a problem:

It is more difficult to remember and internalise Skype sessions . . . I took really copious notes. It's not really how I work [in a shared environment]. It helped me to stay on track and keep it somehow, not just in note form, but in me, it was a way to stay with [the patient] . . . especially during long silences, when I felt I might come unmoored. I don't have a problem with that in person, but with a machine, I'm thinking, writing something like "long pause; I'm thinking x, y, z", was a way to stay connected with him.

This analyst compensates for the difficulty in retaining two-dimensional screen sessions by introducing a sensorimotor component, a way to interact physically with his environment rather than making an internal representation of his environment, like a photograph. Memory, as well as learning and cognition, is inextricably connected to our three-dimensional audio-visual, tactile interactions with our surroundings and using a pen and paper enhanced this analyst's perception and recall of the session.

The three scientists who won the 2014 Nobel prize in Physiology and Medicine, John O'Keefe and May-Britt and Edward Moser, suggest that navigation, knowing how to find one's way in physical space, is intimately related to the way memories are created and stored (Moser & Moser, 2014). They discovered place cells and grid cells, two types of neurons in the brain that enable us to navigate our environment. These cells, which have been dubbed an inner "GPS", give animals and humans the survival skills necessary to find their way through the physical world, knowing where they are, where they have been, and where they are going. The scientists suggest that the same neural systems and algorithms support both physical travel and the mental travel of memory (Buzsáki & Moser, 2013, p. 130). "Essentially, while your brain is making mental maps to help you navigate, it is also overlaying memories—experiences, smells—onto those maps" (Moser & Moser, 2014, p. 2).

The cells connected with navigation and the cells connected with memory are both located largely in the hippocampus region of the brain. "Place and memory are intimately related," says University of Pennsylvania computational psychologist Michael J. Kahana. "Space forms a powerful context in which our memories are encoded . . . That's why this model of how the brain maps the world is so important to who we are as human beings" (Healy, 2014, par. 10). We have seen that when we link movement to experience, we remember it better. If "Memory is deeply and physically connected to our perception and encoding of space" (Moser & Moser, 2014, p. 4), then it is possible that sitting stationary in front of a screen and engaging with a two-dimensional image does not as actively involve those neurons that are engaged when travelling to a session or moving through space in a consulting room.

Episodic memory, explicit autobiographical memory (that is, related to words) is far more fragile and less reliable than implicit memory, which is non-verbal and seated in the body (Clayton et al., 2007). It might be that not having all the cues and implicit communication of a body-to-body relationship affects what we are able to absorb and retain, if that which is embodied and implicit underpins memory.

Those analysts who start work in a shared environment and transfer to computer-mediated treatment, or who continue to meet co-presently with their patients intermittently while also using technology, observe that their memories of working in a shared environment with their patients better enable them to continue a sensitive connection with them in a technologically mediated communication. Anna, a London analyst, speaking of a patient who had moved abroad, refers to it as "an inner template being laid down".

> I had to carry over the quality of knowing her for real as opposed to virtual . . . the quality of being with her in the room had a three-dimensional quality to it and a plastic quality . . . which allows the unconscious to communicate itself. You could almost say that it is a fourth dimension that works between us in that real situation, and in the screen-to-screen [situation] we were both working hard to try and use every ounce of what we knew about that. That is what I would think she was doing, as well as I.

Implicit and explicit memory of co-presence, being bodies together, might help the therapeutic couple to bridge the relational gap. Research needs to be done to examine and evaluate memory processes as they carry over from embodied relational encounters to technologically mediated encounters, and as they affect the thread of experiential continuity between screen-to-screen sessions.

Between the lines: implicit factors in the psychoanalytic process

For almost two decades, the members of the Boston Change Process Study Group (BCPSG) have been exploring and attempting to define the mechanisms of change in psychoanalytic therapy (BCPSG, 2007, 2008; Lyons-Ruth, 1998; Nahum, 2002, 2008; Stern et al., 1998). Basing their thinking on both infant observational research and experiences in adult therapy, they have applied a developmental perspective to clinical material. They have identified two realms, or "domains", of human interaction: that which is implicit and that which is explicit or "reflective-verbal" (Nahum, 2008). Implicit interaction is not primarily language-based, and neither is it normally translated into symbolic form, while explicit interaction involves the transformation of experience into verbal expression.

They describe implicit experience as rooted in the body and cite the concept of the "embodied mind" as the domain from which the verbal/explicit emerges.

> Movement and language (although different modes) are largely integrated during evolution and ontogeny. One cannot think or feel or imagine or have sensations without the direct participation of one's body. Conversely, to move or to act is inherently an expression of mental intention. (Nahum, 2008, p. 134)

Implicit processing begins at birth and continues throughout life. This implicit processing informs the moment-to-moment exchanges that occur in all relating, including psychoanalysis and psychotherapy. It is not replaced when language appears; neither is it inevitably converted to language later in development. It is not necessarily more primitive than the reflective-verbal domain and continues to grow alongside it, when that stage has been reached. It is intuitive and based on action and affect rather than language and symbol. It is not conscious, but not repressed. In development, language is intrinsically grounded in implicit relational experience (BCPSG, 2007). The BCPSG distinguishes it from non-verbal:

> The implicit can be revealed through verbal as well as nonverbal forms of interaction. However, the implicit aspects of meaning are not in the content of the words themselves. The implicit meaning exists, so to speak, *between the lines* . . . (BCPSG, 2007, p. 851 my italics)

In their seminal paper, "Non-interpretive mechanisms in psychoanalytic therapy: the 'something more' than interpretation", Stern and colleagues (1998) suggest that implicit relational knowing is part of "the shared implicit relationship", the area of overlap in each partner's implicit knowledge about their relationship. They define it as implicit procedural knowledge (as in procedural memory, above, such as riding a bicycle or playing tennis), non-symbolic, and outside conscious verbal experience. It specifically involves knowing about interpersonal and intersubjective relations: how to "be with someone" (Stern, 1985).

> It is an intuitive sense, based on one's history . . . based on affect and action, rather than word and symbol . . . By design, everything that the pre-verbal infant knows about interactions with others is contained in his implicit knowledge. Implicit knowing also makes up the majority of what we, as adults, know about social interaction, including transference. (BCPSG, 2007, p. 845)

Clinically, implicit relational knowing is significant in making up what the analyst and patient know of what is in the other's mind, and the current state of their relationship. The shared knowing may remain implicit, or it may be made conscious through interpretation. If the implicit relational knowledge is transformed into explicit conscious knowledge, it is not the same as making the repressed unconscious conscious. The BCPSG describe a developmentally informed model based on processes in which implicit knowledge can lead to long-lasting therapeutic change. This model involves what they call "moments of meeting" in which something new is created in the mutual analytic relationship which alters the intersubjective environment, resulting in new behaviour and experiences (Stern et al., 1998).

A detailed analysis of the above process can be found in the BCPSG's paper, "Forms of relational meaning" (2008). The relevant foundations of the BCPSG's theory are summarised as follows. Like Gallese (2006), they discuss intention, and assign it significance as "the fundamental psychological meaning" (Nahum, 2008). Intentionality is the sense of acting, or being acted upon, toward a goal, or construing that an other is similarly acting or being acted upon. They describe sequences of intentions as giving motivated human behaviour coherence and meaning, whether they are encountered in actions or in language. All phases of an intention—its formation phase, its execution, and its aim—comprise "the intention unfolding process". The "intention unfolding process is a nonsymbolic process-representation of motivated experience that is grasped implicitly" (Nahum, 2008, p. 129). This intuitive grasp of one's own or another's intention is linked to physical experience, action, and emotion. The most rudimentary form of this concept could be connected with Gallese's research into mirror neurons. The intention unfolding process, which happens in seconds, is dynamic, unpredictable, and widely distributed in the body. We are embodied beings and language is deeply interwoven with movement and gesture. Intentions can be expressed and read both implicitly and explicitly. The verbal version of the intention unfolding process is grounded in the non-verbal implicit domain. It is the intuitive perception of that totality which allows us to comprehend the dynamic embodied meaning of a communication (Nahum, 2008, pp. 142–145).

Philosophers such as Heidegger and Merleau-Ponty also believed that the experience of existing is centred on intentionality, and that intentionality is embedded in an embodied experience of the world (Riva et al., 2006). "It is the relationship of embodied, intentional experience and action toward a situation which constitutes embodied being-in-the-world" (Beck, 1976, quoted in Meissner, 1998a, p. 90). Merleau-Ponty connected the embodied experience of existing and acting in space with the capacity to move through space, thus continually changing our perceptive and proprioceptive experience of the world (Meissner, 1998a). Meissner, applying Merleau-Ponty's philosophy to psychoanalysis, writes,

> Motility becomes a form of intentionality in the sense that it substitutes the possibility of action for the Cartesian *cogito*. Motility is not simply the handmaiden of consciousness, the transportation vehicle for consciousness; rather like perception, it is part and parcel of our presence in the world. They are both forms of intentionality which meet the world as embodied presence articulated through space and time. (1998a, p. 91)

Sheets-Johnstone (2011) suggests that we discover our selves and the world through the "primacy of movement", proposing that our embodied consciousness leads to embodied concepts and representations as well as kinaesthetic ones. Following the theories of embodied cognition, corporeal and kinaesthetic images are activated as we speak: we are embodying our words. Indeed, research into gesture that accompanies speech finds that the gesture we use to accompany speech does not require either a model or an observer, but seems integral to the speaking process itself. It suggests that these gestures might reflect, or even facilitate, the thinking that underlies speaking (Iverson & Goldin-Meadow, 1998).

The BCPSG proposes that our language flow is embedded in our bodies and formed by implicit relational knowing, which informs its meaning. They submit that in the consulting room, the analyst/patient hears the verbal message and gathers the underlying implicit experience that engenders the words, and feels the difference between the two. The listener grasps a "gestalt" and must then, in an act of reflection, make a whole meaning of this gestalt (Nahum, 2008). This process comprises three steps of the "intention unfolding process".

1. The intention is implicitly experienced.
2. A verbal version of this implicit experience is rooted in the non-verbal mental/body concepts contained in the implicit domain.
3. There is an inevitable disconnection between the implicit and the verbal, which needs to be considered and embraced as part of the "gestalt" of the communication (Nahum, 2008, p. 145).

The gestalt of the implicitly experienced intention, the verbal version of this implicit experience, and the unavoidable disconnection between the two, is communicated as a whole in the intention unfolding process.

Communication is the vehicle of relationship. Communication conducted in our most intimate relationships, based on developmental observation of infants, contains a significant implicit component, arguably equal or carrying more weight than the explicit component. Both the implicit and explicit domains of human communication are embodied, and our sense of self and embodied experience of existing is dependent on intentionality, moving and acting in space. Much of the intricate interaction between analyst and analysand does not receive explicit verbal focus, making procedures of the shared implicit relationship crucial in the process of therapeutic change. Technologically mediated therapeutic communication is inherently two-dimensional, with narrowed and differently processed sensory communication, and with limits on the potential of moving and acting in a shared space. Can it act as a sufficient conduit for the complexity of this implicit component of communication that lies at the heart of our deepest relational transactions, and from which explicit communication emerges?

The right brain and implicit processes

Concurrent with the BCPSG's research into what constitutes change in psychoanalysis, Allan Schore also focuses his extensive work on the role of implicit affective processes in effecting psychotherapeutic change (2005, 2010, 2011; see www.allanschore.com/index.php for a full review). He highlights the central role of implicit cognition, implicit affect, communication, and affective regulation in the psychotherapeutic model with particular attention to right brain unconscious mechanisms. A psychoanalytic pioneer in integrating a substantial amount of interdisciplinary evidence, Schore cites current neuroscientists in asserting that the right hemisphere of the brain gives birth to the implicit self, the framework of the human unconscious (2005, 2011). He suggests, as does the BCPSG, that the therapist manoeuvres through the moment-to-moment affect-laden therapeutic interaction "not by left brain explicit secondary process cognition, but [by] right brain implicit primary process affectively driven clinical intuition" (2011, p. 75). He stresses that access to these right brain implicit processes by both patient and therapist is essential for effective treatment.

As the BCPSG describes the implicit domain as continuing to grow and develop alongside the reflective-verbal/explicit realm throughout life, Schore depicts the early-forming implicit self as also continuing to develop, although functioning in qualitatively distinct ways to the later-forming conscious explicit self.

Locating this implicit realm lateralised in the right brain, Schore argues,

> in addition to *implicit cognition* (right brain unconscious processing of exteroceptive information from the outer world and interoceptive information from the inner world) the implicit concept also includes *implicit affect*, *implicit communication*, and *implicit self-regulation*. (2011, p. 77)

Schore quotes neuroscientists as contending that the right hemisphere is centrally involved in "maintaining a coherent, continuous and unified sense of self" (Devinsky, 2000, quoted in Schore, 2011). While the left brain mediates most linguistic, conscious, explicit, secondary process behaviours, including explicit analytic reasoning, the right brain is crucial for wider aspects of communication, including free association and reverie, mediated by a "relational unconscious" (Schore, 2011 p. 78). This would include clinical intuition, which Schore considers a major factor in therapeutic effectiveness.

Schore offers a model of implicit communications within the therapeutic relationship, involving right-brain-to-right-brain transference and countertransference communications, representing interactions of the therapeutic couple's unconscious primary process systems. While secondary process communication is conveyed explicitly by words, primary process information, which is largely affective and embedded in the relationship, is communicated non-verbally. This non-verbal communication can include body posture and movements, gesture, facial expression, tone of voice, and speech rhythm (Dorpat, 2001, p. 451). Schore adds,

> In light of the fact that the left hemisphere is dominant for certain aspects of language but the right for emotional communication, I have proposed the psychotherapy process is best described not as "the talking cure" but "the communicating cure". (2005, p. 840)

This "communicating cure", involving both mind and body, comprises a wide range of implicit non-verbal actions that might require co-presence to be conveyed and comprehended.

Using interdisciplinary studies from infant research and neuroscience (i.e., Brancucci et al., 2009; Minagawa-Kawai et al.; Papousek, 2007), Schore suggests that the implicit relational processes that occur in mother–infant interaction and in the consulting room are transmitted in psychobiological exchanges.

> During spontaneous right brain-to-right brain visual–facial, auditory–prosodic, and tactile–proprioceptive emotionally charged attachment communications, the sensitive, psychobiologically attuned caregiver regulates at an implicit level, the infant's states of arousal. (2011, p. 79)

Throughout life "the neural substrates of the perception of voices, faces, gestures, smells and pheromones, as evidenced by modern neuroimaging techniques, are characterised by a general pattern of right-hemispheric functional asymmetry" (Brancucci et al., 2009, cited in Schore, 2011). Schore proposes that relational information is transmitted non-consciously and intuitively, through many psychobiological channels that are dependent on right-brain functions laid down during the formation of early attachment processes and continuing as a mode of communication throughout life.

These implicit psychobiological exchanges affecting attachment processes are what underlie the establishment of the therapeutic alliance. Research by neuroscientists Jean Decety and Thierry Chaminade describes right-brain operations as essential for interpersonal relating. These are the same ones that are specifically utilised in the therapeutic alliance:

> Mental states that are in essence private to the self may be shared between individuals . . . It is interesting to note that our ability to represent one's own thoughts and represent another's thoughts are intimately tied together and may have similar origins in the brain . . . Thus it makes sense that self-awareness, empathy, identification with others, and more generally intersubjective processes, are largely dependent upon the right hemisphere resources, which are the first to develop. (Decety & Chaminade, 2003, p. 591)

Schore theorises that fast, spontaneous transference–countertransference communication of embodied emotion at a preconscious–unconscious level illustrates right brain-to-right brain non-verbal exchange between patient and therapist. This is analogous to BCPSG member Karlen Lyons-Ruth's description of relational processes "[occurring] at an implicit level of rapid cuing and response that occurs too rapidly for simultaneous verbal transaction and conscious reflection" (2000, pp. 91–92).

He goes on to explain that this "dyadic psychobiological mechanism" allows for the detection and communication of unconscious affects. He connects Freud's description of "evenly suspended attention" to the operation of the right hemisphere of the brain which employs a broadly focused global perception and conceptual scope, rather than the left hemisphere of the brain, which is associated with a narrow local focus and conceptual scope (Förster et al., 2008, p. 592; Schore, 2011, p. 84).

> On a moment to moment basis the therapist must both remain psychobiologically attuned to the patient in a state of right brain

evenly suspended attention and at the same time access an intuitive, fast, emotional, and effortless right brain decision process to navigate through the stressful intersubjective context. (Schore, 2011, p. 88)

Schore connects right brain implicit processes to clinical intuition, which is "expressed not in a literal language but is 'embodied' in a 'gut feeling' or an initial guess that subsequently biases our thought and inquiry" (2011, p. 88). He describes it as "an affectively charged embodied cognition that is adaptive for 'implicit feeling or knowing,' especially in moments of relational uncertainty" (2011, p. 89). It is in these very moments of uncertainty in the consulting room that the process of therapeutic change can take place in a patient (see also Stern et al., 1998) if the therapist is able to "implicitly and subjectively be with the patient . . . during affectively stressful moments when the 'going-on-being' of the patient's implicit self is dis-integrating in real time" (2011, p. 94).

Schore points out that (clinical) intuition presents itself in the form of kinaesthetic sensations, feelings, images, and metaphors, which are all properties of right brain processes.

> Here the solution, which has an emotional quality, is revealed, but in a veiled nonverbal form . . . in contrast to the left brain's deliberate, conscious analytical search strategies, the right brain generates the subjective experience of insight, whereby a novel solution is computed unconsciously and subsequently emerges into awareness suddenly. (2011, p. 89)

The rapid, non-conscious use of clinical intuition, rooted in an embodied experience and communicated to the patient in a moment of attunement, can create deep structural change in the patient. Schore posits, "the implicit functions of the emotional right brain are essential to the self-exploration process of psychotherapy, especially of unconscious affects that can be potentially integrated into a more complex implicit sense of self" (2011, p. 94). He stresses the clinical and theoretical necessity of understanding the implicit psychobiological right-brain system, contrasting it to existing studies of explicit action in the consulting room:

> Just as studies of the left brain, dominant for language and verbal processing, can never elucidate the unique nonverbal functions of the

right, studies of the output of explicit functions of the conscious mind in verbal transcripts or narratives can never reveal the implicit psycho-biological dynamics of the unconscious mind. (2010, p. 179)

The unconscious dialogue between analyst and patient is being described through infant observation and cognitive neuroscience as implicit and rooted in the body. In addition, to move is inherently an expression of mental intention (Nahum, 2008). Whether one is referring to the BCPSG's concepts of implicit relational knowing, or Schore's models of implicit right-brain-to-right-brain communication, both models suggest that the therapist manages the moment-to-moment movement of the therapeutic relationship by "implicit primary process affectively driven by clinical intuition" (Schore, 2011). Neuroscientists, such as Gallese (2006), describe the direct unmediated experience of a shared body state via "intentional attunement", so that we are hardwired to respond with empathic understanding.

While technologically mediated treatment clearly can be utilised for the left-brain "analytical search strategies" that Schore describes above, the function of all relationships also depends on moments of right-brain insight, underpinned by non-verbal, embodied, sensation-based perception. The intensely focused effort analysts describe of "peering at the screen" when doing technologically mediated treatment recalls the function of the locally focused left hemisphere of the brain. This narrowed scope of perceptual and conceptual focus might be at the expense of the operation of the right brain's holistic scope of attention that Schore connects to evenly suspended attention.

Can this right brain communication, based on finely nuanced, non-conscious information such as gestures, smells, and pheromones, be conveyed through technologically mediated communication? Can "the communicating cure" which is so richly expressed through such kinaesthetics as posture, gesture, facial expression, as well as speech rhythms, patterns, and the subtle transmission of as-yet unidentified cues be digitally carried?

The evolutionary currency of all relationships, mother–infant, lovers, and therapist–patient, involves two bodies together. Children cannot be parented, much less conceived, from screen-to-screen interaction. How much physical togetherness does a therapeutic relationship need, and how much of a sense of togetherness can technology provide?

CHAPTER SIX

From the second laboratory: technologically mediated communication

There are no research studies published specifically on psychoanalytic treatment conducted via video-conferencing. This is significant because, as outlined above, psychoanalytic communication and the efficacy of treatment depends on different modes of communication and models of treatment delivery than, for example, cognitive–behavioural therapy (CBT), supportive therapy, psychiatric interventions, and short-term, goal-orientated cognitive therapy. A group of researchers from the University of Haifa (Barak et al., 2008) published a comprehensive literature review and meta-analysis of the effectiveness of Internet-based therapy. Their collection of empirical articles published up to 2006 covers a wide range of Internet-mediated forms of communication, including automated software, online chat groups, email and chat-based counselling, self-help interventions, and video-conferencing for problems as diverse as encopresis in children, panic disorder, weight loss, smoking cessation, depression, and anxiety. The meta-analysis performed on ninety-two diverse studies determined that "in most cases, online therapy can be delivered effectively, by using various Internet applications and exploiting several online communication options" (Barak et al., 2008). The wide variation of the forms of Internet-based mediation, models of therapeutic intervention, and patients in treatment decreases the usefulness of this study for application to psychoanalytic practice, since they include instructive, prescriptive, and didactic treatments not dependent on the analyst–patient relationship as is psychoanalysis, and patients with an extensive range of diagnoses, for whom psychoanalysis would not be the treatment of choice. In addition, there is no in-depth assessment of what makes the online therapy delivery effective. The Centre for Reviews and Dissemination at the University of York, an independent research evaluation service, assessed this paper as follows: ". . . the uncertain quality of the included studies, potential for bias and variability across studies mean that the authors' conclusions should be interpreted with caution" (DARE, 2010).

In a far more cautious, but equally comprehensive review, Richardson and colleagues (2009) write,

> In general, efficacy studies have focused on general psychiatric services . . . rather than delivery of psychotherapy, and most of the psychotherapy studies reviewed have failed to use manualised or replicable interventions. (p. 332)

In an interview with Todd Essig for Forbes.com, Lisa Richardson, the lead author states, ". . . the evidence base to support the clinical efficacy of tele-mental health interventions remains underdeveloped" (Essig, 2011).

These reviews and more general reviews on telepsychiatry (e.g., Hilty et al., 2004) lack the specifics applicable to an analytic context. Most research in technologically mediated communication takes place outside of the psychoanalytic field, in such disciplines as behaviour and information technology and human–computer studies, and that is where we need to begin in order to explore the foundations of effective computer-mediated communication.

The majority of the work done in the area of computer-mediated communication originated with the aim of providing effective communication channels in work situations. Increased globalisation means that organisations require employees to communicate across distances and time zones. Early research focused on written or audio-only communication, as that was the technology most easily available at the time.

There is extensive and sometimes contradictory literature comparing face-to-face with video-mediated, telephone, or text communication (O'Conaill et al., 1993, Whittaker, 2003a), but all these studies are aimed at situations of task-orientated information exchange: for example, finding locations on a map or jointly construct-ing a physical object. Whittaker (2003a) describes the "bandwidth hypothesis", in which it was predicted that communication would be less effective with fewer sensory cues. Counterintuitively, this proved not to be the case: adding the visual mode to the auditory mode did not improve communication performance. Because these studies were specifically task orientated, the results cannot be usefully applied to the psychoanalytic situation, where the mode of communication is not limited to manipulating physical items or exchanging concrete infor-mation. In fact, Whittaker adds that there has been no work in the effects of sensory modes other than sight and hearing, and that find-ings from one sort of task cannot be generalised to another.

Isaacs and Tang (1994) differ in that they find, when comparing collaboration via video-conferencing to audio only, interactions became more subtle, natural, and easier. They point out that while it might not make a group complete a task more quickly (the measure used to assess effectiveness in these studies), it provides an important channel for social communication.

Significantly, other studies find that although audio-only and video inclusive systems are equivalent, *only full physical co-presence* makes a difference in the participants' style of language and relating (O'Conaill et al., 1993; Rutter et al., 1981; Sellen, 1995). In one inter-esting study, Rutter and colleagues (1981) studied subjects in less task-focused situations in which they conversed about sociopolitical issues. They were divided into four groups: face-to-face, audio communication only from separate rooms, audio–video link from separate rooms, and co-presently in a room divided by a curtain preventing visual communication. The face-to-face communication was shown to be superior to the other modalities studied, as cues were available both visually and from physical presence. This was followed on a decreasing scale by the audio–visual and co-present curtained off situations, which were roughly equivalent. Finally, the subjects who used audio only from separate rooms ranked lowest in richness of communication.

It is interesting that the quality of communication where the subjects were co-present but out of sight was ranked at least as high as full audio–visual communication. These research studies support the reports of analysts I interviewed, who stressed that even if the whole body could be visible on screen, their experience of relating differed radically from that of physical co-presence. This was particularly underlined by Maria Celano, who described her vivid experience of her analyst's presence when they shared the same environment as very different to her technologically mediated experience of her analyst, despite not being able to see in either condition.

Common ground

Shared perspective with mutually viewable objects in a common physical environment is a crucial non-verbal aspect of relational understanding, and disjointed visual perspectives can undermine communication processes (Olson & Olson, 2000; Whittaker, 2003a). This research comes from the studies in human–computer interaction in which researchers have identified various constraints that mediated communication places on participants, including failure to establish common ground without physical co-presence (Kirk et al., 2010).

The theory of common ground, a very important precursor to trust, comprises the collection of "mutual knowledge, mutual beliefs, and mutual assumptions" that is essential for communication between two people (Clark & Brennan, 1991). This theory acknowledges that the constraints of a medium might impose limits on communication, causing participants to adjust to those constraints in order to establish common ground (Hildreth et al., 1998). There are various constraints that mediated communication places on participants, including those on co-presence (not sharing the same physical environment, not having access to the same objects in the environment that allow mutual reference and a shared context), visibility (though video-conferencing allows participants to see faces, it does not provide the same information and richness of cues as co-presence, such as what the other is looking at), audibility, co-temporality (an experience of different circadian contexts) and simultaneity (lags in communication affect shared experience), individual control (each participant cannot freely choose what to attend to in the environment and change attentional focus easily), implicit cues, and nuanced information through multiple channels—voice, facial expression, body posture (Clark & Brennan, 1991; Olson & Olson, 2000, p. 149).

... Behavioural studies instead suggest that videoconferencing systems fail to support an adequate sharing of the physical frames of reference that make mutual actions and interaction intelligible ... [There is the difficulty] of framing of people in relation to the objects they are interacting with. Most video systems fail to adequately support awareness of people's relative views of objects and other collaborators requiring the participants to reconcile images and perspectives of others to understand relative orientations. A final issue concerns establishing shared perspectives more generally. ... Video systems [create difficulty] in establishing reciprocity of awareness amongst collaborators. Being mutually aware of perspectives and orientations is fundamental to a *shared physical* space but is difficult to recreate in a *shared video* space. (Kirk et al., 2010, p. 136)

The capacity for joint attention has importance for communication in general, technologically mediated communication, and psychoanalytic communication in particular. George, a musician who uses computer-mediated communication with his analyst when he travels to perform, explains, "When I am in the same room with my analyst, looking at things in her office is a way of engaging. I can look at her face, but that can be distracting, so I look at things we can both see. On Skype, I can only see her face, but in the room we share the understanding that we see the same things."

Goldberg (2012) suggests that a shared, communal perception between analyst and patient contributes to an inherently transformative experience for the patient,

something not found in the act of an individual perception alone, or in the context of relating to an object. The distinctive thing about being jointly alive in the act of shared perception is that one is, in a sense, sharing the sensorium-of-the body of the other ... what is at stake is the expansion of individual consciousness. (p. 796)

George continues, "[Skype] feels very different [to the consulting room]. It is much easier to dissociate when I look away from the screen and set eyes on something on my desk that my therapist can't see, only I can see. In that moment I retreat. I don't feel it occurs the same way in the consulting room. I look at things we can see together."

The therapeutic couple engage in a shared sensory experience, "a kind of perceptual commons". This shared sensory experience enables the patient to use objects in the external world in a new way. It lays the foundation for a "communal dreaming" (cf. Ogden, 1996), making possible Winnicott's concept of "apperception", which leads to a sense of self and of feeling real (Goldberg, 2012, pp. 796–797).

The static and limited view of the webcam makes for a greatly different experience of bodies to that in a shared environment: "Not seeing the whole body makes a big difference. The patient's face is either very close or very far away, depending on where she put her laptop . . . she moves a lot. She's a very physical person, she can't sit still . . . movement would be picked up in an exaggerated way by the camera . . . It felt, almost, ghostly, in a way: ghostly in terms of seeing body parts—I'm glad we're talking about this: I've never thought about this before—not having a complete perception," comments an analyst.

Apparent distance (proxemics) affects behaviour. Normally, in a co-present situation, we would move our bodies closer or farther from each other to adjust volume and image. The virtual world has disconnected these physical features, requiring us to move the microphone, the camera, or the monitor (or, in the case of a laptop, the whole device) (Olson & Olson, 2000).

When the visual distortion of bodies with views often limited to only parts of bodies occurs, with frequent poor transmission and delays, the perception of the "gestalt" of the other is obstructed: "Not seeing the whole body makes a big difference"; "You are working with a part object: literally the head and shoulders . . ."

George, the musician, compares his screen therapy experience to remote music lessons: "It is impossible easily to see both hands playing a guitar on a screen. They have solved this problem by introducing a split screen so that you can see both your teacher's hands simultaneously. This is better than nothing, but the student is not experiencing the complete physical and musical gestalt. There is a disconnection. It is not like having the teacher in the flesh."

Recent research has found that during peak intensities of emotion, positive and negative affects were successfully discriminated from isolated body postures, but not isolated faces. The facial expression alone in periods of peak intensity is inherently ambiguous. It shows an overlap in the expression of positive and negative emotions, and does not convey diagnostic information about a specific affect. In the study, it was the posture of the whole body that was crucial in conveying affect. This was true when participants were viewing images of a face without a body, a body without a face, a body with a congruent face, or a body on which a "Photoshopped" face is displaying an incongruent emotion. In each case it was the posture of the body that communicated the accurate emotional information. These findings are counterintuitive and, in keeping with that, the viewers reported that their perceptions were dependent on the facial expressions, despite the fact that it was the body from which they actually gleaned the information. These results challenge the standard models of expression of emotions and highlight the crucial role of the whole body in expressing and perceiving emotion (Aviezer et al., 2012).

Lack of a shared perspective and the potential for joint attention and only partial or distorted views of bodies impede communication and the establishing of mutual common ground. Without common ground, it is difficult to develop a sense of trust, crucial to any functional relationship.

Trust

Trust is very tenuous in the world of technologically mediated communication. Yet, it is a necessary condition not only in the work environment, but in all relationships. Trust allows one to be honest, sincere, and vulnerable. Shared experiences encourage the development of trust. In a study of trust in group interactions, Rocco (1998) found that trust broke down during group collaborative activities when using electronically based formats. In a two-stage experiment, she analysed the effect of face-to-face interaction *vs.* electronic communication and found that trust between participants succeeded only with face-to-face communication. In the second stage of the investigation, she found that a face-to-face meeting prior to a group interaction promoted trust in the electronic context. The findings were that face-to-face communication promotes socialisation. Although she did not use video-conferencing in the study, Rocco included it in her examples of communication that required prior face-to face contact to establish trust.

In a later study including video-conferencing, researchers found that including video and audio in communication significantly increased the sense of trust between participants (in the case of audio only, less so), though trust built more slowly in the mediated condition and it took some time for the video-conferencers to "catch up" with the face-to-face participants. In addition, their data indicated that the trust built up between mediated participants was more fragile: quickly built up, but not lasting (Bos et al., 2001, 2002). Like Rocco, later researchers confirmed that meeting face-to-face prior to communicating with technology helped people to establish and maintain trust (Olson & Olson, 2006). These results are significant for those who use technologically mediated communication for treatment. They indicate that establishing a foundation of co-presence is useful prior to communicating with technology. This makes intuitive sense and has been supported anecdotally by therapists and patients.

> I think the unconscious in the verbal communication can be picked up and made use of and there is still an atmosphere between you, even on Skype, at least after having seen the person for real, because *there's a residual trust and understanding* which allows for the other person to be more free associative than they otherwise might be.

Therapists who spoke to me agreed that their memories of working with their patients in a shared environment better enabled them to continue a perceptive and receptive connection with them using technologically mediated communication.

Gaze

Mutual gaze is impossible with current video technology. While mutual gaze may be infrequent when two participants are engaging in a task, the exchange of social affective information is dependent on facial expression and gaze. People tend to evaluate each other by their patterns of gaze (Whittaker, 2003a). We are adept at perceiving other's gaze direction and, along with other contextual indicators, interpret the other's state of mind though gaze. Sherry Turkle (2011), psychologist and Professor of the Social Studies of Science and Technology in the programme in Science, Technology, and Society at MIT, speaks of this very issue when she describes using Skype with her daughter, "On Skype you see each other, but you cannot make eye contact . . . My daughter has the expression of someone alone" (p. 299).

The rules that govern the use of gaze in communication are complex and culturally dependent (Donath, 2001), but there is no question that eye to eye contact and mutual gaze are behaviours that are established very early in an infant's development and continue to create input and output of communicative information throughout life. Philosophy professor Kim Maclaran (2008) writes that gaze between mother and infant confirms humanity and intentionality. Seeking eye contact is an attempt to be in relation with the other. By taking up the baby's gaze, the adult confirms that he/she is indeed relating to the baby as a communicating intentional being and that the baby is also a communicating intentional being (p. 86).

> Bringing gaze to the mediated world is difficult because gaze bridges the space between people—and the people in a mediated conversation are not in the same space. Addressing this problem requires not only a means for the participants to signal meaningful gaze patterns but creating a common, virtual space for them to gaze across . . . with videoconferencing, the basic problem is that no common space is shared by the participants. (Donath, 2001, p. 381)

At the present state of technological development, the only way to *appear* to be meeting the other's eyes in a technologically mediated communication is to gaze at the camera, which, in fact, precludes the experience of mutual gaze. "You have to look at the camera to make your gaze appear to connect, but it is a simulation of a connection anyway," an analyst tells me.

The use of the screen in mediated communication isolates the head and shoulders and potentially enlarges the view of the face and eyes. At the same time, the frequent poor quality of transmission adds to the distortion by introducing delays and representing gaze as off-centre. Peripheral vision is limited or impossible. Even with the most advanced equipment, the gaze does not match our real world expectations.

Simon Baron-Cohen (2011), Professor of Developmental Psychopathology at Cambridge University, points out the importance of being able to make eye contact in order to make judgements about people's emotions and mental states. He cites a study of a patient whose damage to her amygdala specifically limited her ability to make contact with people's eyes and thereby interpret their emotions (Spezio et al., 2007). The amygdala is a small region of the brain located deep in the temporal lobes. It processes sensory information and is connected with emotional processing, as well as memory and decision-making. It is involved in the "empathy circuit". The eyes are key to interpreting people's emotional states, and the inability to make eye contact limits the ability to recognise emotions in others (Baron-Cohen, 2011, p. 39).

While it may be the model for some psychoanalysts' patients to use the couch during treatment, there is still potential for direct facial contact between the analytic couple during the session before and after the use of the couch, along with peripheral vision and all the differences of both being embodied in the room. These are joint embodied communications that have the potential to go on regardless of a temporary posture.

Attention

The brain retains plasticity throughout life, and it has been demonstrated that the way we use the Internet reroutes our neural pathways. The use of the Internet encourages rapid skimming of the surface of incoming data and picking out the relevant details (Carr, 2011, Small & Vorgan, 2008). While the brain regions that enable people quickly to scan, search, and evaluate, processing multiple sensory stimuli are improved, the capacity for making rich mental connections and contemplative thinking is under-stimulated. "The more we use the Web, the more we train our brain to be distracted—to process information very quickly and very efficiently but *without sustained attention*" (Carr, 2011, p. 194, my italics). The immediately accessible technology, upon which, in fact, the therapist and patient are dependent to communicate remotely, imports the possibility of an "always on" divided attention into the session.

Linda Stone, a former senior executive with Apple and Microsoft Research, calls this "continuous partial attention" (2009). The process of continuous partial attention, familiar to most people who use the Internet, involves paying synchronous attention to a number of sources of incoming information, but at a superficial level. If you have teenage children, you will have seen them in front of the screen doing their homework on a Word document, while at the same time maintaining a number of windows open to chat with friends, check out Facebook, listen to music, and watch their incoming email. They might also have their mobile phones sitting next to them, on which they are receiving and sending numerous texts. When you attend a conference, you and your colleagues might be listening to the speaker while checking your smartphones for calls, texts, and emails. This use of attention differs from multi-tasking in that multi-tasking is defined by the wish to be more productive, automatically and with very little cognitive processing. It is an activity with the aim of producing more time at a later point, in order to do something different. Continuous partial attention describes a state in which attention is engaged in multiple activities that all require cognition (e.g., reading an email and participating in a conference call). It also involves being involved in a primary task

> whilst at the same time scanning for other people, activities, or opportunities and replacing the primary task with something that seems, in this next moment, more important . . . Continuous partial attention is always an "on," anywhere, anytime, any place behavior that creates a sense of crisis . . . We are demanding multiple cognitively complex actions from ourselves. (Stone, 2009)

When teaching at New York University, Stone noticed that her graduate students were in a state of hyper-vigilance with their technology, existing in a constant artificial state of emergency. The capacity to be "always on", to immediately respond to any number of communications, leads to a feeling of over-stimulation and feeling overwhelmed. "We are so accessible, we're inaccessible" (Stone, 2009). This is the activity stimulated by having several windows at once on a screen, all feeding different information simultaneously.

> On the Net, there are windows within windows within windows, not to mention long ranks of tabs primed to trigger the opening of even more windows . . . [this] has become so routine that most of us would find it intolerable if we had to go back to computers that could only run one program or open only one file at a time. (Carr, 2011, p. 113)

This is the way computers are designed to be used and this is the way the tool shapes the user. This is what my analytic colleague, who was thrilled to work from a hotel, and Melissa Weinblatt from the *New York Times* article, who was thrilled to work from the poolside, celebrated: you can connect anywhere, any time.

My conversations with patients and clinicians reveal that the possibility of leaving multiple windows open on the screen, or an undetected smartphone on the desk, distracts from evenly suspended attention and derails shared reverie. Some members of the therapeutic couple give in to the temptation of continuous partial attention, while others are unable to "simply listen, and not bother about . . . keeping anything in mind" because of the intense concentration required to screen out distraction (Freud, 1912b). The associations to the nature of the technology's other uses creates an unconscious expectation in the users.

A recent study, published in the journal *Environment and Behavior*, suggests that the mere presence of a mobile or smartphone on a nearby table or held in the hand can lessen the quality of a co-present conversation, lowering levels of empathy between the participants, especially if they already have a close relationship (Misra et al., 2014). The phone does not have to be actively checked for it to affect the quality of attention, it just has to be within the participants' visual field. The Virginia Tech research team (Misra and colleagues) writes,

Mobile phones hold a symbolic meaning in advanced technological societies. Even when they are not in active use or buzzing, beeping, ringing, or flashing, they are representative of people's wider social network and a portal to an immense compendium of information. Their mere presence in a socio-physical milieu, therefore, has the potential to divide consciousness between the proximate and immediate setting and the physically distant and invisible networks and contexts. In their presence, people have the constant urge to seek out information, check for communication, and direct their thoughts to other people and worlds. Even without active use, the presence of mobile technologies has the potential to divert individuals from face-to-face exchanges, thereby undermining the character and depth of these connections. Individuals are more likely to miss subtle cues, facial expressions, and changes in the tone of their conversation partner's voice, and have less eye contact. (Misra et al., 2014, p. 17)

The authors describe this divided attention as a constant "state of poly-consciousness" because of the continuous awareness of the possibility of instantaneous connection. They advance the idea that the proximity of a technological device, which represents relational networks, will increase the user's emotional arousal level causing "distraction conflict". Distraction conflict is defined as the attentional conflict which occurs when a person attempts to give attention to multiple stimuli at the same time (Misra et al., p. 7). This is significant for analysts and patients using technological mediation, because the vehicle of communication, itself, represents a gateway to instantaneous information, as well as a container of a multiplicity of relational networks. Even without the smartphone on the table (and it so often is), the computer holds the same significance and, thus, the same potential distraction.

The rapid scanning, processing, and multi-tasking encouraged by technologically mediated environments is at odds with the exploration of deep and complex feelings, driving society toward abbreviated "sound-bite" communication (Gergen, 2002; Misra et al., 2014; Turkle, 2011). It need hardly be pointed out that the quality of communication typically supported by technological mediation is the antithesis of the evenly suspended attention or reverie required for the psychoanalytic process. In addition, the compensatory intensely focused attention employed by some analysts to avoid distraction or surmount technical connection difficulties also impedes free-floating attention.

Antonio Damasio did a study that revealed that the higher emotions, such as empathy and compassion, emerge from neural processes that "are inherently slow" (Marziali, 2009). His findings, in one of the first brain studies to concentrate on emotions connected with moral decision-making, suggest that digital media might be more appropriate for some mental processes rather than others. Introspective thought processing leading to empathy takes more time compared to the brain's quick processing of multiple sensory stimuli when using technology. In an interview for the University of Southern California News, USC Annenberg media scholar Manuel Castells said, "Damasio's study has extraordinary implications for human perception of events in a digital communication environment. Lasting compassion in relationship to psychological suffering requires a level of persistent, emotional attention" (Marziali, 2009).

It would seem that the very tool we use, hoping to enable a process of "surrendering [ourselves] to our own unconscious . . . to catch the drift of the patient's unconscious" (Freud, 1923a, p. 239), encourages and accustoms us to the inverse use of the mind.

Distance still matters

"I see a patient in China," says a North American therapist. "Because of the time difference, the session is very early in the morning for me, and late at night for him. At the end of a session he said, 'I have been watching the sun rise in the window behind you.'"

Therapists use technologically mediated communication to see patients who live in dramatically different geographical areas, different time zones, and cultures. But even therapeutic couples who live in the same country one or two time zones away are affected by the difference in time and weather. Sessions often begin with a sort of alignment or orientation. "You look tired; it is very dark." "It looks like it is cold there." "I read in the news that you are having floods." A UK therapist describes her first moments of a session with her patient in the USA: "She's just got out of bed and switched me on, as if she hadn't lived at all that day . . ."

Technology has shrunk the world, and bridged vast distances. Not only can I meet with my son in London in my morning and his evening, but he can give me a tour of his flat, in which I have never set foot. Cairncross (2001) argues in her book *The Death of Distance: How the Communications Revolution Is Changing Our Lives* that new communications technologies are quickly making geography, borders, and time zones irrelevant to how we conduct our personal and business lives. Does technology, as psychoanalyst Ricardo Carlino suggests, decouple the feeling of closeness from the significance of the effect of geographical distance (2011, p. 103)? What does it mean to the analytic relationship when the therapist and patient do not share the same points in their circadian rhythms or a common experience of climate? Is it enough to make contact mind-to-mind, without sharing a joint experience body-to-body?

Gary and Judith Olson, psychologists and professors of information and computer science at the University of California, Irvine, have spent more than two decades studying computer-mediated group work. They state,

There are characteristics of face-to-face human interactions, particularly the space–time contexts in which such interactions take place, that the emerging technologies are either pragmatically or logically incapable of replicating . . . Differences in local physical context, time zones, culture and language all persist despite the use of distance technologies. Some distance work is possible today, but some aspects of it will remain difficult if not impossible to support even in the future. (2000, pp. 140–141)

While improvement in technology might solve some communication problems, the Olsons feel that some challenges will never be met. For example, their research finds that "tightly coupled work" is very difficult to do remotely. Tightly coupled work is highly interdependent work that requires complex communication between participants, a capacity for rapid back and forth conversation, and the ability to be aware of, and repair, uncertainty or misunderstanding (Olson & Olson, 2000, p. 163). It requires an effortless fluidity of participation. The static nature of the webcam and its restricted view means that ease of rich communication (communication with numerous social cues) is limited. The effort to communicate clearly becomes quite intense, and participants develop new communication styles to compensate for these shortcomings. Guiseppe Riva, John and Eva Waterworth, and Fabrizia Mantovani, researchers in informatics, propose that we experience a strong sense of mediated presence when there is no conscious attentional *effort* to access information (Riva et al., 2009). Our awareness of the technology disappears and we perceive and often act as if unmediated. The intensity of effort of access decreases the degree of sense of presence, the vital experience of being in the world with another (Campanella Bracken & Skalski, 2010, p. 187). This recalls the experiences of intense attention reported by clinicians and patients using technological mediation that disrupted their free ranging flow of thought. Their highly concentrated focus was an attempt to compensate for the reduction in rich multisensory information and maintain a sense of connected presence. Paradoxically, this kind of concentration undermines both freefloating attention and the experience of a natural sense of presence.

The Olsons found that people required to do tightly coupled work together ultimately opted to arrange working in a co-present setting, rather than to continue to work remotely. "The work was reorganized to fit the geography" (Olson & Olson, 2000, p. 163). While the remote communication was better than nothing, it was not the communication of choice.

The hardware itself affects perceptions of intimacy and distance, and therapists observe that their experiences can be confusing and counterintuitive. They sometimes make the choice to use headsets because the potentially improved clarity, decreased echo, and noise-screening option provides more affective information. "My patient chose to use a headset and asked me to do the same 'because she felt closer to me.' If I had a headset on and my analysand had a headset on I got a much better feel for how they were breathing, certain kinds of emotional tonalities . . . that I found was a better approximation of being in the room . . ." However, this analyst adds, "That is an issue in some sense. In a regular analysis, your mouth is not next to the ear of the person, but you are there in the room, so I do think there is something about keeping aware of the level of intimacy . . . which even has a sexual component to it."

Alex, an intern who uses technological mediation to continue an analysis started in medical school, tells me, "Using a headset does not feel like a step towards a deeper reality—it's more like a step away. There is something precarious about the feeling of a voice in your head, as if it weren't another person, but an internal conversation." Scharff (2012) writes, "When it enters the headset, the voice of the analysand is delivered inside the analyst's mind in a more total way than in the room where there is more space between them . . ." (p. 81). She suggests that the voice broadcast direct to the ear fosters a sense of connection that supports containment. Another analyst has different views: "A voice in the ear can be too close, a sort of perverse closeness, a *simulated* closeness." Whether one's experience of the voice delivered direct to the mind is one of aural totality, perverse closeness, or, from the patient's point of view, unreality or containment, it is significant that the relationship of voice to ear is *different* to that in the co-present consulting room. The effect of that difference, on both the analyst and the analysand, needs to be taken into account. What does the increased closeness mean? What does it mean to *change* the experience from that of a voice in the room where there is more space between the participants to that of a voice down a wire delivered straight to your ear?

The experience of perspective on the screen is confusing and paradoxical: "I see his head and shoulders, in a chair . . . he is miniaturised on the screen, so even though the camera is closer than I would have been in the room, because he is miniaturised it doesn't seem closer." The size of the image on the screen greatly affects the way participants relate. Work in the laboratories of researchers in human–computer interaction shows that the smaller the image, the more stiff and formal the conversation and the larger and closer the image, the more relaxed and natural the interaction (Olson & Olson, 2000, p. 154).

Technology quirks and limitations are not the only influencer of technologically mediated communication. Gloria Mark, a professor in the Department of Informatics at the University of California, Irvine, and her colleague, Erin Bradner, did an intriguing study of the psychological significance of distance (Bradner & Mark, 2002). They initiated three experimental tasks measuring interactive behaviour between two participants, one a volunteer and one, unbeknown to the volunteer, a paid collaborator. One task measured persuasion, one measured deception, and one measured cooperation. The volunteers were told either that their participating partner was communicating with them from the same city or from a distant city, approximately 3,000 miles away. In reality, the collaborator was sitting in a neigh-bouring room. They connected via audio–video (in another version of the experiment, they used instant messaging). The amount of network delay was no different in either the same or distant city conditions.

Their results are surprising. They challenge the assumption that once a communication channel is established, the geographical dis-tance between the participants is irrelevant. The volunteers interacted with the collaborator differently, depending upon whether they believed she was in the distant or the same city. They were less likely to trust, much more likely to deceive, and less likely to cooperate if they believed she were in the distant city. Cooperation seemed to build up over time; however, the researchers wonder if this trust is a phenomenon called "quick trust", which is a tendency exhibited by remote communicators who quickly form an initial trust which is ephemeral (Bradner & Mark, 2002, p. 232).

Bradner and Mark propose that social identity theory and social impact theory could explain their data. Social identity theory suggests that people consider the skills of those nearby to be superior to the skills of those who are distant. Social impact theory suggests that people at a distance feel less able to influence the other (thus leading to a deceptive enhancement of their self-description). In addition, they put forward the idea that the possibility of meeting the collaborator in person might influence the behaviour of the volunteers.

These findings bring up important questions for technologically mediated treatment. What impact do different time zones and different circadian rhythms have on the attunement of the therapeutic couple? Olson and Olson suggest it makes a difference to collaborative work. How do the limitations of present-day technology affect the necessary effortless fluidity of therapeutic work, especially as research indicates that participants have to make a great effort to communicate, and adapt their normal styles of communication? Finally, how does distance affect the reliability of the communication? It is significant that the test subjects had never met. Would a previous relationship have changed the results of the findings? How does this affect those therapists who agree to see patients they have never been with in the same consulting room? Deception does occur between technologically mediated participants, and more easily than with people who meet face-to-face. How does distance affect trust and honesty in the treatment relationship?

PART III
ON THE SCREEN

CHAPTER SEVEN

The mediating device

I'm ready for my close-up

"Jane, darling, don't you look lovely! How do you do it?" Jane Jetson, the mother in the 1960s futuristic animated sitcom *The Jetsons*, receives an early-morning videophone call from her glamorous friend Gloria. Panicked at facing Gloria because she is still in a bedraggled morning state, she grabs her "morning mask", a perfectly made-up simulation of her face. When I Google Skype and make-up, I come up with 706,000 results, mostly tips for looking your best for a Skype job interview. Writers give guidance on background, lighting, clothes (both style and most video-friendly colour) and make-up ("like you are preparing for your television debut"). The camera distorts the view of the face "A bad angle can make your jaw look wider, create a double chin, or give viewers an up-the-nose shot", advises a make-up artist on beautyriot.com. They counsel that women should wear more make-up than usual, as it does not tend to show up well on camera, and remind us that the camera makes us look ten pounds heavier. There are even suggestions for specific high definition make-up brands designed to look best on high quality close-up video. Home-based workers who attend virtual meetings are enjoined to learn video-production skills such as controlling background noise and framing camera shots.

Things look different when you are looking or being looked at on a screen eighteen inches away. "We look like two huge heads." It is significant that this analyst is aware of how she, too, looks on screen. Video-conferencing software usually includes a small frame showing the user's face somewhere on the screen, as well as a large view of the person to whom you are talking. Although with some software this small frame can be turned off, there is really no way to avoid at least a momentary glimpse of your own face, a form of potential visual scrutiny and self-consciousness not present in the traditional consulting room.

"When I first started using a web-cam," Jessica, a newly qualified analyst from Seattle tells me, "I tested it out with a colleague. She told me I looked unhealthy and washed-out on screen. Now I always put on a bit more blusher and lipstick when I work [in a technologically mediated session]." "I look a lot heavier," says Joseph, an analyst in Los Angeles. "When I met my patient for the first time, he commented on how much thinner I was in person."

Barbara, an analyst who is very experienced in using technology comments, "If you have one hair out of place it is obvious. I always check myself out on the screen before I start the session. It [the screen] gives you an unwelcome and unusual consciousness of your appearance." On the other hand, another analyst remarks, "I sometimes find it interesting to notice my reactions . . . how my face appears to my patient."

Whether one looks at it as a necessary adjustment, a disturbing intrusion, or an interesting source of information, there is no denying that this added input does not exist in a co-present consulting room. What does it mean to apply make-up in a way you normally would not? How does it affect the analyst when he/she decides to tilt the screen for a more flattering angle, sit further back to avoid closer scrutiny, turn on or adjust the aim of a desk light, not for a clearer picture, but for a softer or more complimentary one? What does it mean to prepare for a session, however subtly, with the same frame of mind you have when you are going on stage or television? What does it mean when we simulate health by accentuating make-up? Who is the person we are presenting to the patient, an authentic "other" firmly rooted in herself, or an actor representing a therapist on the screen?

This added dimension is confusing and distracting. Is your patient genuinely seeing him/herself reflected back in your eyes, or does your awareness of your own image somehow intrude into that experience? (As one cannot truly meet someone else's eyes using a webcam, I am referring to the flow of internal thought processes of the analyst.)

The patient, too, can see him/herself. "I see my patient's eyes darting to the side, to the little window with her picture, as she talks. She often watches herself and checks out how she looks as she speaks to me." The added prospect of viewing one's own face must intrude upon both the analyst's and patient's potential for joint reverie. Even if you are able to exclude that view from the screen, at some point you will see it and consider the screen image you are projecting. This prospect detaches us from the immediacy of *being there*. Both the analyst's and the patient's sense of presence is imperceptibly affected by the potential feeding back of information about ourselves in real time. Our attention is divided between ourselves and the other with whom we are interacting.

These questions point to the fact that this property of the screen radically differs from our experience of co-present therapy. They are special features of the simulation and need to be recognised as such. Both the patient and the therapist may find it difficult to think freely when there is a constant awareness of the fact that you are appearing on a screen, and that your appearance is a distorted representation of your real-life self.

The other side of the coin of artificially heightened reality is the latitude that not being co-present confers on the participants. There are myriad articles warning home-workers to be aware of their surroundings and attire. Many home-based workers dress for meetings from the waist up, as do news presenters. Sue Shellenbarger (2012), a columnist in the Work and Family section of the *Wall Street Journal* writes, "My customary attire for Skype interviews is a suit jacket and dress shirt over yoga pants and running shoes. That isn't necessarily a problem unless you have to rise from your seat." She goes on to tell the rather ubiquitous story (everyone seems to know someone who has done this) of a consultant in a video meeting from his home office, apparently in business attire. Interrupted by a knock on the door, he stood up to get it and was wearing only boxer shorts on the bottom. Home-based workers consider casual attire a perk of the job and are often reluctant to dress formally for a remote meeting.

"Late night calls from home are very common," says a Hewlett-Packard remote worker, "[I] prefer to dress in any attire, walk around the room, multi-task" (Hirsh et al., 2005).

I talked to many analysts who feel the same way. "I would rather work with the video off so I can wear my pyjamas," says one analyst. Another describes,"I will wear a more formal jacket and shirt with my old jeans on the bottom." "I like to keep my feet bare, and sometimes I wear tracksuit bottoms with a work-type top." Early in my techno-logically mediated experience, I spoke to a group of analysts about countertransference issues when using computer mediation. When I mentioned the issue of dressing the top half of the body for the camera, like newscasters, many in the audience nodded and laughed. This is the paradox of working with one foot at home and one foot in the virtual consulting room. One might say that in the choice of dress there is a simulation of formality, with an underlying private contradictory message.

When we dress for play and relaxation, we inhabit an emotional space that is very different from the way we are in the consulting room, where we try, for a designated time, to be more reliable than people in ordinary life and at the service of the patient (Winnicott, 1955). The interesting point enacted by the therapists above (and the newscasters and remote workers) is that what you see is not the whole story. While the top half is appropriately professional, the bottom half is secretly transgressive.

It can be lonely, frustrating, and difficult working in "the impossi-ble profession". Having to be more reliable than people in ordinary life and at the service of the patient can be taxing. Wearing pyjamas and tracksuit bottoms, unbeknown to the patient, is a silent gesture of defiance both to the demands of the patient and the exacting require-ments of the psychoanalytic training itself.

When I started training in the 1980s, I remember one of my super-visors telling the new group of candidates that you should reserve particular clothes for wearing only to work. What she was emphasis-ing was the idea of "putting on your professional hat". This "uniform" helped to distinguish between work and everything else in the daily isolation of working one-to-one, especially if your consulting room was at home.

"Dressing is a commitment to the day," says Lucy, the nineteen-year-old university student we met earlier. She tells me that she decides not to wear pyjamas to her session (though, as she is a patient, she is perfectly entitled to do so). "There is a difference between going out with your teeth brushed or unbrushed or face washed or un-washed." The routine of getting dressed establishes the separation between the night and day and the private and public self. When a therapist dresses in play clothes or sleep clothes for a session, his/her commitment to the seriousness of the session is weakened. Because one can only do that with technologically mediated sessions, it calls into question the analyst's view of the comparative seriousness of that mode of communication to do work.

Dressing deceptively is even more complex. If it is about the secret thrill of "breaking rules", the nature of the device enables us to do so. We do it because we can. It is a statement about being in two places at once, which also puts one "in two minds". It is also a statement about simulation. We are not really in the consulting room; we are in a simulated consulting room. What you are seeing is not a complete and authentic therapist; he/she is a simulation of the real embodied thing, like Jane Jetson's morning mask. The implicit knowledge that what you are projecting and what you are seeing is a simulation enables the deception. All you need to know about is what you can see. The reality of the rebelliously dressed "bottom half" means you are not "all there" for the patient.

Of course, this does great damage to the therapeutic relationship. Just as children know all sorts of things about their parents that the adults think they are keeping secret, the patient must gather, on some level what is going on. The therapists, themselves, have to carry the knowledge that they are using the technology as a sort of sabotage, to inhibit their devotion and withhold their commitment. They are main-taining the "emotional illusion" of telepresence for their patients, but not for themselves.

Acknowledging the fact of the simulation, both to oneself and to one's patient, might go some way to allowing the therapist and patient to join together in their perception of the process. Openly discussing the limitations of what can be accomplished with this modality of treatment allows both participants to step out of the simulation. Then they may be able to work with mutual awareness that there are fundamental differences between screen relationships and embodied ones. They might have some idea of how much might be done thera-peutically before bodies need to be together again.

Loose connections

For those of us who grew up with *Star Trek*, it is amazing that science fiction has become science fact with the advent of software such as Skype or ooVoo, providing free and easy availability of computer-to-computer video and audio communication. The characters on the USS Enterprise's bridge could communicate through deep space with crystal clarity face-to-face over wide-screen monitors. Any visual or audio distortion signalled an impending disaster. Unfortunately, software like Skype, ooVoo, and FaceTime are not so reliable. Depending on the quality of computer, speed of connection, volume of Internet traffic, and the stability of a power source, technologically mediated communication software can vary wildly in the quality of the audio and video service it provides, sometimes in the space of a few seconds. Users become expert at adapting to the vagaries of video-conferencing tools, turning off the video to increase bandwidth and improve the audio, calling back any number of times until a connection is clearer, or rebooting their computers. For Ruth, a psycho-analyst in Chicago, the poor connection disrupted an international treatment enough to end it: "I became very angry at the device—and at times with the patient—and she became very angry with me and felt I didn't 'get her.' But the [Internet connection] was so bad in that case, the transmission was so poor, and therefore the holding [environment] was all screwed up. I would get really mad at the computer and I would talk with her about the technology—and wasn't there any alternative—couldn't we improve the device? And for her it was all about the psychological, the wounding of me not 'getting' her."

Often the therapeutic couple simply puts up with a poor connection, disjointed synching, echoes, freezing picture, lags in transmission, and actual breaks in connection as long as words are somewhat comprehensible. Because our drive to connect is so strong, there is a danger that the disruptions simply become incorporated into the fabric of the session, without their impact being acknowledged and examined. Fieldwork in the area of human–computer interaction shows that participants are *unaware of the difficulty* they are having with the communication device and adapt their behaviour to accommodate it rather than fix the technology. They develop new behaviour to compensate for the deficiencies of the technology, behaviour that takes effort and is less natural and spontaneous (Olson & Olson, 2000).

When Essig talks about therapists' blindness to breaks in functional equivalence, that lack of awareness might, in part, be connected to this documented behaviour of ignoring breaks in communication and adapting to their occurrence.

A delay, or "latency", is inherent in the technology that transmits audio over the Internet. The time and distance it takes for a signal to travel, zigzagging through myriad nodes, and the signal processing that occurs along the way affect the quality of communication in sometimes subtle but significant ways. For example, audio latency over the Internet is too high for real-time coordination and collaboration of musicians. Humans can accurately perceive audio interval as short as 4–5 milliseconds. Any delay greater than 500 milliseconds will severely disrupt conversational flow (de Menil, 2013; Olson & Olson, 2000).

Karen Ruhleder and Brigitte Jordan (1999, 2001), who were researchers at the Xerox Palo Alto Research Center, did a fascinating analysis of the consequences of delay in technology mediated interaction. These consequences were not apparent to the remote participants and only evident following a microanalysis of transcripts. What is said and heard on either side of the communication is different, but neither participant is aware of the disparity. They observed that the lack of conversational alignment caused by the delay contributed to potentially serious shifts in meaning. Delay-induced silences were misinterpreted and timing of utterances meant there was speech overlap or unintended interruptions. Turn taking, the precise implicit and explicit anticipation of when one speaker's conversational turn is ending, so that another might reply, broke down. In co-present face-to-face conversation, if there is misunderstanding, both parties understand that something has gone wrong and must be repaired. In technologically mediated communication, the origin of the problem might not be apparent to either participant, as the conversation will be heard differently by each side. The misalignment cannot be identified by the participants. Therefore, they are not able to repair the miscommunication in real time. The participants are left with a pervading and inexplicable sense of uneasiness. A "now moment" becomes a "near-now moment" (Stern et al., 1998; Summersett, 2013).

The imperfection of the technology is a very real problem. Breakdowns of communication, and the possibility that one might not even be aware of these breakdowns have tremendous implications for those treating patients via technological mediation. While it is true that co-present treatments can be interrupted or intruded upon, the extreme rarity of this occurrence can make it useful grist to the analytic mill. Many therapists who use technologically mediated communication find this sort of disruption, as well as very unclear video and poor audio, a dismayingly frequent event. Therapists joke that the opening words of a session are "Can you see me? Can you hear me?"

> My patient was weeping and sharing with me a most intimate story. At that moment, the connection was broken. The disruption to the flow of our interaction and the distress caused by the abrupt loss of connection felt terribly intense and violent for both of us. It took some minutes to reconnect, and by then the session could not be resumed where we left off. The tear in the fabric of the session was impossible to repair at that time. Yes, we could explore what the loss of connection meant to her and analyse its deeper meaning, but that could not really repair the impact of the hiatus, especially as it was not an isolated occurrence.

"The technology is such a problem," Ajia, a patient, tells me. "I have such a high level of anxiety that something is going to go wrong. It stops the flow."

The loss of connection affects the fragile feelings of mutual presence, "being together with", and shared reverie between the therapeutic couple. "The more the breakdown, the less is the level of presence-as-feeling, the less is the quality of experience, and the less is the possibility of surviving in the environment," write Riva and colleagues (2006, p. 69), describing the evolutionary function of the feeling of presence as feedback to the self about the status of its activity. What these researchers in human–computer interaction propose is that when we experience variations in presence, in our experience of being-in-the-world, it signals to the self the need to overcome the breakdown in a search for more favourable experience. "A breakdown occurs when, during our activity, we are forced to stop the use of intentions-in-action" (Riva et al., 2006, p. 75). If sequences of intentions give motivated human behaviour coherence and meaning, then a breakdown of "the intention unfolding process" has serious consequences. Riva and co-authors write of the breakdown of presence-as-feeling as indicating a threat to survival, bringing to mind John Bowlby's focus on fear and the search for safety. Slade (2013) writes about Bowlby,

> For Bowlby, the drive to survive—not just physically, but psycholog-
> ically—was the key to understanding the organization of mental life.
> To couch this in more contemporary terms—our biology, core
> elements of our neural make-up, our arousal systems, our cognitive
> apparati, our representations of self and other are organized, at least
> in part by our instinct to survive . . . Relationships are the remedy for
> fear—of loss, annihilation, of psychic emptiness . . . (p. 41)

Slade (2013) describes the search for safety as a basic experience
that drives all human beings, not just those who are traumatised. Fear
for her survival sends a child back to the carer who offers a secure
base, regulating her fear. The secure child is then enabled to go out
into the world again, with freedom to explore and develop. Un-
regulated fear inhibits exploration, including the development of a
mental life and a full recognition of the other. By extension, clinically,
the therapist must provide for the patient a secure base where the
therapist is able to contain her anxieties, from which the patient may
eventually feel free to venture out in exploration of self and other.

What happens when a therapist cannot provide a secure base
consistently enough, when there is no way to insure that the connection will not be suboptimal or broken? "Just exactly as my patient was
talking about the pain of feeling lonely and disconnected, the Internet
connection was broken," recounts a therapist working with a patient
who is a relief worker in Africa. "The extreme weather in the remote
place she lives meant that we could not make contact again to resume
the session. Although I was able to follow up with an email that she
received when power was restored, I felt frustrated and impotent. I
could not be present with her to hold those feelings or to make sense
of them. By the time we met for the next session so much had
happened that the moment was lost."

Winnicott wrote about continuity of being:

> The holding environment . . . has as its main function the reduction to
> a minimum of the impingements to which the infant must react with
> resultant annihilation of personal being. Under favourable conditions
> the infant establishes a continuity of existence. (Winnicott, 1965, p. 47)

When there is a breakdown in presence, the breakdown in connection
for many patients is a literal re-enactment of previous traumas. The
search for, and discovery of, the sense of self, finding an identity, is the

aim of psychotherapy, and there must be a good-enough holding environment to achieve this. Yet, the possibility of "breakdown" of the good-enough environment and the connection to the mother/therapist is always there in a technologically mediated communication. Without good-enough holding, the baby/patient does not have the opportunity to "be", and can only react to impingement. Winnicott would describe this reaction as annihilation, a feeling of falling forever, leading to an inability to distinguish between inside and outside, me and not-me—in fact, as we shall see, the lack of a sense of presence (Winnicott, 1965).

Clearly, we need to give further thought to the effects of the unreliability of the technology in its present state. Preparing a patient in advance for that possibility might go some way to modifying the shock or frustration when it occurs. Exploring the significance of breaks in transmission or poor connections in the transference and countertransference is useful. However, consideration must be given to the accumulated impact of repeated impingements, small and large, on a treatment. In a co-present consulting room, we make every effort to maintain continuity and a safe space in which to work. Most of the time we are successful in doing so, making the times in which we fail fruitful moments to explore. We are able to be "good-enough mothers". However, the instability of the technology is, at this point in its development, often beyond our control, despite using the most-up-to date equipment and fastest connections possible. Both members of the therapeutic couple experience the frustrations, disappointment, and distress with the therapist's inability to provide a secure base.

Fantasies and quick fixes

Properties of the device change the nature of analytic sessions in other ways. "The digital clock is always visible on a computer screen," remarks Charles, the psychoanalyst in Boston. "My patients are much more tuned in to the timing of the session. They frequently bring the session to a close. With face-to-face work, even with a clock in room, patients are not usually so aware, and I generally bring the session to an end."

As mentioned previously, using technologically mediated software one can often see a "window" with one's own video transmission simultaneously to seeing the person with whom one is talking. Therapists tell me they find this distracting and some opt to use a function, if available, that showed the patient's video picture only.

Patients, too, can simultaneously see themselves and the person to whom they are talking. The analyst has no way of knowing what the screen set-up of the patient is. This can lead to both distraction and deception. One therapist found, through a chance remark, that for the first year of treatment the patient had been looking exclusively at himself, his own video picture blown up on the screen, throughout every session. Another therapist belatedly discovered that a patient, who could be seen just from the waist up, was wearing only underwear from the waist down. When I give him these examples, Todd Essig comments to me, "The fact that those fantasies can be acted on in reality shows how different the experience of technologically mediated communication is."

Therapists, themselves, might find that they are more easily distracted when using the computer: "I found myself wondering all the time what my email was. I think the nature of the device encourages us to think about multi-tasking," said one. Another confessed, "I'm ashamed to admit to surreptitiously checking my email during a session . . ."

Personal computer use is varied, and, as mentioned above, the kind of attention required is quite different to that of analytic practice. Patients' associations and habitual use of the computer, outside of sessions, can colour the tenor of the sessions. "My patient used the computer extensively for shopping and porn: I felt the associations bled over into the therapy experience. The same computer screen he used to watch porn, he used to interact with me." Of course, it is beneficial to explore these associations. However, it is important to acknowledge the difference between having a multi-purpose mediating device converting your voice and image into packets of digitalised data to be reassembled on the other end and an unmediated body-to-body communication.

The device itself is the vessel for many projections and fantasies, and adds an additional layer of complexity to a therapeutic transaction. "My patient has an extensive virtual identity online, including a different name. I was never sure how he regarded our interaction: was it a simulation, were we just personas or avatars?" Ruth, who is a senior analyst with many years' experience, remarks, "When my patient terminated therapy [prematurely], he told me that it was not as satisfying as those things online that he could control, like porn and video games." Patients approach the use of a computer with expectations and memories (some implicit) formed from past experience. This is also how patients approach their therapist and becomes the basis for an analysis. But a patient's expectations of a therapist (or the image of a therapist) on a screen can be confusing. Charles, the Boston psychoanalyst, points out, "Some patients wonder if Skype sessions are less expensive. The implication is that it is less valuable as you are not getting the real thing." While Charles feels that the patient's fantasy is that being co-present has more worth than working via a screen, from a different angle one could say that it is less of a fantasy for the patient and more of a perception. It could be said that it is the analyst's fantasy that the two ways of working are worth the same that needs to be explored.

Therapists, too, have to work through their previous experiences of computer use: "Because [the computer] is used for less intimate, less sensitive, less high-end communication, changing that into a living conversation is a radical shift in the use of the machine for me."

Another association to the computer, for therapists and patients, was that of a source of endless information. "In my childhood, when there were no computers," says a San Francisco psychoanalyst, "I had a fantasy of a big book with all the answers that I could consult whenever I wanted . . . and here it is [she gestures toward the computer]. I look things up all the time." "I have had patients who treat me as if I am an oracle residing in the computer," adds her colleague, "I feel like I have to pay attention to both my own and my patient's fantasies about the computer's capabilities. I love my computer: I use it mostly as a word processor, and in terms of rapidly [obtaining] information."

Patients and therapists alike comment on the instantaneous aspect of computers. The words "quick fix" come up repeatedly. An analyst who is also an artist says, "I really love the computer, but at the same time I feel that it's so much left brain stuff that it kind of dampens my right brain and the 'quick fix' of the computer does feel as though it has a very nasty effect on my own creativity."

The notion of the quick fix permeates our society. People send texts and emails and expect immediate replies. My supervisees receive texts from patients and feel pressured to respond rapidly, unable to take time to consider how best to communicate. Our rhythms have changed and the space for cogitation has shrunk. The ease and speed of connection sets up an expectation of immediate gratification, and waiting and frustration become difficult to bear. The time it takes to have relationships with depth has become problematic. However, relationship is central in psychoanalysis. Patients expect a quick fix and find it hard to understand how long psychoanalysis and psychoanalytic psychotherapy might take. They turn to medication and time-limited therapies, treatments that do not require a relationship, for a magic solution.

Lucy, the university student, uses Skype for her sessions when she is away from her therapist in the summer and during holidays. She tells me that she uses her computer for "quick fixes": YouTube, Facebook, Wikipedia. She grapples with the notion that therapy is not a quick fix. She muses, "I guess you can analyse like a quick fix in a Skype session, but it would come undone when you disconnect." Lucy talks about how difficult it is to square her quick fix use of the computer and the slow, thoughtful time it takes to build a therapeutic relationship and make the internal shifts required for psychic change. She worries that her instantaneous experience of connection will not be lasting. The rapidity and simplicity of technological connectivity does not feel to her like the effort of diligence that leads to an experience of continuity built in a shared environment.

CHAPTER EIGHT

The problem of presence

I n facilitating developmental change and growth, whether for a baby or a patient, the goal is to establish an authentic sense of self. The sense of self is deeply connected to a sense of presence. Winnicott describes this concept of the beginnings of the separate self with the term "unit status". For Winnicott, "unit status" designates the achievement of whole personhood, with the ability to distinguish between "me" and "not-me" and inside and outside:

> I wish to mention a form of development that especially affects the infant's capacity for making complex identifications. This has to do with the stage at which the integrating tendencies of the infant bring about a state in which the infant is a unit, a whole person, with an inside and an outside, and a person living in the body, and more or less bounded by the skin. Once outside means "not-ME" then inside means ME, and there is now a place in which to store things . . . Now the infant's growth takes the form of a continuous interchange between inner and outer reality, each being enriched by the other. (1965, p. 91)

The achieving of identity is included in the process of establishing a separate selfhood.

Grotstein (1978) writes that the capacity to experience space is "a primary apparatus of ego autonomy" originating in infancy when the neonate begins to experience skin as a boundary between self and non-self (cf. Bick, 1968). "Man exists and thinks in spatial terms. He seems to correlate external spatial phenomena with a template of inner space corresponding to this external space. Space becomes the context and perspective for thought and the road-map of experience" (Grotstein, 1978, p. 56). He believes that the maturing awareness and tolerance of the "gap", the space in distance and time between the going and coming of the primary object (mother/therapist), constitutes a "baptism of space". The infant's ability to "contain" the space in the absence of his/her carer (or therapist), allows him/her to instigate a sense of space and begin the process of separation. The sense of external space through separation also initiates a sense of internal psychic space, and an internal place where representations, memories, and images can be contained.

Celenza (2005) asks, "*Where* is analysis?" Although she is referring more specifically to where it takes place in an embodied way between the analytic couple in a shared environment, the question is a generally pertinent one, as she adds,

> The physical presence of both the analyst and the analysand is the foundation through which the experience of the analytic process is mediated ... making the location of bodies a potentially anchoring metaphor for therapeutic action. (p. 1647)

The physical bodily presence of the analytic couple is intrinsic to the reality that each brings to the analytic encounter as real participants: "the presence and engagement of the self in the analytic process is inherently bodily in all its manifestations" (Meissner, 1998b, p. 278). Both the self as intentional agent giving meaning to behaviour and the behaviour itself as expressive of meaning regarding the self's inner world operate in the analytic process. Therefore, the perception of presence is deeply rooted in the development of interiority/exteriority, self, identity, and the whole personhood that Winnicott called "unit status".

Layers of self

Damasio, in the field of neuroscience, also tracks the emergent self as developing through experience of interaction with an object or environment, located in space and time (Damasio, 1999, 2012). He divides the self into three layers: the proto-self, the core self, and the autobiographical or extended self. He defines the proto-self as the level of the self that gathers information regarding the state of the body. It is developed in the brain stem and it generates feelings that signify our existence. It is the necessary foundation of the overall self, creates basic consciousness, and is solely concerned with homeostasis. Damasio suggests that primordial feelings, feelings that occur continuously and automatically when one is awake, are the primary production of the proto-self. They provide a non-conscious direct experience of the living body.

The second level of self Damasio calls the core self. He hypothesises that this level of awareness allows most animals, and humans to be conscious of, and react to, their environment. This level of consciousness requires the interaction of the organism with an object and gives a sense of "here and now", the awareness of the present moment, independent of language, reasoning, and memory.

> [It] provides the organism with a sense of self about one moment— now—and about one place—here. The scope of core consciousness does not illuminate the future, and the only past it vaguely lets us glimpse that which occurred in the instant just before. There is no elsewhere, there is no before, there is no after. (Damasio, 1999, p. 16)

The third layer of self is the autobiographical (or extended) self, which allows for reflexive self-consciousness. Extended or autobiographical consciousness gives one a coherent picture of history, a narrative that "is now connected to the lived past and the anticipated future" (Damasio, 1999, p. 196). The narrative is formed from real events, imaginary events, past interpretations, and reinterpretations of events. A continuous identity situated in time emerges from the autobiographical self.

"The presence of *you* is the feeling of what happens when your being is modified by the acts of apprehending something" (Riva & Waterworth, 2003). Extended consciousness emerges from the gradual build-up of the subject's memories, experienced from the core self. It allows the creation of an internal world, including the imaginary, learning from the past, and the consideration of future possibilities not present in the current situation, as compared to the perceptual world experienced as outside the self (Damasio, 1999).

Damasio suggests that combination of the core and autobiographical selves within the mind produce a "knower", a sense of subjectivity that he elegantly expresses in the title of his book *Self Comes to Mind* (2012, p. 24).

In *The Interpersonal World of the Infant* (1985), Stern proposes a very similar development of selfhood that involves a delimiting of inside, outside, self, and other. In a series of overlapping stages, the infant develops from an early emergent self with a sense of "physical cohesion" (p. 7), to a core self, in which the infant creates an organised subjective perspective. This stage involves intense interaction with the carer, who acts as a "self-regulating other" for the infant (p. 102). The stage of the subjective self follows, in which there is an intersubjective exchange of affect with the mother, followed by the verbal stage, which initiates more abstract thinking. Later Stern added a "narrative self" in which the child creates autobiographical representations to create an identity.

In psychoanalytic thought, the development of ego autonomy, independent selfhood, is dependent on the locating of the self in space and the defining of the boundary between me and not-me. In neuroscience, Damasio (1999) proposes that the self and consciousness can be divided into three layers emerging from the proto-self, the inchoate feeling of self that arises from the brain's detailed map of the body, through the core self that registers the here and now "feeling of what happens" and requiring the organism to experience interaction with an object or environment. Finally, the extended, or autobiographical consciousness emerges, located in time, utilising memory, and blending knowledge with immediate experience.

Layers of presence

Researchers in the fields of information and communication technology and cyberpsychology have done fundamental work on defining the sense of presence in practical terms because they wish to propose the parameters on which to base the development of the best tools for communication technology and, particularly, in the realm of immersive virtual reality (Lombard & Ditton, 1997; Mantovani & Riva, 1999; Riva, 2006, 2009; Riva & Waterworth, 2003; Riva et al., 2004, 2006, 2009; Waterworth & Waterworth, 2003b).

Newer views from cognitive and neuroscience suggest that our cognition is influenced and possibly determined by our experiences in the physical world. No longer simply a matter of the manipulation of abstract symbols isolated in the brain, it is, instead, firmly lodged in the bedrock of sensorimotor processing. Just as our minds are situated in the body, our sense of presence is also situated, and related to our intentions and the actions we can take in space. The location of our bodies in space—and what we can do in it—is key to our sense of presence.

Space is defined by action. People experience presence if they are able to act in an external world where they can successfully transform their intentions into actions. Actions are defined by intentions, a person's specific purpose in acting, an end or goal he/she aims at.

> It is through the development of a common spatial and temporal framework with external objects, that the agent becomes a self, able to differentiate between internal and external intentions/action . . . the emergence of the Self also leads to the recognition of the "Other" as "another intentional Self". (Riva, 2008, p. 107)

Further, his or her experience of intersubjective or social presence is connected to the capacity to interact with the Other in the world, sharing intentional attunement with others. Communication and technology researchers state that the extent to which these experiences of levels of presence are integrated in a technologically mediated environment correlates with the intensity of experienced presence (Riva & Waterworth, 2003).

A person's capacity to locate him/herself in space according to the action he/she can do in it gives a sense of basic presence. Presence is the perception of successfully transforming an intention into an action (Riva et al., 2009). This "cyberpsychological" definition of presence, rooted in cognitive and neuroscience, is crucially significant to the study of technologically mediated treatment if one remembers two things. First, there is no potential to successfully transform an intention into an action in today's technologically mediated treatment that takes place in two separate environments, rather than a shared space. Thus, the intensity of the sense of presence, according to their definition, is greatly diminished. Second, without that sense of presence in a shared arena where intentions can be enacted, a patient will never be able to experience the analyst as real, surviving, and external. Without even the potential to act on intention, the patient can never experience the analyst as outside his/her omnipotent control in a shared reality.

We can see that these theories put forward by scientists involved in virtual reality research, linking presence to an internal and external sense of self and the potential to enact intentions in a shared space, closely align with both infant observation studies and psychoanalytic thought. The concepts of acting in the world of one's intentions and sharing intentional attunement with others recall the psychoanalytic theory of mentalization: the capacity to understand our own and other's behaviour in terms of intentional mental states, such as goals, needs, desires, beliefs, purposes, and reasons. The development of this capacity leads to the subjective experience of self and body as separate, with a sense of agency and the experience of the other as subjectively and physically separate and with a sense of agency (Fonagy et al., 2003).

In early presence research, the word presence was a contraction of the term "telepresence", first coined by MIT cognitive scientist Marvin Minsky in a 1980 article on remote-controlled technology. Lombard and Ditton (1997), in their fundamental paper on the concept of presence, defined it as a perceptual illusion that a technologically mediated experience was not mediated. The technological medium disappears from the conscious attention of the user and he/she behaves as if the mediation were not there. They enumerated six different conceptions of presence, including social richness, a sense of realism, a sense of transportation, a sense of immersion, a sense of interactivity or control, and a sense of the medium itself as a social actor. They suggest that all these definitions of presence are linked by the central idea of the experience producing an illusion of non-mediation. Among the most important variables in determining a sense of presence are sensory richness and the number and consistency of sensory outputs: the greater the number of human senses for which a medium supplies stimulation, the greater the capacity for the medium to produce a sense of presence. Lombard and Ditton also pointed out the importance of media user variables, such as the willingness to suspend disbelief and familiarity with the technology (1997).

The International Society for Presence Research provides a definition that was synthesised during discussion among their members and allows for various dimensions of presence ranging from those human perceptions that are not technologically mediated (i.e., face-to-face) to fully immersive virtual reality where the technology seems to become invisible.

> Presence (a shortened version of the term "telepresence") is a psychological state or subjective perception in which even though part or all of an individual's current experience is generated by and/or filtered through human-made technology, part or all of the individual's perception fails to accurately acknowledge the role of the technology in the experience. (2000)

Riva and Waterworth elaborated and extended this theory of [tele]presence to encompass the concept of presence, itself, regardless of whether it was technologically mediated. They remind us that while the design of virtual reality technology brought the theoretical issue of presence into focus, no one can argue that ". . . the experience of Presence suddenly emerged with the arrival of virtual reality" (Biocca, quoted in Riva, 2009, p. 159). Instead, they posit that presence is a basic state of consciousness, a fundamental neuropsychological phenomenon the goal of which is to produce a sense of agency or control (Riva et al., 2006). They propose a theory of presence based on four positions:

1. Presence has evolved as a defining feature of the self. The sense of presence enables the nervous system to recognise the separation between external events that may act upon the self in a shared physical world and an internal world where events occur solely within the self. This allows the organism accurately to interpret its perceptions, thereby ensuring its survival.
2. Although the experience of presence is an integrated feeling, theoretically it can be divided into three developmental layers.
3. Each level of presence elucidates a particular aspect of internal–external world separation and is distinguished by individual properties.
4. In humans, the sense of presence "is a direct function of these three layers: the more they are able to differentiate the self from the external world, and the more they are integrated, the more we experience a sense of presence" (Riva & Waterworth, 2003; Riva et al., 2004).

Interestingly, Riva and Waterworth hypothesise that there is a direct link between the development of the three layers of presence with the development of Damasio's (1999) layers of the self: the proto-self, the core self, and the extended or autobiographical self.

Proto presence (self vs. non-self): Damasio says that the proto-self consists of an organised collection of neural patterns that non-consciously maps the ongoing physical state of the organism (Damasio, 1999, p. 154). Each time the proto-self encounters an object, it is changed because, in order to map the object, the brain must adjust the body, signalling those adjustments and the mapped image back to the proto-self (Damasio, 2010, p. 215). Movement plays a central role in this process, which allows any organism automatically to regulate and adapt to its internal and external environment, ensuring the organism's survival. Riva and Waterworth propose that, through the comparison of sensory referred properties of the external world with separate internal sensorimotor representations of those properties, the organism is able to transform that information into appropriate responsive movement. Every perception is relevant to the well-being of the organism and is detected as such by the proto-self. The operations of sensing the state of the organism and acting are closely related. They suggest that the more the proto-self is in the body, the more it is differentiated from the external world. From this concept of proto-self, Riva and Waterworth derive a definition of proto presence.

> We can define *proto presence* as an *embodied presence related to the level of perception–action coupling*: the more the organism is able to couple correctly perceptions and movements, the more it differentiates itself from the external world, thus increasing its probability of surviving. (Riva & Waterworth, 2003)

Proto presence is embodied and based on the accurate matching of perception to movement.

Core presence (self vs. present external world): If the proto-self is changed by an encounter with an object, the core self takes this process a step further by connecting that changed proto-self to the external object that changed it. This object becomes the focus of attention (Damasio, 2010, p. 215). The core self exists in the here and now, continually re-created by each object with which it interacts. It has a sense of subjectivity, including perspective, ownership and agency on top of the proto-self's primordial feelings. Damasio hypothesises that one of the core self's chief functions is to enable the subject to recognise the present moment.

> The present is signaled by real time stimuli from the senses; but as perceptions are 90% or more stored knowledge, *the present moment needs to be identified for behavior to be appropriate to what is happening out there now.* (Gregory, cited in Riva & Waterworth, 2003, Section 2.2, par. 4)

Riva and Waterworth describe the process by which this is achieved as a complex neural mechanism that produces a shift in attentional focus. This shift in perceptual attention enables an organism to identify the external present moment and to differentiate between dreaming and waking. Connecting the core self to the process of core presence, core presence can be thought of as

> *the activity of selective attention made by the self on perceptions*: the more an organism is able to focus on its sensorial experience by leaving in the background the remaining neural processes, the more it is able to identify the present moment and its current tasks, increasing its probability of surviving. (Riva & Waterworth, 2003, Section 2.2, par. 6)

Core presence depends on an ongoing perception of being in an external world and discerning its state.

Extended presence (self in relation to present external world): The extended or autobiographical self encompasses more than just the here and now. Our memories are constructed into a narrative of our past, as well as the imaginable future. To anticipate the future involves planning and deliberation. In the extended self, consciousness has developed to the point where it can not only comprehend the meaning of experience in the here and now, but can attach significance to it. Riva and Waterworth highlight that characteristic of Damasio's extended or autobiographical self: the autobiographical self comprehends the external world with a meaning that has significance, imbuing an event in one's life with worth or value. In their vision, extended presence "[verifies] *the significance of the experience for the self. The more the self is present in the significant experiences, the more it will be able to reach its goals, increasing its possibility of surviving*" (Riva & Waterworth, 2003). The degree to which we can consider the consequences and significance of events in our current external situation equals the degree to which the sense of presence will be reinforced (Riva et al., 2006, p. 84).

Riva and Waterworth (2003) specifically suggest that *the more integrated these layers of presence are* (focused on the same events), *the higher the intensity of experienced presence* (in section 3.1, par. 2). When considering the impact of technological mediation on our sense of presence, it is significant that most media, with the exception of immersive virtual reality, only influence a limited number of layers.

In this view of presence based on Damasio's theory of the layers of self, motility, the differentiation of the internal from the external world (including dreaming and waking), and the creation of a sense of the significance of experience all combine to create a sense of reality in the world.

The discovery of mirror neurons and hypothesising about how perception, action, and intention share the same neurological language led Riva to elaborate further on the psychology of presence. As we saw in Chapter Five, mirror neurons, situated in the area of the brain next to motor neurons, fire in the brain when we observe another's actions, mimicking the exact pattern that our brains would use if performing the action ourselves. We experience the actions of the other as if we were performing the same action, having the same emotion, or utterance (Gallese, 2006; Gallese et al., 2007). The same neural substrates are activated whether acts are performed or simply perceived. In addition, it has been observed in both monkeys and humans that even when actions are partially hidden from the observer, mirror neurons can code the action based on *anticipation* of the final goal. This facilitates the ability to predict and understand action intention. When an act is performed, the pathway from the brain to the spinal cord is triggered, leading to movement. When an action is simply observed or imagined, the movement is suppressed: the action is simulated neurally, but not enacted (Gallese, 2009).

Presence locates the self: primary and social presence

Riva suggests, based on the above hypothesis, that it is the sense of presence that enables people to distinguish between a perceived action, an intended action, and a performed one. By being able to locate oneself in space and separate what happens internally from what is happening externally, the distinction between that which is perceived, that which is intended, and that which is enacted is clarified.

People experience presence if they are able to enact in an external world of their intentions. The experience of presence enables the control of agency and social interaction through the unconscious separation of both "internal" and "external" and "self" and "other" (Riva, 2006, 2008, p. 97). "What we need for presence are both the affordance for action (the possibility of acting) and its enaction (the possibility of successfully acting)" (Riva, 2009, p. 161). He defines presence as *"the non mediated (prereflexive) perception of successfully transforming an intention into an action (enaction) within an external world"* (2008, p. 110).

Like Gallese, Riva is interested in the infant observation studies of Meltzoff (2007), in which he determines that infants monitor their own bodily acts via proprioception and can detect cross-modal equivalents between their own acts-as-felt and acts-as-seen by others. The perception, as well as the execution, of action is perceived within the same internal frame. Infants can relate what they feel, for example, to what they see. Meltzoff observes newborns' ability to imitate the facial expression and simple manual acts of others, despite not being able visually to monitor their own movements. The infants possess a "like-me" framework enabling them to identify the similarities between self and other. Young infants make a basic self/other equivalent connection. "The other is *like* me but is not confused with me" (Meltzoff, 2007). Further, Meltzoff demonstrates that infants are able to detect intentionality in their carers. They are able to understand adults' attempted goals, even if the adults failed to fulfil them. When the infants observe the adults "accidentally" overshooting or undershooting a target, or failing to pull apart a dumbbell-shaped toy, the infants themselves are able successfully to achieve the adults' intended goals, despite the fact that the adults had failed in the execution. Meltzoff (2007) determines that, from nine to fifteen months, infants are able to infer the goals and intentions of an adult, even if the observed adult is unsuccessful in achieving them. Infants' self-experience allows them to perceive goals, plans, and intentions beyond surface behaviour. Infants use themselves as a framework for understanding the subjectivity of others, and reciprocally learn about the potentials for their own action by observing other's actions (p. 39).

Riva connects Meltzoff's observations that infants understand the goal-directedness in human acts, without yet being able to recognise "whose" intention it is, with the concept of basic presence. He describes the experience of basic presence as the identification of the other as an intentional self.

> It is through the development of a common spatial and temporal framework with external objects, that the agent becomes a self, able to differentiate between internal and external intentions/actions. However, the emergence of the *Self* also leads to the recognition of the "Other" as "another intentional Self". (Riva, 2008, p. 107)

Meltzoff's studies suggest that infants have goals and act intentionally. When an infant sees another act in the same way, his/her own basic experience would suggest that the other has a goal or intention beyond his/her perceived behaviour, even if he/she fails to achieve that goal. It is through interaction with external objects in a shared environmental context from which the basic self and the sense of basic presence emerge (Meltzoff, 2007; Riva, 2008). Thus, basic presence is a state of recognising an intentional other. It is significant that both Riva and Meltzoff emphasise the importance of "a common spatial and temporal framework" (Riva, 2008, p. 107) or "behavioral envelope" (Meltzoff, 2007, p. 12) for the emergence of a sense of both a basic self and basic presence.

From basic (inner) presence emerges social presence (co-presence): "*the non-mediated perception of an enacting Other within an external world*", in which there are also three layers (Riva, 2008, p. 107). The infant develops from recognition that there is an intentional Other, through interactive social presence where there is the recognition of the intention of the Other toward the Self, to shared social presence, where the Self and Other share the same intention and the infant is able to identify intentional attunement in other selves (Riva, 2008, p. 110).

Riva connects experience of higher levels of presence and social presence to higher and more complex potentials for intentions and their enactions.

In summary, Riva inextricably connects the development of the self to the development of a sense of primary and social presence. In fact, he identifies the growing experience of presence as that which facilitates the sense of separation of internal and external and self and other, leading to the feeling of agency and social interaction in the world. He describes the infant at birth, supported by such research as that of Meltzoff, as being able to recognise intention without being aware of whose intention it is. This stage equates with Daniel Stern's "early emergent self", and the process of separation described by Winnicott and Grotstein.

"Presence-as-process," the seating of the self internally and the perception of the external world as outside us, is achieved by neural development included in the three stages of proto presence (the subject locating the self in the body, as opposed to the external world: inside/outside; self/non self), core presence (self within the present external world), and extended presence (self in relation to the present external world). The outcome of this process is *"presence-as-feeling*: the non mediated (intuitive) perception that an intention is enacted successfully ... [and] experienced indirectly (prereflexively) by the self through the characteristics of action and experience" (Riva et al., 2006, p. 70). These intentions do not have to be "pre-meditated", but can be "intention-in-action" formed instantaneously and non-consciously impelling movement, as with the intention unfolding process formulated by the BCPSG.

This developmental journey from the basic recognition of the inside of self *vs*. the outside of self to the self in relation to the present external world provides the foundation for infants to use themselves as a reference to understand the internal world of others and, at the same time, learn about the potentials of their own actions by observing those of others. Through this type of relational interaction with intentional others, infants develop more complex social and relational intelligence (Meltzoff, 2007, p. 26).

The development of the self facilitated by the experience of presence leads to the recognition of the other as another intentional self, the outcome of which is "social-presence-as-feeling", the non-mediated perception of other's intentions, including empathy and attunement (Riva et al., 2006). Significantly, this would equate with Winnicott's "unit status", when a person is capable of a separate selfhood participating in a rich interchange between self and other. The achievement of personhood, the beginning of a separate self, depends on the ability to distinguish between "me" and "not-me", and inside and outside (Winnicott, 1965). Without the experience of presence, this would not be possible.

Being in the world with

Spanning disciplines, our sense of self is described as an embodied experience of existing, dependent on intentionality, moving and acting in space. Psychoanalysts talk of the birth of the self in terms of the experience of the skin as a boundary between self and other. The "baptism of space" is the recognition of the space in distance and time between self and other. The sense of external space through separation initiates a sense of internal psychic space (Grotstein, 1978).

The bodily presence of the analytic couple, inseparable from their minds, is the basis through which the intersubjective relationship in the analytic encounter is mediated. We have seen that Damasio, in the field of neuroscience, also tracks the emergent self as developing through experience of interaction with an object or environment, located in space and time (Damasio, 1999).

To summarise, researchers in information communication theory and technology are concerned with understanding and defining the concept of presence as precisely as possible in order to develop media which support this experience. Their hypotheses are founded on the features of being. These include defining spatiality (space around us and within us), and "being in the world with" (how we experience our existence in reference to others). The perception of presence is deeply rooted in the development of interiority–exteriority, self, and identity, creating a sense of reality in the world. People experience presence if they are able to enact in an external world of their intentions. A person's capacity to locate him/herself in space according to the action he/she can do in it gives a sense of basic presence. Further, the subject's experience of social presence is connected to the subject's capacity to interact with the Other in the world, sharing intentional congruence and attunement with others. These definitions of presence parallel the theoretical and clinical preoccupations of psychoanalysts, whose concerns are to enable a patient to achieve a sense of identity, a separate selfhood, in a relational interchange with the external environment. Both disciplines' concerns intersect most precisely at the point where the practice of psychoanalysis meets the utilisation of communication technology.

We have learnt that the extent to which experiences of levels of presence are integrated in a technologically mediated environment correlates with the degree of experienced presence (Riva & Waterworth, 2003). However, designers of present communication technology cite the numerous ways in which technology cannot fulfil these requirements (Donath, 2001; Olson & Olson, 2000; Ruhleder & Jordan, 1999, 2001; Sellen, 1995; Whittaker, 2003a,b). Why is this important?

The development of a sense of self might require both embodied perception *and* interaction with others. Maclaren (2008) describes the emergence of self in relation to other as a process which takes place over months and is never, even in adulthood, wholly complete. She describes the way that, through an "ongoing negotiation of boundaries" we come to know our own individual selfhood through actively relating to an embodied other. People are embodied intentional beings, orientated *toward* others, and other people's intentionality orientates us. "[The infant's] seeking out the gaze of the other enacts the implicit proposal that the other is an intentional communicative being—someone who is not an inanimate object but an active *relating-to-me*" (p. 86).

The intentionality of gaze and the solidity of the body both contribute to the recognition of self through the other. Maclaren suggests that our intercorporeal relations are a condition of the achievement of selfhood and illustrates this through a series of mother–infant studies in which infants respond with a tense fixed distress to an inanimate object and with smooth free cycling in and out of attention with a human being (Maclaren, 2008). It is only through perceiving others who recognise them that infants are able to conceive of themselves as a self. Of course, this recalls Winnicott's question, "What does the baby see when he or she looks at the mother's face? I am suggesting that, ordinarily, what the baby sees is himself or herself" (1971a, p. 112). Mirroring interactions between mother and the child provide a foundation for a sense of self.

Fonagy (2003) writes of "marked mirroring", the mother's ability to reflect the infant's feelings while also making clear that the feeling she is expressing is not hers, but the infant's (p. 231). He links it to Bion's concept of containment. What goes on in therapy is verbal, nonverbal, physiological, conscious, and unconscious. It is all directed toward patients becoming able to know themselves and their feelings, to feel fully present inside and outside, to be whole selves. Presence researchers such as Riva state that one feels present if one is acting in a shared temporal and spatial framework with external objects. Presence requires both the possibility of acting and of successful enacting. It is through interaction with external objects in a shared environmental context, from which the *basic self and the sense of basic presence emerge*. Sense of self and sense of presence are inextricably entwined.

What happens when there is no prospect of the therapeutic couple sharing a temporal or spatial framework? Screen-to-screen, there is no *possibility* of interacting with external objects in a shared environment. As Heeter (2003), Professor of Telecommunication at Michigan State University says,

> The perceived potential for interaction (affordances) acting upon or being acted upon may increase presence . . . the video draws attention to a lack of shared physical space, possibly inhibiting rather than enhancing social presence. *The Telewindow presents proof of not being there.* (p. 14, my italics)

So, how do psychoanalysts who are thinking about, writing about, and conducting technologically mediated treatments think about the issues of telepresence and co-presence? How do they conceive of a patient making use of an analyst when the potential to use is confined to the imagination rather than seated in the body? Enid Balint said, "the core of psychoanalysis is, in brief, the understanding of intrapsychic processes and states, and their relationship, or lack of it, with external reality" (cited in Parsons, 2009). If there is no external object in a shared environment with whom to interact, can a patient come to understand a relationship with the other, and external reality? What process do we think is happening when we do a mediated treatment?

PART IV
MAKING A PLACE FOR
SCREEN RELATIONS

CHAPTER NINE

Sometimes it works . . .

There is no doubt that some practitioners and patients do experience technologically mediated psychoanalysis as effective. Laura treated a patient in a remote area where there was no prospect of obtaining psychotherapeutic help:

> When I began I had no idea whether or not transference would occur in this medium or whether an analytic process could take place. I was wary of the limitations of the medium, having used Skype before in non-analytic situations, and the reassurances of another analyst that transference occurs regardless of the medium did not really reassure me. I was willing to give it a try, but I was prepared for failure. The reason I was willing to give it a try was because there was no other option, and this patient was suffering. I used Skype during separations with my in-person analysands only subsequent to my experience with this analysand because I had practice with the medium and because I knew that a process could develop and be sustained.

Laura feels strongly that the treatment she mentions above was transformative and that the results for her patient are long lasting. She tells me that she feels that, even if it is easier in a co-present treatment to pick up non-verbal elements, the signals of unconscious communication that are necessary for the analytic process to develop can be picked up in a technologically mediated situation. "I know my unconscious and my analysand's unconscious were in communication when we began having similar dreams during one phase of the analysis, something that happens during my in-person analyses as well." She distinguishes between the concepts of desirability and necessity when choosing modes of treatment and asks me, "Is it possible that computer-mediated psychoanalysis can be efficacious, even given the limitations you describe?" This is a crucial question, one that is echoed by Patrick, who asks, "If there are exigent reasons to offer computer-mediated treatment, are there ways to transform or substitute for the subtle communication one might lose in mediation?" It is interesting that he chooses the words "transform" and "substitute" because then what he is referring to is a *different* process than that which takes place in co-present treatment. Essig adds, "I totally agree that this is a vital question. And to it I would want to add an additional condition: if not [possible to transform or substitute], is it still possible to be helpful and effective even if the processes involved are substantially different that what takes place in-person? Without this additional condition, we risk biasing our descriptions so that they will justify current practice rather than deepen our understanding of what we are actually doing." What is important here is the necessity to understand exactly what is taking place when we treat another human being via technology: what succeeds in getting through, what gets "transformed" into something different, and what is degraded or lost along the way.

> Screen versions of reality will always leave something out, yet screen versions of reality may come to seem like reality itself. We accept them because they are compelling and present themselves as expressions of our most up-to-date tools. We accept them because we have them. They become practical because they are available. So, even when we have reason to doubt that screen realities are true, we are tempted to use them all the same. (Turkle, 2009, p. 17)

We need to know what *exactly* is left out and be able to distinguish between simulation, the "screen version of reality", and reality itself. Much points to the probability that when we use simulations, we might be unaware of exactly how they affect our essential experiences of intimacy.

"My experience of people is that they want to connect in some way and that way might be very painful, it might be unsatisfying . . . but there is an *underlying connection hunger and it is because of that we can use other media*," says Boston psychoanalyst, Charles. Turkle (2011) writes about how humans are wired to relate, describing a student interacting with Kismet, a robot, exclaiming, charmed, "You're adorable!" Myriad experiments confirm that people socialise with communication technologies as if they were people. In one "politeness study", participants asked to evaluate a computer unconsciously made an effort not to offend it with their criticisms (Blascovich & Bailenson, 2011). Because of our evolutionary hardwiring, we make the most of what we are offered. Our drive to connect can lead us to perceive minds even where no minds exist, in inanimate objects, like a robot or a computer programme, attributing human characteristics to those things (Mitchell, 2009).

In 1966, Joseph Weizenbaum, a computer scientist at MIT, designed a comparatively simple software programme called ELIZA, which would engage humans in conversation. ELIZA was modelled on the dialogue style of a Rogerian psychotherapist. Weizenbaum was not intending to do any exploration into computer-assisted psychotherapy; he was interested in creating a programme that could perform natural language processing. He was deeply shocked to find that participants began talking with ELIZA as if it were a real person. They quickly began to confide personal information to the simulation and became anxious about the limits of the programme's confidentiality. Imbuing ELIZA with human qualities, the users unconsciously tailored their answers to preserve the illusion. "What I had not realized," said Weizenbaum, "is that extremely short exposures to a relatively simple computer program could induce powerful delusional thinking in quite normal people" (Weizenbaum, 1976, p. 7).

A group of psychiatrists enthusiastically believed that the ELIZA programme could be developed into a therapeutic tool that could be made widely available to mental hospitals and clinics suffering a shortage of psychotherapists. Weizenbaum's co-worker on the programme, a psychiatrist named Kenneth Colby, seriously endeavoured to create a similar programme specifically for psychotherapy. In doing so, he wanted to create a formalised computer therapy that was precise and cognitive. His view of psychotherapy was inimical to psychoanalytically informed therapy. He modelled computer therapy on the computer itself and suggested that the therapist was an information processing machine. Weizenbaum felt that he was adjusting his therapeutic system to the limitations of the computer rather than to human needs (Turkle, 1995). "What can a psychiatrist's image of his patient be when he sees himself, as therapist, not as an engaged human being acting as a healer, but as an information processor following rules . . ." (Weizenbaum, 1976, p. 6).

We have seen how users of technological mediation unconsciously adapt their behaviour to the limitations and deficiencies of the screen. Weizenbaum observed how the users of ELIZA modified their questions to conform to the programme's parameters, as well as how Colby fitted his model of therapy into the way computers operate. Turkle (2011) calls this willingness to engage with the inanimate the wish to fill in the blanks. There is something inherent in us that compels us to connect, to bridge the gaps, and fill in the blanks. We do whatever we must to maintain our relationships, primed by an instinct to survive physically and psychologically. When we assess the limitations of technologically mediated treatment, it is very important not to automatically adjust our perceptions to fit the limitations of the tools.

When analysts talk to me, they often distinguish between their experiences of working with patients they have never met "in the flesh" and how it feels when they use mediated communication as an adjunct to a treatment that already exists in the shared consulting room. They uniformly say that their memories of working with their patients in a shared environment better enabled them to continue a sensitive connection with them using technologically mediated communication. They cite "residual trust and understanding" as facilitating this process, which is supported by Rocco's (1998) studies on trust being reinforced in computer-mediated communication following previous face-to-face interaction. Both explicit and implicit memory may help the therapeutic couple to bridge the relational gap. Many analysts agree that the longer a patient has been seen in a shared environment, the easier it is to refer to those explicit and implicit memories. What one analyst called "an inner template" links with the BCPSG's concept of implicit relational knowing, a significant component in how the analyst and patient intuit what is going on in each other's mind. This form of implicit experience of the other, rooted in the body, or, as Schore (2011) says, "right-brain-to-right-brain", may be sustained for some time, despite the narrowed channels of technological communication. As Anna said, "I had to carry over the quality of knowing her for real as opposed to virtual . . . You could almost say that it is a fourth dimension that works between us in that real situation, and in the screen-to-screen . . . we were both working hard to try to use every ounce of what we knew about that." However, because the "intention unfolding process" in which the "gestalt" of the conscious verbal and unconscious implicit intention involves embodied as well as reflective verbal communication, implicit memory may only go so far in filling in the gaps to make a whole meaning of the "gestalt" when technologically mediated (Nahum, 2008).

If clinical intuition, driven by right brain primary process, is what leads the analyst to ultimately communicate explicitly to the patient, and this intuition, essential for effective treatment is based on unconscious processing of exteroceptive and interoceptive information, then implicit memory to "fill in the blanks" might have a limited period of utility. "Secure attachment makes the insecurity of detachment bearable," says Jeremy Holmes, "but the mental representation of security fades without reinforcement. Absence makes the heart grow fonder—but only for a while; out of sight, out of mind all too easily takes over" (2010, p. 143). It would be a useful future study to examine and evaluate the resilience of memory processes as they carry over from embodied relational encounters to technologically mediated encounters.

The majority of the trainee psychoanalytic psychotherapists I teach and supervise in China also have their own training analyses and therapies via technological mediation because of the current scarcity of local psychoanalysts and psychoanalytic psychotherapists. Although they may have co-present clinical supervision connected with their workplace, their training supervision is online. As this is a model that is very familiar to them, many do not hesitate to treat their own patients via technological mediation. This is usually because a current patient has moved away or is studying abroad. Occasionally, they have patients who do not have therapists available in their area of the country referred to them by colleagues.

When they bring these cases into a continuous case supervision class or to individual supervision, they are often struggling with issues specifically related to technologically mediated work. They are puzzled by their difficulties in using their countertransference and in picking up nuanced communication. They feel distanced from patients with whom they once felt connection. They encounter impasses in the treatment, and feel unable to move it on. They feel it is more difficult to make an impact or have an impact made upon them by their patients. However, they do not connect their problems with the fact that they are working in a different medium. Because, for most of them, that is all they know, they do not think to wonder about the differences that might occur in a treatment when it transfers from co-presence to technological mediation. They do not talk with their patients about the differences they are experiencing using a screen, or interpret significant fantasies and meanings the patient might make of it. When I ask them to think about things such as how it feels when they are not in the same room, cannot see the whole body, are separated by screens, and what that might mean to both of them, they suddenly have a look of dawning recognition and relief. They do not consciously anticipate that the co-present treatment they have been doing will differ from the mediated one, as this is not something they have personally experienced. But when the possibility of this is pointed out, they all nod in vigorous acknowledgement.

One student talks about the difficulty a patient has in feeling a sense of continuity and connection to her after the patient has transferred to a university in another city. The patient talks about missing being with her therapist in the same room and feels she is "living on fumes of the past". She places her hand on the screen, each finger stretched out, longingly. She describes how flat and unreal the therapist feels. She tells the therapist that something solid is missing, that something is lost. The student therapist reports how she feels she has to learn to have a new relationship with the patient in therapy when working online. Because the student's experience of her own therapy has been online, there is a disconnect for her between the patient's expressions of loss and the newly adopted use of technology.

It transpires that it is perfectly possible for the patient being treated technologically to return to her former city and see the therapist co-presently about once a month. We talk about how this might affect the patient and the therapist, how their sense of connection might possibly be "refreshed" by those visits. When the therapist takes this up with the patient, they are both tremendously relieved, and then able to have a conversation about what the distance, the screen, and the loss of being bodies together means for them both. This was not something that had occurred to the student or her fellow classmates. Yet, when I suggested the possibility that something might be *different* about screen relations, it was almost as if I could see the wheels turning in their minds. They recognised something of their own experience and began to have words to describe it.

The idea of living on "fumes of the past", as described by the patient, makes me wonder how the process of having a memory of an embodied experience operates and how exactly it informs technologically mediated treatment. Does familiarity with the embodied presence of the other simply deepen an emotional bond? Does memory in some way actually enliven and reinforce a sense of presence? Does it intensify the capacity to imagine, are we "filling in the blanks"? How does it alter mediated perception in the here and now? Is the periodic possibility of potential action in the room together enough to allow the patient to test the analyst's capacity to survive? Is intermittent contact enough to foster the perception of the object as real in a shared reality? If embodied contacts revive a connection between people, how often and how long is required? What implications does this have for screen treatments where the participants may never meet?

When an analyst is aware that working on a screen is a simulation, fundamentally different from working in a shared environment, then he/she may be capable of experiencing moments of presence without becoming entrapped. Discriminating between the properties of screen relating and co-present relating might enable the analyst to make successful interventions with the patient. This depends upon keeping the limitations of the screen in mind. Patients have differing needs and sometimes the limited potential of a screen treatment may be just good enough for them. As an analyst says to me, "Sometimes you get lucky." However, this is a very different treatment schema to that which evolved from one hundred years of psychoanalytic development. The process by which we work using mediation by technology is not the process that occurs between two physically present people in the traditional consulting room. When both analyst and patient are clear about the nature of technological mediation, it makes a space for informed thinking and attention to the impact of the screen on the analytic process.

Our training analysis has the largest impact on what we do in the consulting room, followed by supervision. What are the implications of candidates being analysed in one modality and proceeding to work in another, with no basis for comparison? Yet, as I write, not only are there several organisations training psychoanalytic psychotherapists remotely, but also at least one institute in the USA that is a member of the IPA and APsaA that does distance training and more institutes in negotiation for this type of programme. Distance candidates are willing to invest a tremendous amount in these trainings, not only money, but, because of the time difference, sometimes staying up all night to attend classes. Training institutes should be obliged to discuss transparently with their students the potential limitations of this kind of training. I am not saying that technologically mediated training should not be done. There might be very good reasons why a mental health professional without immediate access to such a training may wish to have what is possible and on offer. What I am saying is that the institutes need to reflect carefully about exactly how their trainees are being prepared if they are experiencing simulated personal treatments via technology and intend to practise with their own patients co-presently.

In the same vein, candidates who are attending co-present trainings have lobbied to be allowed to see their own training patients via computer mediation. There has been an increasing difficulty over the years for candidates to fulfil institutes' requirements for experience in providing intensive analyses. It is a struggle for candidates to find and keep patients who will commit to an open-ended analysis meeting multiple times per week. Getting training patients who are enabled to attend sessions more easily remotely, or who are abroad without any other option for treatment, goes some way to ameliorating this problem. Yet, again, there is the issue of training in a mode that involves an inherently different process to that of co-present psychoanalysis. It is not simply a matter of importing or exporting.

One analyst who had been prominently active in this campaign shares his personal experience of this issue during his training. "I was very enthusiastic about my institute 'ok-ing' distance work. I had lost two patients during my training and was very anxious about losing more time. I felt that if I could cast a wider net, I might be able to fulfil my requirement." Although at that time his training institute did not give him permission to treat a training patient via technological mediation, the analyst had other opportunities to treat patients remotely. "After my experience of using Skype [to work with] patients, I can understand why my institute was hesitant. It is not at all the same thing as working in the same space with a patient. I have definitely revised my opinion."

The possibility of technologically mediated treatments comes at a time when psychoanalytic trainings are having immense difficulty attracting trainees. Patients are in short supply for established practitioners. As that source shrinks in all venues, "clinical survival methods" come into play for both training institutes and practising analysts (Carlino, 2011). A training institute might decide to solicit students from abroad who must attend the training remotely. Analysts might decide to provide technologically mediated treatment and list it on their new websites as an option. Survival methods might affect clarity of vision. This takes us to the next chapter, on the growing economic pressures to use, and rely on, technology.

CHAPTER TEN

The elephant in the room

The rise of technology-based treatments is not merely the consequence of emerging technological possibilities meeting clinical need, as some suggest. Simply put, many highly trained mental health professionals are looking for work. The economics of treatment at a distance cannot be ignored.

Following the heyday of the practice and teaching of psychoanalysis from the 1950s through the 1970s, the popularity of psychoanalysis and psychoanalytic psychotherapy has waned dramatically in the western world. Third-party payers, whether it is private insurance companies or governments subsidising health care, have capped the number of sessions available to patients and support cheaper, time-limited behavioural therapies and psychopharmacological treatments. The limits set by payers reinforce patients' expectations of a "quick fix". Many people who would significantly benefit from psychoanalytic care find themselves increasingly pressed for time, distracted by technology, and economically challenged. They prefer short-term treatments, with less time and financial commitment and what they perceive as quicker results.

Applications to psychoanalytically based trainings, where excellent candidates once competed for admission to highly selective institutes, have declined considerably. Trainees do not want to risk the commitment of time, money, and emotional and intellectual devotion to train in a profession with an uncertain future where the pool of patients is drying up. In 2013, three major London institutes providing training in psychoanalysis and psychoanalytic psychotherapy merged into one, after some years of struggle to attract trainees. Institutes in the USA, too, are finding it difficult to survive, as psychoanalysis continues to be marginalised in favour of less expensive, short-term, supportive or solution-focused therapies. Senior analysts in training institutes, who used to be able to depend on the influx of new candidates as training patients, find this source of patients ebbing as well. Psychoanalytically orientated training in psychology graduate programmes and psychiatric residency programmes has all but disappeared, replaced by a focus on psychopharmacology and time-limited behavioural therapies for which the practitioners know they will be reimbursed (Eisold, 2005).

The marketplace has been flooded with an oversupply of therapists, especially in large cities. There is increased competition among practitioners and a decrease in patient referrals. In the USA, many senior practitioners are medical, because of the American Psychoanalytic Association's former policy of requiring psychoanalytic trainees to have medical degrees. Having done an extended training totalling an average of sixteen years, they would expect to earn the equivalent of American doctors. Newly qualified therapists, who could once look to their teachers and peers to make enough patient referrals to start a healthy practice can no longer do so, as their senior colleagues face increasing financial uncertainty. While there are still pockets of professional prosperity in large cities such as Manhattan, analysts at all stages of their careers speak of lowering fees and the difficulty of making a living comparable to other professional groups. It has been suggested that the standard "fifty-minute hour" had been widely reduced to forty-five minutes in the USA, in order to bill enough hours to make up for reduced reimbursement (Kevin, 2013). Many practitioners find themselves practising in non-analytic modalities in order to survive financially (Silver, 2003). An *ad-hoc* committee of the IPA, set up to examine the extent and character of the crisis in psychoanalysis, described the decline in patients, candidates, and psychoanalytic presence in university and medical trainings as leading to "demoralization, anguish, [and] paralysis" (Connolly, 2008,

p. 481). So, it is into this bleak state of affairs that technologically mediated, distance psychotherapy has appeared, and, in the light of the foregoing, it is disingenuous for its advocates to hide behind an indiscriminate defence of its clinical worth, when it is so obviously being adopted wholesale as the apparent cure for sick practices.

Here are a few examples of what our profession is subjected to. *Online Therapy: A Therapist's Guide to Expanding Your Practice* assures the reader that rather than debating the merits and pitfalls of using the Internet in therapy, the book "moves directly to implementation. After all, online therapy is already here!" (Derrig-Palumbo & Zeine, 2005). The book *Psychotherapy 2.0*, part of the United Kingdom Council for Psychotherapy Series, is described on the publisher's website thus:

> [It] blows open the consulting room doors and shows successful pathways for attracting new clients to gain access to psychological help, as well as demonstrating that despite initial scepticism, working online as a psychotherapist or counsellor can be as effective as "face2face" work. (Weitz, 2014)

The Telemental Health Institute offers online "evidence-based professional training for best practices in Telemental Health" including legal and ethical issues, reimbursement strategies, and telepractice documentation guides. Their web page urges you to "Expand Your Practice/Substantially Reduce Overheads/Be on the Growing Edge" (Maheu, 2012). It offers continuing education credits for psychologists, nurses, counsellors, and doctors.

Lest one object that the above books and website (only a small selection among many) are too broadly referring to psychotherapy and psychology, a quick Google search of the key words "psychoanalyst" and "Skype" brings up in the first two pages the websites of five IPA psychoanalysts who all routinely make Skype available as a service to their potential patients. "People are often short of time and are sometimes increasingly reluctant to get in a car to drive through country lanes or busy city streets," explains one. The books *Distance Psychoanalysis* and *Psychoanalysis Online* also come up in the search, both of which look to a future of screen treatment as convenient and possibly preferable in some situations (Carlino, 2011; Scharff, 2013a). The American Psychoanalytic Association's search facility to find an analyst on their website includes in its search criteria "offers distance analysis by phone/by Skype". My registering body, the British

Psychoanalytic Council, has posted a call for BPC registrants who use Skype for long-distance clients in its Members area on its website.

"There is no doubt," an analyst tells me, "that much of the rush to adopt Skype is economically driven. If you have empty hours to fill and patients more willing to Skype than to show up at your door, you'll consider doing it." A newly trained analyst says, "It is the only way I have filled up my practice. It greatly expands the possibilities for getting patients. Because I practise from California, I have to call it 'life coaching' if I see someone out of state." Josh, an analyst in Australia, says, "Technology allows you to break out of the consulting room. It gives you a worldwide mandate."

An argument that has been put forward in support of technologically mediated treatment is that co-present treatment is a luxury reserved for the urban elite and not something to which the common masses can aspire. Online psychoanalysis is seen to be the more democratic solution. As the current market is oversupplied with practitioners from a wide range of the mental health professions, this would not seem to be a problem, except for those who are in stiff competition with their colleagues. While outreach to those in need is a worthy goal, care should be taken as to how one represents what is offered. This is particularly true when psychoanalysts and psychoanalytic psychotherapists are breaking new ground, offering treatment and training in countries where there is, as yet, no established psychoanalytic tradition. Is technologically mediated treatment being described as equivalent to co-present psychoanalysis in these new territories?

Unpalatable as it may be to hear these sentiments, access to technologically mediated treatment is seen as a way to revive the dying economy of a profession in peril. I say this as one of the members of that profession, and someone who has used and does use technology for treatment and supervision. Competition for patients and the difficulty of making a living already forces analysts to work unhealthily long hours to make ends meet. "You feel like you may as well try it," an analyst shrugs, "because one of your colleagues certainly will." The consequence of these analysts' positions is a powerful critique. There is no cost-free choice, even though the cost is paid by others and not by the online psychoanalyst.

People who rely on technological mediation as a first-line treatment are ignoring the economic damage done to traditional co-present psychoanalysis. This results in two significant effects. First, a substitution effect, where an hour online is an hour less in the consulting room: there is no net gain. Second, if we accept that technologically mediated treatment is experimental and unproved, with limitations as compared to co-present treatment, then it is akin to marketing a fine dining experience and, because people want fast food, opening a MacDonald's because if you do not someone else will.

This view is voiced rather extremely by John Grohol, a clinical psychologist who sits on the editorial board of the journal *Cyberpsychology, Behavior and Social Networking*, on the subject of potential state legislation of online therapy in the USA:

> Legislatures which do limit such online services are only shooting themselves in the foot. Other states, or even other countries, will become the e-therapy capitals of the world, catering to millions of Americans every year.

> This is not a prediction, this is a simple fact of business and economics on the Internet. Markets which have a great demand for them do not shut down, they simply move. Any legislature or licensing board which thinks it can legislate economic forces with restrictions on practice has a limited understanding of economics and the new global economy. It may be your task to try and educate them so they make the right decisions in this area. If you don't, nobody else will. (Grohol, 2011)

He emphasises that he is referring to "e-therapy" and later suggests that one call it that in order to avoid the legal issues of calling it online psychotherapy.

But wait a moment: there are *not* "millions of Americans" just waiting to take advantage of putative therapeutic opportunities, here or anywhere else in the world. These kinds of fanciful and extreme points of view do not serve us well. On the contrary, they merely point out to all (and this includes the many detractors of psychoanalysis) the desperate and panicky tone emanating from some segments of our profession that this whole topic has provoked.

Thinking about working with technology in a simulation of a session forces us to confront systems outside of our comfort zone. These issues, connected as they are to "clinical survival" and professional status and identity, ignite dramatically extreme emotional responses when discussed by groups of psychoanalysts.

There are additional important factors that also need to be considered. If you are going to use technological mediation you do need to know how the tools you use affect the work you do. You cannot expect to have it both ways. To wit, the majority of analysts who spoke with me charge the same fee scale for technologically mediated sessions as they do for co-present sessions (I am aware there are some analysts who do not do so, but this is less common). If one acknowledges that technologically mediated treatment is an experimental process with limitations and constraints that differs from co-present sessions (and one has a duty to inform patients of this), then one must charge accordingly. "After all," a medical doctor says to me, "a CAT scan costs less than an MRI. And it gives you less information."

It is difficult for therapists to acknowledge to themselves and to their patients the uncertain and sometimes unsatisfactory treatment we offer when we depend on technology. Therapists are either unaware or reluctant to suggest that the mode of treatment they are offering is not the same process as that which they offer in a shared environment. Patients who may be desperate for help which is unavailable elsewhere will take it in any case. In my experience, they give a quick consent and do not have enough understanding of the therapeutic process to really consider the implications. Analysts who choose to use technology for economic reasons are particularly resistant to discussing its experimental nature and limitations with their prospective patients. Patients who are opting for this mode of treatment because of comfort and convenience are not willing to think about alternatives.

Analytic training organisations that offer trainings via technological mediation should also be obliged to alert their candidates to the differences between having a training analysis or therapy on the screen and in a shared environment. By not doing so, they are implicitly stating that what they offer is identical to a co-present training (and they might be charging the same tuition fees).

"You are accusing me of unethical behaviour," an analyst says to me indignantly. In fact, I am not. What I am making is a plea for awareness. If we use this unproved method of communication for treatment, be cognisant that it is both experimental and different, not a direct replication of bodies being together in the consulting room. If we choose to use technology for treatment, know exactly what are our motivations and what are the possible consequences. Understanding the particular characteristics of screen-to-screen relations can help clinicians make better choices. In the case of a patient who might not otherwise receive any help at all, it could be the treatment of choice. In the case of a patient who is too panicked by intimacy to be able to function with a therapist co-presently, it might be a temporary way to work that paves the way for a safe transition to the consulting room. Unless we can understand how the two contexts differ, we cannot begin to make informed decisions about how and when we use them. But, do not let "demoralization, anguish, [and] paralysis" caused by the current crisis in psychoanalysis and psychoanalytic psychotherapy dictate our choices in treatment.

"If you can't beat 'em, join 'em," says Josh. But the *them* is *us*. It is *our* profession and we are a part of it; we have responsibility for its future. If we make uninformed decisions, impulsive decisions, or resigned decisions, we not only affect the direction of our profession's future, we affect the quality of our patients' care.

CHAPTER ELEVEN

The toothpaste and the tube

I t is a popular assumption that there is an unbridgeable genera-
tional divide between "digital natives", those people who grew up
with digital technology and are comfortable using it, and "digital
immigrants", whose brains and thought patterns developed before
the existence of digital technology. This gap between generations
seems to require "digital immigrants" (people born before the 1980s)
to adapt to the radical technological advances in this new era of
connectivity or risk falling behind both socially and economically.
Psychoanalysts, who are a generally older cohort, are keenly aware of
this pressure to keep abreast of technological advances. Naturally,
they display a curiosity and wish to understand the impact of this
sea change as it affects their patients' personal lives and wider main-
stream culture. If they did not do so, they would be trapped in "simulation avoidance", the inability to think about the significance of the
immense technological shifts that affect our culture.

Having said that, there seems to be a rather uncritical assumption
that the apparently ubiquitous technological practices of the younger
generation must somehow be actively incorporated into a new form
of analytic communication—an attitude of "adapt or die". Psychoanalysts write confidently of the day when technologically mediated

communication will be the treatment of choice by "digital natives", no matter what their distance from an available analyst. They accept that while for "digital immigrants" the idea of knowing an other is connected with an embodied experience of the other, for "digital natives" the concept of knowing is quite different. It is still understood as a meeting and a knowing, despite the fact that all contact with that person is disembodied through mediation. They suggest that those people who have learnt new habits of communication have little difficulty in conducting a mediated treatment (Carlino, 2011). They cite digital natives' customary and habitual use of technology for intimate and business communication: "Technology is driving their choices, and their lifestyle is driving their need for technology, including the need for technology assisted psychoanalysis to maintain the optimum frequency of analytic sessions for in-depth analytic work". They suggest that there has been a radical transformation of the mind and its perception of the body, ". . . to which psychoanalysts must now adapt their treatment approach" (Scharff, 2013a, p. 65).

This is a rather curious attitude to the culture of the Internet, which is in the comparatively early days of its development and, as yet, largely unexamined—especially in the realm of relationships. It seems premature to make sweeping predictions such as "there is no going back, and just as we cannot put toothpaste back in the tube, psychotherapy practice is changed for ever with the advent of the digital age" (Weitz, 2014, p. 227). One must ask why there is such an intense demand by psychoanalysts that they adapt their approach to suit the technology-driven lifestyles of digital natives when technologically mediated treatment is still in an experimental stage. Many patients start psychotherapeutic treatment asking for fortnightly or even once-monthly sessions, ostensibly because it suits their lifestyle and/or financial situation. However, we know that analytic treatment cannot progress with large gaps of time between sessions. Do we agree to those immense gaps because it suits the patients' lifestyle? Sometimes, people want what, in the end, is not best for them. So, we try to explain why, in our professional opinion, more frequent and regular sessions forward the therapeutic process. Before we scramble to join a perceived technological land rush, we need to know and be able to explain exactly what we are offering to patients and why.

In the past ten years, the digital generation gap—and some argue that this distinction is spurious—has become less wide. Over the past twenty years, Internet statistics show that the average adult spends more time online than the average child (Carr, 2011, p. 227). Sherry Turkle interviews children and teens who despair of their parents' attention, as they pore over texts and emails on their mobile phones in the car, at the dinner table, breastfeeding babies, at funerals, and in the playground (Turkle, 2011). Nursing homes and retirement homes are full of media stations for the residents to use, and they do. Both young and old who use technology adapt to the rhythms of continuous partial attention, to rapid instantaneous jumping from one piece of information to the next, to constant connection, thereby forming new neural connections and new cognitive habits. Yet, somehow, the analysts I talked to disowned the value of their own experiences, pre and post the coming of the digital age, as if those who were born immersed in technology, rather than knowing differently, know best.

There is an uncomfortable feeling that psychoanalytic psychotherapies are seen as anachronistic and old-fashioned, and that they must "move with the times" in order to remain relevant and utilised. "I was trained in the 1970s," says Joanna, "I don't feel I can possibly understand the experiences of texting, emailing, Facebook and FaceTime that my young patients bring to my office in the same way they inherently do." Lawrence, an analyst nearing retirement who has written prolifically on sociocultural issues tells me, "We [digital immigrants] have to respect their culture and adapt to it, as if we were visiting a foreign country and learning its language and customs. We need to keep abreast of the times." Essig comments on this devaluing of a whole generation's sensibilities:

> [We] just may know (and value) things crucial for being fully human. We are among the last generations to have participated in both worlds (the pre- and post-digital) and that gives our generation special status. Our generational sensibilities just may turn out to be wisdom we cannot afford to lose. In fact, I think our generational sensibilities need to be revered, in part because our generation is among the last who will know it natively. Some of the young journalists I've gotten to know via Forbes are acutely aware of the limitations of screen relations. Several of them have responded with a "yuck response" when I told them about analysts flocking to the screen to treat patients in other locations and countries. Digital natives often yearn for the old country only us digital immigrants remember.

There is a difference between the desire to understand the nature of something profoundly, and to incorporate it wholesale into our lives. While we certainly should not dismiss or deprecate technology, we do not need to allow it to "drive our choices". We need to find a way to approach it appreciating the differences it produces in our perceptions and in our relationships, critically and thoughtfully.

When we read that for digital immigrants the idea of knowing a person is intrinsically connected with an embodied experience of the other, as opposed to another kind of disembodied mediated knowing, is that something we want to give up? As we are irrefutably and irreversibly embodied creatures, do we want to give up, *can* we give up, that to which we are inextricably bound as human beings? How are we changed by knowing in a disembodied way? It certainly is different, and, as creatures who intimately interact with others, it behoves us to understand that difference.

A 2010 University of Michigan study found that college students today have had a marked drop in their capacity to empathise with other people. Absorbed in their disembodied, controllable connections, they lose the ability to relate to unpredictably whole and present people. Increasingly, psychotherapists report that patients who "present in their consulting room . . . [are] detached from their bodies and unaware of the most basic courtesies" (Turkle, 2011, p. 293). Despite the impact of technology on our ability to relate, it is the digital natives, like the ones who said "yuck" to Essig about screen treatments, who may be leading a nascent Internet backlash. Danah Boyd, a researcher at Microsoft Research, discovered that young people would much rather be with their friends in person than mediated by technology. However, increasingly isolated, teenagers are not only tethered by technology, but by helicopter parents concerned with safety, decreased mobility with school and schoolmates often located far away, and societal limitations (Bilton, 2014). Young people are painfully aware of the damage of constant connection, even if they have difficulty managing the position of being "always on". They express dismay at never receiving their parents' and friends' full attention. They have a dawning awareness of the potential violations of their privacy on the Internet, even with purportedly encrypted applications like Skype (Carr, 2011; Turkle, 2011).

If we know that the younger generation and our generation, too, are increasingly disconnected through hyper-connection, is simulation the way we want to model ourselves as mental health practitioners? Is it all right not to "be there" when you are perhaps treating someone for the damage done in a relationship with someone who was not fully there? What does it mean that we are offering ourselves, with whom the patient is invited to have a transformative relationship, as disembodied? Is it reasonable to expect our patients to *imagine* what it is like to have real embodied relationships when they might be coming to us because that is an area in which their lives have broken down?

Sherry Turkle points out the potential risks of providing substitutes for human care, when people propose that robots take over the simpler chores in life such as feeding or changing babies.

> ... children fed their string beans by a robot will not associate food with human companionship, talk and relaxation. Eating will be come dissociated with emotional nurturance. Children whose diapers are changed by robots will not feel that their bodies are dear to other human beings. (Turkle, 2011, p. 292)

If we offer a screen analyst instead of an embodied analyst, with what will the patient associate that relationship? If a patient chooses technologically mediated communication as treatment of choice regardless of their distance from a consulting room, what does that say about the patient—and about us if we are willing to treat him or her under such circumstances?

Turkle describes the concept of "sacred space" as a place where people can hold themselves apart from simulation, in order to feel most fully themselves. Architects at MIT in the 1980s, using the new tools of computer simulation, reserved for themselves the continuing experience of drawing by hand, which personalised their creations and connected them physically to that process. This was done by even the most eager supporters of computer-assisted design. Today, some designers keep on their desks in front of their design screens the components for cardboard models, checking their computer designs against their cardboard ones that they consider "more real". An architect explains how hand drawings and models "preserve my physical intuitions" (Turkle, 2009, pp. 47–48). The architect's expression of the "more real" connects to her perception of being able to enact bodily in an external world of her intentions. She has a perception of her presence in the spatiality of the external world rather than in a simulation.

The sacred space, a connection between creative conception and physical expression that the architects chose to safeguard, is reminiscent of Winnicott's (1971c) notion of the "third area" of potential space. It is that intermediate area between the internal psychic reality and the external world of the physical environment where creative living resides. It is the area where "everything we do strengthens the feeling that we are alive, that we are ourselves" (Winnicott, 1990, p. 43). It is that creative sacred space that we hope to offer our patients for potential psychic growth, located between the patient's inner world and the external world of shared perception. "The special feature of this place where play and cultural experience have a position is that *it depends for its existence on living experiences . . . they take up time and space*" (Winnicott, 1971c, pp. 108–109).

The young MIT postgraduate students understood that while computer-assisted design was introduced "experimentally" in the 1980s, it was actually a given that it would be incorporated into their programme.

> One architecture student said that when she asked her professor why no one was trying to compare how structures designed "manually" actually "stacked up" against structures designed on the screen, she just got a shrug. As she put it: "It was just assumed that the computer would win." From the time it was introduced, simulation was taken as the way of the future. (Turkle, 2009, p. 12)

This is the same way technologically mediated treatment is being adopted into analytic practice, with a sense of inevitability and a veneer of being in the vanguard of "the greatest moment of change since Freud" (Weitz, 2014). Books such as *Psychotherapy 2.0* claim that "despite initial scepticism, working online as a psychotherapist or counsellor can be as effective as 'face2face' work" without actually asking how co-present therapy actually "stacks up" against screen therapy (Weitz, 2014).

In response to the "crisis in psychoanalysis", analysts are desperately searching for ways to redirect the profession. Smarting from accusations both internally in the field and externally in wider society that "we are sectarian zealots engaged in self-perpetuating delusions", analysts are attempting to be more responsive to the cultural and socio-political spheres in which they are embedded (Eisold, 2003, p. 579). Fearful of being labelled inward looking and isolated, there is a push to bring thinking and practices into the twenty-first century. After all, who would want to appear to be against progress, change, and flexibility in considering the patient's needs? Who would want to be identified as a Luddite, standing on the side of rigidity and dogmatism? "We psychoanalysts are 'playing catch-up'," an analyst explains to me. "Activities with computers are part of a larger cultural paradigm shift." Analysts seem to be resigned (or enthusiastic) to accepting the necessity to practise mediated treatment as part of that cultural shift. This is despite urgent calls from scholars in human–computer relations to reassess the impact of technology on our most intimate relationships (Carr, 2011; Turkle, 2011).

It is significant that Sherry Turkle, a psychologist and one of our foremost experts in the social implications of technology, has moved from speculations on how the Internet can expand one's sense of identity to deep concern about the costs of technological communication for direct human connection. Far from being a Luddite, she calls for a reclaiming of our direct human ties and a re-evaluation of the place of technology in our lives. As psychoanalysts and psychoanalytic psychotherapists, it is the capacity for full, authentic human experience that concerns us. What do we sacrifice, and what blind alley do we go down, when we hasten to "play catch up" without reflection and awareness? Essig comments,

> I must say that I don't agree screen relations based treatments are necessarily here to stay, especially as a routine, functionally equivalent replacement for in-person treatments. After all, psychoanalytic history is replete with practices thought to be a good idea at the time that we've learned to jettison: treating one's daughter, never mixing meds and the talking cure, interpreting a psychosomatic cause for ulcers, taking countertransference to be problem not data, viewing the analyst as a neutral objective blank screen, the ubiquity of penis envy in women. And when we add in rapidly developing technologies, we just don't know what the future of computer-mediated treatment will be.

As Turkle (2011) cautions, we have created "inspiring and enhancing technologies, and yet we have allowed them to diminish us" (p. 295). Rather than unhesitatingly jumping into the fast-moving current of the moment at the precise time when there are calls for reconsideration of the impact of technology on our cognition and our most intimate relationships, we need to step back and take stock of our position. Already, observations are being made of how technology can degrade our human relationships, reducing them in complexity and richness in ways of which we are not even conscious and that we now take for granted. How, then, does the technology of simulation affect the psychoanalytic relationship, into which patients enter in order to locate a genuine sense of self? Until we know this clearly, neither we nor our patients can make informed decisions on how best to proceed together.

CHAPTER TWELVE

To be in the presence of someone

Speaking of the unique value of bodies together, other than the well-known possibilities for human bodily interaction that have nothing to do with psychotherapy per se, although it may be very therapeutic, just what empirical data do you have about the "unique value of bodies together in psychotherapy?" To my mind, sorry to use the term mind, but I think in psychoanalytic therapy we think what really matters is the unique value of two minds together. As I wrote in an earlier post, it's not the 20th century anymore and the idea that people actually have to physically meet in an office is a passé understanding reserved for people whose existence is in large urban centers with plenty of high priced therapists. Surely, if people can reasonably be expected to meet together I have nothing against office mediated psychotherapy.

So posts a psychoanalyst on the forum of Division 39, the psycho-analysis division of the American Psychological Association. Are co-present bodies indeed *passé*? Have we reached the point where, as Fortunati (2005) says, body-to-body communication is an increasingly ephemeral prototype? Are we losing, as she predicts, the social memory of the qualities of co-present communication as we progress in the twenty-first century?

Two minds together are, as we have seen, only half the story. This particular inconvenient truth is that bodies cannot be left out of the equation, although it continues to interest me that human beings persist in wishing to do so. The mind is inextricably rooted in the body, and all our emotional experience is bodily based, arising in the body before conscious awareness (Damasio, 1999). Communication is both explicit and implicit, and the implicit realm is highly nuanced and highly dependent on physicality. It requires the whole body with its complex array of non-verbal language.

"The relation between outside and inside is as central to psychoanalysis as breathing" (Parsons, 2007, p. 1444). Just as Winnicott said there is no such thing as a baby, there is no such thing as a mind. The external and internal are connected, just as the body and mind are connected. You cannot have a disembodied mind; neither, for long, can you have an internal setting without the checks and balances of a shared external environment.

Working in a simulation is fraught with difficulties. There is a tremendous amount of thinking involved to maintain the illusion of telepresence. It can be sustained in fits and starts, but the effort of concentration impedes the ease of moving between internal and external that promotes reverie. Having the freedom to dream together requires a sense of safety for both the analyst and the patient. Both must have a continuing sense of the other's presence to refer back to in order to be permitted the latitude to explore. Ignoring the "telewindow" is like ignoring the man behind the curtain in *The Wizard of Oz*. The moment the technology intrudes, the illusion is lost. It is hard to connect the "functionally equivalent" moments into a flow, partly because of the highly unreliable state of our technology and partly because it takes such concentration—a concentration which is the inverse of reverie—to maintain a suspension of disbelief.

As studies in technological communication show, there is a danger that the participants stop themselves from knowing when the technology fails and when the functional equivalence ends. In that state, one is not occupying an internal space from which psychoanalytic understanding can emerge. It is a far shallower place, without the possibility of natural silences and the capacity to wait for the patient to discover how to make use of the analyst. There is a real danger of missing the shift and not knowing that it has happened.

Presence requires the sense of bodies together. We know that it is dependent on recognising the other as an intentional self, located in a shared physical space with the potential to interact with the other. That sense of presence, as defined by researchers in such fields as informatics and virtual reality, contributes to the capacity to use an object, which is perceived as external and part of a shared reality. The development of this capacity is central to the maturation of both infant and patient.

Very early in my training, I brought a session with a young patient to supervision. The patient had said, with great conflict, that she wanted to pick up a nearby pencil and throw it at me. I remember my supervisor saying, "You will know that she is getting better when she is able to pick up the pencil, throw it at you, and *just* miss you." You cannot throw a simulated pencil and risk hitting your analyst. The act of suspension of disbelief suspends something else. Imagination is a wonderful thing, but when exercising it you do not truly test the resilience and separate existence of the other. Yet, it is essential that the analyst survive. "The subject is creating the object in the sense of finding externality itself . . . this experience depends on the object's capacity to survive" (Winnicott, 1969, p. 714). Bodies need to be together to test that capacity to survive. It cannot be done with two minds alone.

Parsons (2014) writes about implicit transference interpretations. Referring to a paper by Ronald Baker (1993, which he quotes), he suggests that the actual survival of the analyst is therapeutic because it is an implicit transference interpretation, just as the analyst's providing a safe environment is an implicit interpretation that the patient is not in his/her original emotionally damaging environment.

> These implicit interpretations cannot simply be replaced by verbal interpretations. If the analyst tries to tell the patient that the analyst is surviving, or draws the patient's attention to the safety and reliability of the setting, the patient still has to decide whether what the analyst is saying, or the motivation behind it can be trusted. (Parsons, 2014, p. 175)

Not only is Parsons referring to communication between analyst and patient that is not transmitted in words, but he is also pointing out the necessity that the patient experience the analyst's survival and the fact that the environment is safe. This is not possible screen-to-screen in two separate environments. This is where, as the psychoanalyst Hannah said to me, "You hit a wall."

Parsons compares "states of mind" with "states of being", reminding us that the traditional psychoanalytic familiarity of verbal interpretation leaves out that which is not affected by the explicit.

> To think only in terms of states of mind is to think of psychic growth as resulting solely from understanding which can be put into words. This blocks a more radical opening of horizons to new orders of experience, and new registers of psychic life. (2014, p. 125)

A prime concern with technologically mediated treatment is that the elimination of co-present bodies largely confines the psychoanalytic process to "states of mind" rather than "states of being". It is when one can dwell in a "state of being" that one can take part in the psychoanalytic process of communicating with oneself and the other. Without a true sense of presence, we miss the opportunity to experience a space of internal and external reality, as well as that intermediate space which can be used for joint play and the creation of symbols. Simulation may take the potentially symbolic into the realms of the inauthentic because it is not counterweighted by the experience of body-to-body communication, with all the palpable potentiality that it implies.

We work much more often than not with patients who will need to remain a very long time in areas where words are not available. The days of the "good neurotic" who is highly responsive to verbal interpretations showing up in our consulting rooms seem be over. In any case, neuroscience is telling us that we need our whole bodies with other whole bodies to communicate most deeply and completely.

Asking a patient to provide his/her own safe space is also foreclosing an area of potential healing and growth. Balint (1950) spoke of "creating a proper atmosphere *for* the patient *by* the analyst". The provision of a safe space for the patient, in addition to providing a "good-enough" environment enabling the patient to heal psychic damage and foster psychic change, is akin to Turkle's (2009, 2011) concept of "sacred space". This is the place where people can feel most fully themselves. It is the protected place where both analyst and patient have the freedom to be just as they need to be in order to find joint analytic understanding. The security of the external space makes possible a similarly secure internal space (Parsons, 2014). Significantly, Turkle describes it as a place where people can hold themselves apart from simulation.

There are times when mediated communication can go some way to include a mutual experience of "states of being". There are times when unconscious to unconscious communication can take place, despite the limitations of the medium. Maintaining the illusion of presence could give real moments of deep understanding because our desire to connect is so strong and we instinctively make the most of what material we have. Knowing a patient very well before using mediation might provide a sort of bridge of familiarity on which to travel for some time. It might enable one to be more sensitive to communications because one recognises previous patterns. However, the current state of technology, coupled with the fact that we have evolved to relate as bodies together, militates against it. Although needing further study, the information we have about communication, the limits of technology, and the way we are neurologically wired points to the fact that we need to experience presence to "keep it real". Mediating our relationships degrades them. It is not the same as co-present relating. Being bodies together is neither *passé* nor unnecessary, and making that argument appear as if it were offered in the name of the "common people" is disingenuous.

While making psychoanalytic treatment available via mediation to those who have no other option is certainly better than nothing, it should not be offered with the understanding that it is the same thing as co-present treatment. We cannot justify modelling to our patients that our bodies are just incidental. Neither can we allow them to think that the path to authentically being alive and psychic growth can travel along cables and be confined to two-dimensional screens. At some point, they deserve the experience, many for the first time or they would not be seeking therapy, of the "primacy of safety" (Modell, 1988). At some point, they need to test the analyst's capacity to bear the impact of their love and their hate in the flesh and not protected by the barrier of a screen. The truth of these experiences needs to be lived, not simply described and not simulated. As Tanya said about kicking and kissing, "When not in a shared space, all the physical potential is taken away, but the important thing is to have the *potential . . .*"

In Spike Jonze's near-future film, *Her*, the protagonist, Theodore, is a lonely man whose job is to compose and dictate "beautifully hand-written letters" into a computer for clients who are too busy or too inarticulate to write their own intimate communications. He falls in love with his operating system, artificially intelligent software with the voice of a woman who seems to pass the Turing test.

Negotiating the "limited perspective" of the non-artificial mind, Samantha, the disembodied operating system, engages a human sex surrogate to stand in for her in a physical encounter with Theodore. It ends disastrously for all, because Theodore cannot maintain the illusion that Samantha and the physical surrogate are one.

The love affair is doomed as Samantha evolves beyond the limitations of human beings. In the final scene, Theodore sits on a rooftop overlooking the city with his embodied friend, Amy. She puts her hand on his hand. He puts his other hand on top of her hand and looks at their hands together. He rubs her skin with his thumb. He could not have done this with his operating system, Samantha. The film is about many things, but in the end it is about the constraints and the joys of having a body and about the need to have a real relationship in order to learn to have a real relationship.

People far more experienced than I in the studies of the relationship between human beings and technology are sounding alarms about the costs of technological mediation on intimate human connection. "The well-known possibilities of human bodily interaction", to which the psychoanalyst writing on the Division 39 listserv refers, have *everything* to do with psychotherapy. What is psychotherapy if not a process to realise the depth of one's full humanity? "Discourse without embodiment is ill-fated discourse" (Alessi, 2001, p. 537). The practice of psychoanalysis is to restore discourse, internally within oneself and externally with the other. "The presence and engagement of the self in the analytic process is inherent bodily in all its manifestations" (Meissner, 1998b, p. 277).

I write this from Boulder, Colorado, a university city and an American technology hub offering the fastest cable connections in a dramatically beautiful natural setting. I see a former UK patient, whom I have known for nearly two decades, at my noon and her evening. In a moment of speculative non-fiction, technologically mediated communication makes it possible for us to reconnect. "I wish I were in the States," she says. "I would like to be in the peaceful, calm setting of your consulting room. It was a safe place to be. The memory makes me gravitate toward that thought. There is something very special about being in the presence of someone else. You know, just lounging wordlessly . . . to sit beside someone . . . to be in the presence of someone . . ."

REFERENCES

Alessi, N. (2001). Disembodiment in cyberspace is not a myth. *CyberPsychology & Behavior, 4*(4): 537–538.

Allison, S. E., von Wahlde, L., Shockley, T., & Gabbard, G. O. (2006). The development of the self in the era of the internet and role-playing fantasy games. *American Journal of Psychiatry, 163*(3): 381–385. doi: 10.1176/appi.ajp.163.3.381.

Argentieri, S., & Amati Mehler, J. (2003). Telephone 'analysis': 'hello, who's speaking?' *Insight: International Psychoanalytic Association, 12*(1): 17–19.

Aron, L. (2009). Day, night, or dawn: Commentary on paper by Steven Stern. *Psychoanalytic Dialogues, 19*: 656–668.

Aronson, J. (Ed.) (2000). *Use of the Telephone in Psychotherapy.* Northvale, NJ: Jason Aronson.

Aviezer, H., Trope, Y., & Todorov, A. (2012). Body cues, not facial expressions, discriminate between intense positive and negative emotions. *Science, 338*(6111): 1225–1229. doi:10.1126/science.1224313.

Balint, M. (1950). Changing therapeutical aims and techniques in psychoanalysis. *International Journal of Psychoanalysis, 31*: 117–124.

Balint, M. (1979). *The Basic Fault.* London: Tavistock.

Barak, A., Hen, L., Boniel-Nissim, M., & Shapira, N. (2008). A comprehensive review and a meta-analysis of the effectiveness of internet-based psychotherapeutic interventions. *Journal of Technology in Human Services, 26*(2): 109–160.

Barlow, J. P. (1996). Declaration of independence for cyberspace. Accessed 2012 at: http://wac.colostate.edu/rhetnet/barlow/barlow_declaration.html

Baron-Cohen, S. (2011). *The Science of Evil*. New York: Basic Books.

Bass, A. (2003). "E" enactments in psychoanalysis: another medium, another message. *Psychoanalytic Dialogues*, 13(5): 657–675.

Beebe, B., Knoblauch, S., Rustin, J., & Sorter, D. (Eds.) (2005). *Forms of Intersubjectvity in Infant Research and Adult Treatment*. New York: Other Press.

Bick, E. (1968). The experience of the skin in early object relations. *International Journal of Psychoanalysis*, 49: 484–486.

Bilton, N. (2014). A conversation with Danah Boyd, author of "It's Complicated," about teenagers online. *New York Times*, March 22.

Bion, W. R. (1962). *Learning From Experience*. London: Tavistock.

Bion, W. R. (1967). Notes on memory and desire. *Psychoanalytic Forum*, 2: 279–281.

Bion, W. R. (1970). *Attention and Interpretation*. London: Tavistock.

Blakeslee, S. (2006). Cells that read minds. *New York Times*, October 1, p. C3.

Blascovich, J., & Bailenson, J. (2011). *Infinite Reality: The Hidden Blueprint of Our Virtual Lives*. New York: William Morrow.

Bos, N., Gergle, D., Olson, J., & Olson, G. M. (2001). Being there versus seeing there: trust via video. *CHI'01 Extended Abstracts on Human Factors in Computing Systems, ACM*, 291–292.

Bos, N., Olson, J., Gergle, D., Olson, G., & Wright, Z. (2002). Effects of four computer-mediated communications channels on trust development. *Proceedings of the SIGCHI Conference on Human Factors in Computing Systems: Changing our World, Changing Ourselves*: 135–140.

Boston Change Process Study Group (2007). The foundational level of psychodynamic meaning: implicit process in relation to conflict, defense and the dynamic unconscious. *International Journal of Psychoanalysis*, 88: 843–860.

Boston Change Process Study Group (2008). Forms of relational meaning: issues in the relations between the implicit and reflective-verbal domains. *Psychoanalytic Dialogues*, 18: 125–148.

Boston Change Process Study Group (Ed.) (2010). *Change in Psychotherapy*. New York: W. W. Norton.

Bounds, G. (2010). How handwriting trains the brain. *The Wall Street Journal*, 1 January 2014.

Bradner, E., & Mark, G. (2002). Why distance matters: effects on cooperation, persuasion, and deception. *Proceedings of the 2002 ACM Conference on Computer Supported Cooperative Work*, 226–235.

Brainsky, S. (2003). Adapting to, or idealising technology. *Insight: International Psychoanalytic Association, 12*(1): 22–24.

Brancucci, A., Lucci, G., Mazzatenta, A., & Tommasi, L. (2009). Asymmetries of the human social brain in the visual, auditory and chemical modalities. *Philosophical Transactions of the Royal Society B: Biological Sciences, 364*(1519): 895–914.

Brockman, J. (1999). Philosophy in the flesh: a talk with George Lakoff. Accessed 2013 at: http://www.edge.org/3rd_culture/lakoff/lakoff_p1. html

Bucci, W. (1994). The multiple code theory and the psychoanalytic process: A framework for research. *Annual of Psychoanalysis, 22*: 239–259.

Bucci, W. (1997). Patterns of discourse in "good" and troubled hours: a multiple code interpretation. *Journal of the American Psychoanalytic Association, 45*(March): 155–187.

Bucci, W. (2000). The need for a "psychoanalytic psychology" in the cognitive science field. *Psychoanalytic Psychology, 17*(2): 203–224.

Bucci, W. (2002). The referential process, consciousness, and the sense of self. *Psychoanalytic Inquiry, 22*: 766–793.

Burgoon, J. K., Buller, D. B., & Woodall, G. (1989). *Nonverbal Communication: The Unspoken Dialogue.* New York: Harper and Row.

Buzsáki, G., & Moser, E. I. (2013). Memory, navigation and theta rhythm in the hippocampal–entorhinal system. *Nature Neuroscience, 16*(2): 130–138.

Cairncross, F. (2001). *The Death of Distance: How the Communications Revolution is Changing Our Lives.* Boston, MA: Harvard Business Review Press.

Campanella Bracken, C., & Skalski, P. D. (Eds.) (2010). *Immersed in Media: Telepresence in Everyday Life.* New York: Routledge.

Carlino, R. (2011). *Distance Psychoanalysis: The Theory and Practice of Using Communication Technology in the Clinic,* J. Nuss (Trans.). London: Karnac.

Carr, N. (2011). *The Shallows: What the Internet Is Doing to Our Brains.* New York: W. W. Norton.

Castonguay, L. G., & Beutler, L. E. (2006). Common and unique principles of therapeutic change. In: L. G. Castonguay, & L. E. Beutler (Eds.), *Principles of Therapeutic Change That Work* (pp. 353–369). New York: Oxford University Press.

Celenza, A. (2005). Vis-à-vis the couch: where is psychoanalysis? *International Journal of Psychoanalysis, 86*: 1645–1659.

Clark, A. (1998). *Being There: Putting Brain, Body, and the World Together Again.* Cambridge, MA: MIT Press.

Clark, A. (1999a). An embodied cognitive science? *Trends in Cognitive Sciences, 3*(9): 345–351.

Clark, A. (1999b). Where brain, body, and world collide. *Cognitive Systems Research, 1*(1): 5–17.

Clark, H. H., & Brennan, S. E. (1991). Grounding in communication. *Perspectives on Socially Shared Cognition, 13*: 127–149.

Clayton, N. S., Salwiczek, L. H., & Dickinson, A. (2007). Episodic memory. *Current Biology, 17*(6): 189–191.

Clyman, R. B. (1991). The procedural organization of emotions: a contribution from cognitive science to the psychoanalytic theory of therapeutic action. *Journal of the American Psychoanalytic Association, 39S*: 349–382.

Connolly, A. (2008). Some brief considerations on the relationship between theory and practice. *Journal of Analytic Psychology, 53*: 481–499.

Curtis, A. E. (2007). The claustrum: sequestration of cyberspace. *Psychoanalytic Review, 94*(1): 99–139.

Damasio, A. (1999). *The Feeling of What Happens: Body and Emotion in the Making of Consciousness*. London: Vintage.

Damasio, A. (2005). *Descartes' Error*. New York: Penguin.

Damasio, A. (2012). *Self Comes to Mind: Constructing the Conscious Brain*. New York: Vintage.

Database of Abstract of Reviews of Effects (DARE), & Centre for Reviews and Dissemination. (2010). Review of *A Comprehensive Review and a Meta-analysis of the Effectiveness of Internet-based Psychotherapeutic Interventions*. Accessed 2013 at: www.crd.york.ac.uk/CRDWeb/Show Record.asp?AccessionNumber=12009103993&UserID=0

De Menil, B. (2013). Music collaboration will never happen online in real time. Accessed 2014 at: https://medium.com/race-class/e1c6448fc3d4

Decety, J., & Chaminade, T. (2003). When the self represents the other: A new cognitive neuroscience view on psychological identification. *Consciousness and Cognition, 12*(4): 577–596.

Derrig-Palumbo, K., & Zeine, F. (2005). *Online Therapy: A Therapist's Guide to Expanding Your Practice*. New York: W. W. Norton.

Donath, J. (2001). Mediated faces. In: M. Beynon, C. Nehaniv, & K. Dautenhahn (Eds.), *Cognitive Technology: Instruments of Mind 4th International Conference, CT 2001 Coventry, UK, August 6–9, Proceedings* (pp. 373–390). Berlin Heidelberg: Springer. doi:10.1007/3-540-44617-6_34.

Dorpat, T. L. (2001). Primary process communication. *Psychoanalytic Inquiry, 21*(3): 448–463.

Dreyfus, H. L. (1991). *Being-in-the-World: A Commentary on Heidegger's Being and Time, Division 1*. Cambridge, MA: MIT Press.

Eisold, K. (2003). The profession of psychoanalysis: past failures and future responsibilities. *Contemporary Psychoanalysis, 39*: 557–582.

Eisold, K. (2005). Psychoanalysis and psychotherapy: a long and troubled relationship. *International Journal of Psychoanalysis, 86*: 1175–1195.

Essig, T. (2011). Sloppy (dangerous) journalism at Scientific American MIND undermines promise of telehealth. 20 May. Accessed at: www.forbes.com/sites/toddessig/2011/05/20/sloppy-dangerous-journalism-at-scientific-american-mind-undermines-promise-of-telehealth/

Essig, T. (2012a). Actually connect: A reply to Bonnie Litwotz's "only connect". *Off the Couch, 2*(1): 10–17.

Essig, T. (2012b). Psychoanalysis lost—and found—in our culture of simulation and enhancement. *Psychoanalytic Inquiry 32*(5): 438–453.

Essig, T. (2012c). The addiction concept and technology: diagnosis, metaphor, or something else? A psychodynamic point of view. *Journal of Clinical Psychology: In Session, 68*(11): 1175–1184.

Essig, T. (2015). The gains and losses of 'screen relations:' a clinical approach to simulation entrapment and simulation avoidance in a case of excessive internet pornography use. *Contemporary Psychoanalysis, 51*(3) (in press).

Fishkin, R., & Fishkin, L. (2011). The electronic couch: some observations about Skype treatment. In: S. Akhtar (Ed.), *The Electrified Mind* (pp. 99–111). Lanham, MD: Jason Aronson.

Fishkin, R., Fishkin, L., Leli, U., Katz, B., & Snyder, E. (2011). Psychodynamic treatment, training, and supervision using internet-based technologies. *Journal of the American Academy of Psychoanalysis and Dynamic Psychiatry, 39*(1): 155–168.

Fonagy, P. (2003). Genetics, developmental psychopathology, and psychoanalytic theory: The case for ending our (not so) splendid isolation. *Psychoanalytic Inquiry, 23*: 218–247.

Fonagy, P., & Target, M. (2000). Playing with reality: III. the persistence of dual psychic reality in borderline patients. *International Journal of Psychoanalysis, 81*: 853–873.

Fonagy, P., Target, M., Gergely, G., Allen, J., & Bateman, A. (2003). The developmental roots of borderline personality disorder in early attachment relationships: A theory and some evidence. *Psychoanalytic Inquiry, 23*: 412–459.

Förster, J., Liberman, N., & Kuschel, S. (2008). The effect of global versus local processing styles on assimilation versus contrast in social judgement. *Journal of Personality and Social Psychology, 94*(4): 579–599. doi: 10.1037/0022–3514.94.4.579.

Fortunati, L. (2005). Is body-to-body communication still the prototype? *The Information Society*, *21*: 53–61. doi:10.1080/01972240590895919.

Freud, S. (1905e). *Fragment of an Analysis of a Case of Hysteria. S. E.*, *7*: 7–122. London: Hogarth.

Freud, S. (1912b). The dynamics of the transference. *S. E.*, *12*: 98–107. London: Hogarth.

Freud, S. (1912e). Recommendations to physicians practising psychoanalysis. *S. E.*, *12*: 109–120. London: Hogarth.

Freud, S. (1913c). On beginning the treatment (further recommendations on the technique of psycho-analysis I). *S. E.*, *12*: 121–144. London: Hogarth.

Freud, S. (1914g). Remembering, repeating and working-through (further recommendations on the technique of psycho-analysis II). *S. E.*, *12*: 145–156). London: Hogarth.

Freud, S. (1916–1917). *Introductory Lectures on Psycho-analysis. S. E.*, *16*. London: Hogarth.

Freud, S. (1923a). Two encyclopaedia articles. *S. E.*, *18*: 233–260. London: Hogarth.

Freud, S. (1923b). *The Ego and the Id. S.E.*, *19*: 1–66. London: Hogarth.

Gabbard, G. O., & Westen, D. (2003). Rethinking therapeutic action. *International Journal of Psychoanalysis*, *84*: 823–841.

Gallagher, S. (2005). *How the Body Shapes the Mind*. Oxford: Oxford University Press.

Gallagher, S., & Roy, J. (2011). Philosophy of mind. Accessed 2014 at: http//cfs.ku.dk/summerschool/readings/

Gallese, V. (2006). Intentional attunement: embodied simulation and its role in social cognition. In: M. Mancia (Ed.), *Psychoanalysis and Neuroscience* (pp. 269–298). Milan: Springer.

Gallese, V. (2009). Mirror neurons, embodied simulation, and the neural basis of social identification. *Psychoanalytic Dialogues*, *19*: 519–536.

Gallese, V., Eagle, M. N., & Migone, P. (2007). Intentional attunement: mirror neurons and the neural underpinnings of interpersonal relations. *Journal of the American Psychoanalytic Association*, *55*(1): 131–176.

Gallese, V., Fadiga, L., Fogassi, L., & Rizzolatti, G. (1996). Action recognition in the premotor cortex. *Brain*, *119*(2): 593–609.

Gergen, K. J. (2002). The challenge of the absent present. In: J. E. Katz & M. Aakhus (Eds.), *Perpetual Contact* (pp. 227–241). Cambridge: Cambridge University Press.

Goldberg, P. (2012). Active perception and the search for sensory symbiosis. *Journal of the American Psychoanalytic Association*, *60*(4): 791–812.

Grohol, J. (2011). Best practices in eTherapy. Accessed 2013 at: http:// psychcentral.com/best/best4.htm

Grotstein, J. S. (1978). Inner space: its dimensions and its coordinates. *International Journal of Psychoanalysis, 59*: 55–61.

Grotstein, J. S. (2005). Projective *trans*identification: an extension of the concept of projective identification. *International Journal of Psychoanalysis, 86*: 1051–1069.

Hanly, C., & Scharff, J. S. (2010). Telephone analysis. *International Journal of Psychoanalysis, 91*: 989–992.

Hannaford, C. (2007). *Smart Moves: Why Learning is Not All in Your Head.* Salt Lake City, UT: Great River Books.

Hanselman, S. (2010). Building an embodied social proxy or crazy webcam remote cart thing. Accessed 2014 at: www.hanselman.com/ blog/BuildingAnEmbodiedSocialProxyOrCrazyWebcamRemoteCartT hing.aspx

Healy, M. (2014). Nobel prize honors researchers' discovery of the brain's GPS system. *Los Angeles Times*, October 6. Accessed at: www.latimes. com/science/sciencenow/la-sci=sn-nobel-prize-medicine-20141006-story.html

Heeter, C. (2003). Reflections on real presence by a virtual person. *Presence: Teleoperators and Virtual Environments, 12*(4): 335–345.

Heidegger, M. (1966). *Discourse on Thinking.* New York: Harper & Row.

Hildreth, P., Kimble, C., & Wright, P. (1998). Computer mediated communications and communities of practice. *Proceedings of Ethicomp March 98, Erasmus University, The Netherlands*: 275–286.

Hill, D. (2000). Computer-mediated-therapy: possibilities and possible limitations. *Psychologist/psychoanalyst, 19*(4). Accessed at: www.psybc.com

Hilty, D., Marks, S., Urness, D., Yellowlees, P., & Nesbitt, T. (2004). Clinical and educational telepsychiatry applications: a review. *Canadian Journal of Psychiatry, 49*(January): 12–23.

Hirsch, I. (2008). *Coasting in the Countertransference.* New York: Analytic Press.

Hirsh, S., Sellen, A., & Bokropp, N. (2005). Why HP people do and don't use videoconferencing systems. Accessed 2013 at: http://research. microsoft.com/en-us/um/people/asellen/publications/why%20Hp %20people%2004.pdf

Hoffman, J. (2011). When your therapist is only a click away. *New York Times*, September 23, p. 1.

Holmes, J. (2010). *Exploring in Security.* London: Routledge.

International Society for Presence Research. (2000). The concept of presence: explication statement. Accessed 2014 at: http://ispr.info/

Isaacs, E. A., & Tang, J. C. (1994). What video can and cannot do for collaboration: a case study. *Multimedia Systems, 2*(2): 63–73.

Iverson, J. M., & Goldin-Meadow, S. (1998). Why people gesture when they speak. *Nature, 396*(6708): 228–228.

Jackson, M. (2008). *Distracted: The Erosion of Attention and the Coming Dark Age.* New York: Prometheus Books.

Jacobs, T. (1994). Nonverbal communications: some reflections on their role in the psychoanalytic process and the psychoanalytic education. *Journal of the American Psychoanalytic Association, 42*(3): 741–762.

Jacobs, T. (2005). Discussion of *Forms of Intersubjectivity in Infant Research and Adult Treatment.* In: B. Beebe, S. Knoblauch, J. Rustin, & D. Sorter (Eds.), *Forms of Intersubjectivity in Infant Research and Adult Treatment* (pp. 165–189). New York: Other Press.

Jarrett, C. (2013). A calm look at the most hyped concept in neuroscience—mirror neurons. Accessed at: www.wired.com/2013/12/a-calm-look-at-the-most-hyped-concept-in-neuroscience-mirror-neurons/

Kelly, M., & Tabin, J. (2009). Psychoanalysis in China. *Psychologist-Psychoanalyst, XXIX*(3): 18–19.

Kevin, R. C. (2013). The 45-minute therapy 'hour': a sign of the times? [Letter to the editor.] *New York Times,* October 15, p. A26.

Kirk, D. S., Sellen, A., & Cao, X. (2010). Home video communication: mediating 'closeness'. *Proceedings of the 2010 ACM Conference on Computer Supported Cooperative Work,* 135–144.

Kliner, J. M., & Lemon, R. N. (2013). What we know currently about mirror neurons. *Current Biology, 23*(23): 1057–1062. doi:http://dx.doi.org/10.1016/j.cub.2013.10.051.

Lakoff, G. (1995). Body, brain and communication. In: J. Brook & I. A. Boal (Eds.), *Resisting the Virtual Life: The Culture and Politics of Information* (pp. 115–129). San Francisco, CA: City Lights.

Lakoff, G., & Johnson, M. (2003). *Metaphors We Live By* (2nd edn). Chicago, IL: University of Chicago Press.

Langs, R. (1979). *The Therapeutic Environment.* New York: Jason Aronson.

Lanier, J. (2011). *You Are Not a Gadget: A Manifesto.* New York: Vintage.

Leffert, M. (2003). Analysis and psychotherapy by telephone: twenty years of clinical experience. *Journal of the American Psychoanalytic Association, 51*(1): 101–130.

Loewald, H. W. (1960). On the therapeutic action of psycho-analysis. *International Journal of Psychoanalysis, 41*: 16–33.

Lombard, M., & Ditton, T. (1997). At the heart of it all: the concept of presence. *Journal of Computer-Mediated Communication, 3*(2). Accessed at: http://onlinelibrary.wiley.com/doi/10.1111/j.1083-6101.1997.tb00072.x/full

Lyons-Ruth, K. (1998). Implicit relational knowing: its role in development and psychoanalytic treatment. *Infant Mental Health Journal, 19*(3): 282–289.

Lyons-Ruth, K. (2000). "I sense that you sense that I sense . . .": Sander's recognition process and the specificity of relational moves in the psychotherapeutic setting. *Infant Mental Health Journal, 21*: 85–98.

Maclaren, K. (2008). Embodied perceptions of others as a condition for selfhood? *Journal of Consciousness Studies, 15*(8): 63–93.

Maheu, M. (2012). TeleMental Health Institute. Accessed 2012 at: http://telehealth.org

Mantovani, G., & Riva, G. (1999). "Real" presence: how different ontologies generate different criteria for presence, telepresence, and virtual presence. *Presence: Teleoperators and Virtual Environments, 8*(5): 538–548.

Marziali, C. (2009). Nobler instincts take time. Accessed 2013 at: http://dornsife.usc.edu/news/stories/547/nobler-instincts-take-time

Masson, J. M. (Ed.) (1985). *The Complete Letters of Sigmund Freud to Wilhelm Fliess, 1887–1904.* Cambridge, MA: Harvard University Press.

Meissner, W. W. (1998a). The self and the body: II. The embodied self—self vs. nonself. *Psychoanalysis and Contemporary Thought, 21*: 85–111.

Meissner, W. W. (1998b). The self and the body: IV. the body on the couch. *Psychoanalysis and Contemporary Thought, 21*: 277–300.

Meltzoff, A., & Moore, M. (1977). Imitation of facial amd manual gestures by human neonates. *Science, 198*(4312): 75–78.

Meltzoff, A. N. (2007). The 'like me' framework for recognizing and becoming an intentional agent. *Acta Psychologica, 124*(1): 26–43.

Merleau-Ponty, M. (1962). *The Phenomenology of Perception,* C. Smith (Trans.). London: Routledge & Kegan Paul.

Milner, M. (1969). *The Hands of the Living God: An Account of a Psychoanalytic Treatment.* London: Hogarth Press.

Minagawa-Kawai, Y., Matsuoka, S., Dan, I., Naoi, N., Nakamura, K., & Kojima, S. (2009). Prefrontal activation associated with social attachment: Facial-emotion recognition in mothers and infants. *Cerebral Cortex, 19*(2): 284–292.

Minsky, M. (1980). Telepresence. *Omni,* June: 45–51.

Misra, S., Cheng, L., Genevie, J., & Yuan, M. (2014). The iPhone effect: the quality of in-person social interactions in the presence of mobile devices. *Environment and Behavior,* 1–24: doi: 10.1177/0013916514539755.

Mitchell, J. P. (2009). Watching minds interact. In: M. Brockman (Ed.), *What's Next: Dispatches on the Future of Science* (pp. 78–88). New York: Vintage.

Modell, A. H. (1976). "The holding environment" and the therapeutic action of psychoanalysis. *Journal of the American Psychoanalytic Association, 24*: 285–307.

Modell, A. H. (1988). The centrality of the psychoanalytic setting and the changing aims of treatment—a perspective from a theory of object relations. *Psychoanalytic Quarterly, 57*: 577–596.

Moore, B., & Fine, B. (1990). *Psychoanalytic Terms and Concepts*. New York: American Psychoanalytic Association.

Moser, E., & Moser, M. B. (2014). Mapping your every move. *Cerebrum: The Dana Forum on Brain Science, 4*: 1–10. Accessed at: www.dana. org/Cerebrum/2014/Mapping_Your_Every_Move_1_/

Nahum, J. P. (2002). Explicating the implicit: the local level and the micro-process of change in the analytic situation the Boston Change Process Study Group (BCPSG), listed alphabetically, Nadia Bruschweiler-Stern, Alexandra M. Harrison, Karlen Lyons-Ruth, Alexander C. Morgan, Jeremy P. Nahum, Louis W. Sander, Daniel N. Stern, & Edward Z. Tronick. *International Journal of Psychoanalysis, 83*: 1051–1062.

Nahum, J. P. (2008). Forms of relational meaning: issues in the relations between the implicit and reflective-verbal domains: Boston Change Process Study Group. *Psychoanalytic Dialogues, 18*: 125–148.

Neumann, D. (2012). Psychoanalysis in cyberspace. *The Candidate, 5*(January): 24–35.

O'Conaill, B., Whittaker, S., & Wilbur, S. (1993). Conversations over video conferences: an evaluation of the spoken aspects of video-mediated communication. *Human–Computer Interaction, 8*(4): 389–428.

Ogden, T. H. (1996). Reconsidering three aspects of psychoanalytic technique. *International Journal of Psychoanalysis, 77*: 883–899.

Ogden, T. H. (2004). This art of psychoanalysis. *International Journal of Psychoanalysis, 85*: 857–877.

Olds, D. (2006). Identification: psychoanalytic and biological perspectives. *Journal of the American Psychoanalytic Association, 54*: 17–46.

Olson, G., & Olson, J. (2000). Distance matters. *Human–Computer Interaction, 15*: 139–178.

Olson, J., & Olson, G. M. (2006). Bridging distance: empirical studies of distributed teams. *Human–Computer Interaction in Management Information Systems, 2*: 27–30.

Osnos, E. (2011). Meet Dr. Freud: Does psychoanalysis have a future in an authoritarian state? *The New Yorker*, 10 January, pp. 54–63.

Pacella, B. (1980). The primal matrix configuration. In: R. F. Lax, S. Bach, & J. A. Burland (Eds.), *Rapprochement: The Critical Subphase of Separation–Individuation* (pp. 117–131). New York: Jason Aronson.

Pally, R. (1998). Emotional processing: The mind-body connection. *International Journal of Psychoanalysis, 79*: 349–362.

Papousek, M. (2007). Communication in early infancy: an arena of inter-subjective learning. *Infant Behavior and Development, 30*: 258–266.

Parsons, M. (2007). Raiding the inarticulate: the internal analytic setting and listening beyond countertransference. *International Journal of Psychoanalysis, 88*: 1441–1456.

Parsons, M. (2009). An independent theory of clinical technique. *Psycho-analytic Dialogues, 19*: 221–236.

Parsons, M. (2014). *Living Psychoanalysis.* East Sussex: Routledge.

Prensky, M. (2001). Digital natives, digital immigrants part 1. *On the Horizon, 9*(5): 1–6.

Richards, A. K. (2001). Talking cure in the 21st century telephone psycho-analysis. *Psychoanalytic Psychology, 18*(2): 388–391.

Richards, A. K. (2003). Fruitful uses of telephone analysis. *Insight: International Psychoanalytic Association, 12*(1): 30–32.

Richardson, L. K., Christopher Frueh, B., Grubaugh, A. L., Egede, L., & Elhai, J. D. (2009). Current directions in videoconferencing tele-mental health research. *Clinical Psychology: Science and Practice, 16*(3): 323–338.

Riva, G. (2006). Being-in-the-world-with: presence meets social and cognitive neuroscience. In: G. Riva, M. T. Anguera, B. K. Wiederhold, & F. Mantovani (Eds.), *From Communication to Presence: Cognition, Emotions and Culture Towards the Ultimate Communicative Experience. Festschrift in Honor of Luigi Anolli* (pp. 47–80). Amsterdam: IOS Press.

Riva, G. (2008). Enacting interactivity: the role of presence. In: F. Morganti, A. Carassa, & G. Riva (Eds.), *Enacting Intersubjectivity: A Cognitive and Social Perspective on the Study of Interactions* (pp. 97–114). Amsterdam: IOS Press.

Riva, G. (2009). Is presence a technology issue? some insights from cogni-tive sciences *Virtual Reality, 13*, 159–169. doi:10.1007/s10055–009–0121-6.

Riva, G., & Waterworth, J. (2003). Presence and the self: a cognitive neuro-science approach. *Presence-Connect, 3*(3). Accessed 29 September 2012 at: www.informatik.umu.se/~jwworth/Riva-Waterworth.htm

Riva, G., Anguera, M. T., Wiederhold, B. K., & Mantovani, F. (Eds.). (2006). *From Communication to Presence: Cognition, Emotions and Culture Towards the Ultimate Communicative Experience. Festschrift in Honor of Luigi Anolli.* Amsterdam: IOS Press.

Riva, G., Waterworth, J., & Waterworth, E. (2004). The layers of presence: a bio-cultural approach to understanding presence in natural and mediated environments. *CyberPsychology & Behavior, 7*(4): 402–416.

Riva, G., Waterworth, J., Waterworth, E., & Mantovani, G. (2009). From intention to action: the role of presence *New Ideas in Psychology, XXX*: 1–14. doi:10.1016/j.newideapsych.2009.11.002.

Rizzolatti, G., Fadiga, L., Gallese, V., & Fogassi, L. (1996). Premotor cortex and the recognition of motor actions. *Cognitive Brain Research, 3*(2): 131–141.

Rocco, E. (1998). Trust breaks down in electronic contexts but can be repaired by some initial face-to-face contact. *Proceedings of the SIGCHI Conference on Human Factors in Computing Systems*, 496–502.

Rodriguez de la Sierra, L. (2003). If it helps, why not? *Insight: International Psychoanalytic Association, 12*(1): 20–21.

Rosen, C. (2010). Can you hear me? Can you see me? Conducting a Skype internet analysis in Chinese. *Symposium 2011: Our Practice Today: Treatment and Transformation*, Mount Sinai Medical Center, New York.

Ruhleder, K., & Jordan, B. (1999). Meaning-making across remote sites: how delays in transmission affect interaction. In: S. Bodker, M. Kyng, & K. Schmidt (Eds.), *Proceedings of the Sixth European Conference on Computer-supported Cooperative Work, 12–16 September 1999* (pp. 411–429). Copenhagen: Kluwer Academic.

Ruhleder, K., & Jordan, B. (2001). Co-constructing non-mutual realities: delay-generated trouble in distributed interaction. *Computer Supported Cooperative Work, 10*(1): 113–138.

Rustin, J. (2013). *Infant Research and Neuroscience at Work in Psychotherapy*. New York: W. W. Norton.

Rutter, D., Stephenson, G., & Dewey, M. (1981). Visual communication and the content and style of conversation. *British Journal of Social Psychology, 20*(1): 41–52. doi:10.1111/j.2044–8309.1981.tb00472.x.

Rycroft, C. (1956). The nature and function of the analyst's communication to the patient. *International Journal of Psychoanalysis, 37*: 469–472.

Sachs, D. M. (2003). Telephone analysis—sometimes the best choice? *Insight: International Psychoanalytic Association, 12*(1): 28–29.

Sand, S. (2007). Future considerations: interactive identities and the interactive self. *Psychoanalytic Review, 94*(1): 83–97.

Saporta, J. A. (2008). Digitalizing psychoanalysis and psychotherapy? Possibilities and downsides. *American Psychoanalyst, 42*(2): 1–9.

Saul, L. J. (1951). A note on the telephone as a technical aid. *Psychoanalytic Quarterly, 20*: 287–290.

Scharff, J. S. (2010). Telephone analysis. *International Journal of Psychoanalysis, 91*: 981–992.

Scharff, J. S. (2012). Clinical issues in analyses over the telephone and the internet. *International Journal of Psychoanalysis, 93*: 81–95.

Scharff, J. S. (2013a). *Psychoanalysis Online: Mental Health, Teletherapy, and Training*. London: Karnac.

Scharff, J. S. (2013b). Technology-assisted psychoanalysis. *Journal of the American Psychoanalytic Association*, *61*(3): 491–509.

Schore, A. N. (2005). A neuropsychoanalytic viewpoint: commentary on paper by Steven H. Knoblauch. *Psychoanalytic Dialogues*, *15*(6): 829–854.

Schore, A. N. (2010). The right brain implicit self: a central mechanism of the psychotherapy change process. In: J. Petrucelli (Ed.), *Knowing, Not-Knowing and Sort of Knowing: Psychoanalysis and the Experience of Uncertainty* (pp. 177–202). London: Karnac.

Schore, A. N. (2011). The right brain implicit self lies at the core of psychoanalysis. *Psychoanalytic Dialogues*, *21*(1): 75–100.

Sellen, A. J. (1995). Remote conversations: the effects of mediating talk with technology. *Human–Computer Interaction*, *10*(4): 401–444.

Shapiro, S. (1996). The embodied analyst in the Victorian consulting room. *Gender and Psychoanalysis*, *1*: 297–322.

Sheets-Johnstone, M. (2011). *The Primacy of Movement*. Philadelphia, PA: John Benjamins.

Shellenbarger, S. (2012). Pants required: attending meetings when working from home. *The Wall Street Journal*, May 16. http://blogs.wsj.com/at work/2012/05/16/pants-required-attending-meetings-when-working-from-home/

Silver, C. B. (2003). A survey of clinicians' views about change in psychoanalytic practice and theoretical orientation. *Psychoanalytic Review*, *90*: 193–224.

Slade, A. (2013). The place of fear in attachment theory and psychoanalysis. The Fifteenth John Bowlby Memorial Lecture. In: J. Yellin & O. B. Epstein (Eds.), *Terror Within and Terror Without* (pp. 39–58). London: Karnac.

Sletvold, J. (2014). *The Embodied Analyst*. Hove: Routledge.

Small, G., & Vorgan, G. (2008). *iBrain: Surviving the Technological Alteration of the Modern Mind*. New York: Collins Living.

Smolen, A. G. (2011). The multiple meanings of the electrified mind. In: S. Akhtar (Ed.), *The Electrified Mind: Development, Psychopathology, and Treatment in the Era of Cell Phones and the Internet* (pp. 129–140). Lanham, MD: Jason Aronson.

Snyder, E. (2009). Psychoanalysis and globalization. *International Psychoanalysis*, (September): 1–17.

Spezio, M. L., Huang, P., Castelli, F., & Adolphs, R. (2007). Amygdala damage impairs eye contact during conversations with real people. *Journal of Neuroscience*, *27*: 3994–3997.

Stern, D. N. (1985). *The Interpersonal World of the Infant: A View from Psychoanalysis and Developmental Psychology*. New York: Basic Books.

Stern, D. N., Sander, L. W., Nahum, J. P., Harrison, A. M., Lyons-Ruth, K., Morgan, A. C., Bruschweiler-Stern, N., & Tronick, E. Z. (1998). Non-interpretive mechanisms in psychoanalytic therapy: the 'something more' than interpretation. *International Journal of Psychoanalysis, 79*: 903–921.

Stewart, H. (1990). Interpretation and other agents for psychic change. *International Review of Psycho-analysis, 17*: 61–69.

Stone, L. (2009). Beyond simple multi-tasking: continuous partial attention. Accessed 2013 at: http://lindastone.net/2009/11/30/beyond-simple-multi-tasking-continuous-partial-attention/

Strachey, J. (1934). The nature of the therapeutic action of psycho-analysis. *International Journal of Psychoanalysis, 15*: 127–159.

Suler, J. (2001). Assessing a person's suitability for online therapy: the ISMHO clinical case study group. *CyberPsychology & Behavior, 4*(6): 675–679.

Suler, J. (2004). The online disinhibition effect. *CyberPsychology & Behavior, 7*(3): 321–326.

Suler, J. (2006). The psychology of cyberspace. Accessed 2012 at: http://users.rider.edu/~suler/psycyber/psycyber.html

Summersett, B. (2013). The latency of dialogue. Accessed 2014 at: https://medium.com/how-to-use-the-internet/3fb3669cc794

Turkle, S. (1995). *Life on the Screen.* New York: Simon & Schuster.

Turkle, S. (2009). *Simulation and its Discontents.* Cambridge, MA: MIT Press.

Turkle, S. (2011). *Alone Together.* New York: Basic Books.

Turkle, S. (2015). *Reclaiming Conversation.* New York: Penguin.

Wallerstein, R. S. (1988). One psychoanalysis or many? *International Journal of Psychonalysis, 69*: 5–21.

Waterworth, J. A., & Waterworth, E. (2003a). The core of presence: presence as perceptual illusion. *Presence-Connect, 3*(3). www.8.informatik.umu.se/~jwworth/perceptual%20core.html

Waterworth, J. A., & Waterworth, E. L. (2003b). The meaning of presence. *Presence-Connect 3.* www.informatik.umu.se/~jwworth/PRESENCE-meaning.htm

Weitz, P. (Ed.) (2014). *Psychotherapy 2.0: Where Psychotherapy and Technology Meet.* London: Karnac.

Weizenbaum, J. (1976). *Computer Power and Human Reason.* New York: W. H. Freeman.

Westen, D., & Gabbard, G. (2002a). Developments in cognitive neuro-science: I. conflict, compromise, and connectionism. *Journal of the American Psychoanalytic Association, 50*: 53–98.

Westen, D., & Gabbard, G. (2002b). Developments in cognitive neuro-science: II. implications for theories of transference. *Journal of the American Psychoanalytic Association, 50*: 99–134.

Whittaker, S. (2003a). Theories and methods in mediated communication. In: A. C. Graesser, M. Gernsbacher, & S. Goldman (Eds.), *Handbook of Discourse Processes* (pp. 243–286). Mahwah, NJ: Lawrence Erlbaum.

Whittaker, S. (2003b). Things to talk about when talking about things. *Human–Computer Interaction, 18*(1–2), 149–170.

Wilson, R. A., & Foglia, L. (2011). Embodied cognition. In: E. N. Zalta (Ed.), *The Stanford Encyclopedia of Philosophy*. Available at: http://plato.stanford.edu/archives/fall2011/entries/embodied-cognition/

Winnicott, D. W. (1955). Metapsychological and clinical aspects of regression within the psycho-analytical set-up. *International Journal of Psychoanalysis, 36*: 16–26.

Winnicott, D. W. (1958). The capacity to be alone. *International Journal of Psychoanalysis, 39*: 416–420.

Winnicott, D. W. (1965). *The Maturational processes and the Facilitating Environment: Studies in the Theory of Emotional Development*. London: Hogarth Press.

Winnicott, D. W. (1969). The use of an object. *International Journal of Psychoanalysis, 50*: 711–716.

Winnicott, D. W. (1971a). Mirror-role of mother and family in child development. In: *Playing and Reality* (pp. 111–119). London: Tavistock.

Winnicott, D. W. (1971b). Playing: a theoretical statement. In: *Playing and Reality* (pp. 38–53). London: Tavistock.

Winnicott, D. W. (1971c). The place where we live. In: *Playing and Reality* (pp. 104–110). London: Tavistock.

Winnicott, D. W. (1975a). Transitional objects and transitional phenomena. In: *Through Paediatrics to Psycho-analysis* (pp. 229–243). London: Hogarth Press.

Winnicott, D. W. (1975b). The depressive position in normal emotional development. In: *Through Paediatrics to Psycho-analysis* (pp. 262–278). London: Hogarth Press.

Winnicott, D. W. (1989). *Psycho-analytic Explorations*, C. Winnicott, R. Shepherd, & M. Davis (Eds.). Cambridge, MA: Harvard University Press.

Winnicott, D. W. (1990). *Home Is Where We Start From*. New York: W. W. Norton.

Yamin Habib, L. E. (2003). Physical presence-a sine qua non of analysis? *Insight: International Psychoanalytic Association, 12*(1): 25–27.

Zalusky, S. (2003). Dialogue: telephone analysis. *Insight: International Psychoanalytic Association, 12*(1): 13–16.

INDEX

Adolphs, R., 109
affect(ive), 91–92, 95–96, 106
  attunement, 57, 84
  connection, 57
  contribution, 76
  expression, 85
  implicit, 95
  information, 107, 115
  intensity of, 54
  -laden, 95
  missing, 36
  negative, 15, 105
  positive, 105
  regulation, 54, 95
  relationship, 71
  shift, 25
  state, 47
  unconscious(ness), 97–98
Alessi, N., 182
Allen, J., 139
Allison, S. E., 40
Amati Mehler, J., 46, 48
American Psychoanalytic
    Association, 45, 163–164
American Psychological Association,
    53, 78, 177
anger, 15, 21, 37–38
Anguera, M. T., 31, 81, 93, 128, 137,
    140, 142, 146
anxiety, 8, 28, 41, 46, 59, 62, 100,
    128–129, 155, 160
  economic, 9
Argentieri, S., 46, 48
Aron, L., 7
Aronson, J., 43–44, 48

attachment
  communication, 96
  processes, 97
  secure, 157
  theory, 73
attention(al)
  analytic, 57
  conflict, 112
  conscious(ness), 139
  continuous partial, 109–111, 171
  divided, 112
  effort, 114
  emotional, 112
  evenly-suspended, 5, 21, 74, 97–99,
    111–112
  fluid, 24
  focused, 23, 52, 75, 103, 112,
    141–142
  free-floating, 112, 114
  intensity of, 23, 114
  joint, 104, 106
  perceptual, 142
  selective, 142
  sustained, xiii, 109
  synchronous, 109–110
autonomy, 7–8, 35, 39, 53, 135, 137
Aviezer, H., 106

Bailenson, J., 8, 155
Balint, E., 149
Balint, M., 73, 180
Barak, A., 100
Barlow, J. P., 66
Baron-Cohen, S., 108–109
Bass, A., 70–71

Bateman, A., 139
Beebe, B., 6, 51, 84
behaviour(al), 12, 50, 54, 73, 77, 86,
    92, 101, 105, 108, 117, 126–127,
    135, 139, 156
  cognitive-, 100
  human, 92, 128
  intentional, 84
  interactive, 116
  mother–infant, 74
  non-verbal, 79
  observed, 84
  perceived, 145
  problematic, xii
  science, 65
  secondary process, 96
  studies, 104
  surface, 144
  therapies, 162–163
  unethical, 167
Berninger, V., 88
Beutler, L. E., 78
Bick, E., 135
Bilton, N., 172
Bion, W. R., xi, 22–23, 74–75, 85, 148
Blakeslee, S., 83
Blascovich, J., 8, 155
Bokropp, N., 124
Boniel-Nissim, M., 100
Bos, N., 107
Boston Change Process Study Group
    (BCPSG), 6, 86, 90–92, 94–95, 97,
    99, 146, 156
Bounds, G., 88
Bowlby, J., 73, 128–129
Bradner, E., 116
Brainsky, S., 48
Brancucci, A., 96–97
Brennan, S. E., 103
Brockman, J., 80
Bruschweiler-Stern, N., 80, 91–92, 98,
    127
Bucci, W., 80, 82
Buller, D. B., 76
Burgoon, J. K., 76
Buzsáki, G., 89

Cairncross, F., 113
Campanella Bracken, C., 114
Cao, X., 44, 103–104
Carlino, R., 30, 40, 44–45, 47–50, 56,
    113, 161, 164, 170
Carr, N., xiii, 6, 44, 109–110, 171–172,
    175
Castelli, F., 109
Castells, M., 112
Castonguay, L. G., 78
Celenza, A., 135
Centre for Reviews and
    Dissemination, 101
Chaminade, T., 97
Cheng, L., 111–112
China American Psychoanalytic
    Alliance (CAPA), 4, 55–56, 63
Christopher Frueh, B., 101
Clark, A., 65, 80
Clark, H. H., 103
Clayton, N. S., 90
clinical vignettes
  Ajia, 23, 128
  Anna, 21, 25–26, 34, 39, 90, 157
  Barbara, 122
  Bella, 17–19, 74
  Catherine, 16, 33
  Celia, 27, 34
  Charles, 34, 130, 132, 155
  Claire, 18
  Ellie, 38, 58
  George, 104–105
  Jessica, 122
  Joanna, 63, 171
  Joseph, 122
  Lawrence, 171
  Louis, 26
  Lucy, 20, 32, 36, 74, 124, 133
  Lynn, 16
  Maria Celano, 28–31, 56, 103
  Michael, 52
  Ms A, 61–62
  Nancy, 16
  Patrick, 38, 41, 154
  Peter, 15, 20
  Ruth, 126, 131

Sara, 22
Stephen, 16, 25, 33
Tanya, 27–28, 32, 39–41, 181
Will, 39
Clyman, R. B., 86
communication (*passim*) *see also*:
    attachment
    analytic, 169
    asynchronous, 49
    audio-visual, 44–45, 48, 59, 102
    basic, 50
    body-to-body, xii, 6, 131, 177, 180
    co-present, 7
    countertransference, 96–97
    didactic, 5
    digital, 112
    distance, 48
    embodied, 9, 65
    emotional, 82, 96
    explicit, 28, 77, 95
    face-to-face, 102, 106
    human, 94
    implicit, 25–26, 28, 52–53, 90, 95–96
    infrastructures, 44
    instantaneous, 3, 50
    intimate, 182
    mediated, 4–5, 7–9, 11, 35, 44,
        46–47, 52, 54–55, 57–59, 61, 66,
        90, 99, 101, 103–104, 107–108,
        113, 116, 126–128, 130–131,
        156, 173, 178, 181–182
    meta-, 65
    online, xiv, 100
    personal, 19, 33
    physical, 14
    problems, 114
    psychoanalytic, 66, 100, 104
    quality of, 25
    remote, 115
    right-brain-to-right-brain, 99
    screen-to-screen, 23, 26, 38
    sensory, 30, 52, 56, 94
        multi-, 87
    social, 102
    studies, xvii, 10
    synchronous, 49

technologies, 113, 137, 147, 155,
    157, 175
telephone, 48
theory, 147
therapeutic, 94
unconscious(ness), xi, 5, 56, 181
verbal, 50–51, 79, 107, 157
    non-, xvii, 6, 51–52, 76, 79, 96
video, 44
visual, 30, 102
Connolly, A., 163–164
conscious(ness), 33, 51, 70, 76–77, 80,
    84, 86, 88, 91–93, 95–96, 98, 104,
    111, 114, 136–137, 140, 142, 148,
    157–158, 176 *see also*:
    attention(al), unconscious(ness)
    access, 86
    attention, 139
    autobiographical, 136–137
    awareness, 178
    basic, 136
    core, 136
    decision, 17
        -making, 82
    effort, 83
    expectations, 74
    experience, 81
    extended, 136
    memory, 86
    mind, 99
    non-, 82–84, 97–99, 136, 141, 146
    poly-, 112
    pre-, 71, 97
    reflection, 97
    self-, 30, 122, 136
    sub, 87
    thought, 86
    unusual, 122
Curtis, A. E., 32

Damasio, A., 21, 65, 80–81, 112,
    135–137, 141, 147, 178
Dan, I., 96
Database of Abstract of Reviews of
    Effects (DARE), 101
Decety, J., 97

De Menil, B., 127
deprivation, 25, 27, 32, 48, 52, 56
Derrig-Palumbo, K., 164
development(al), xii, xiv, 4, 30, 36–37,
        53, 66, 70–71, 75, 80–81, 91–92,
        106, 108, 129–130, 134–135,
        137–141, 145–148, 170, 179
    achievement, 36
    change, 134
    ego, 75, 137
    journey, 146
    necessity, 40
    neural, 146
    observation, 94
    perspective, 91
    professional, 61
    psychoanalytic, 159
    technological, 8, 180
Dewey, M., 102
Dickinson, A., 90
Ditton, T., 137, 139
Donath, J., 108, 147
Dorpat, T. L., 96
Dreyfus, H. L., 81

Eagle, M. N., 83–85, 143
Egede, L., 101
ego, xii, 79 see also: development(al)
    autonomy, 53, 135, 137
    body, xii, 79
    -centric, 81
    super-, 75
    -syntonic, 52
Eisold, K., 163, 174
Elhai, J. D., 101
Erlich, S., 9
Essig, T., 6, 19, 23, 33, 42, 46–47, 50,
        57–60, 64, 101, 127, 131, 154,
        171–172, 175

Facebook, 28, 110, 171
FaceTime, 7, 126, 171
Fadiga, L., 83
fantasy, 37–38, 56, 64, 73, 132 see also:
        unconscious(ness)
Ferenczi, S., 70

Fine, B., 77
Fishkin, L., 4, 44, 46, 48, 55–56, 61–63
Fishkin, R., 4, 44, 46, 48, 55–56, 61–63
Fogassi, L., 83
Foglia, L., 80
Fonagy, P., xi, 76, 139, 148
Förster, J., 97
Fortunati, L., 6, 8–9, 177
free association, 5, 30, 70, 74, 96
Freud, S., xi, 22, 41, 50, 70, 74–75, 79,
        86, 111, 113, 174
    Dora, 50
    Little Hans, 59

Gabbard, G. O., 40, 71, 77–78, 80, 82,
        86
Gallagher, S., 65, 81–82
Gallese, V., 65–66, 82–85, 92, 99,
        143–144
Genevie, J., 111–112
Gergely, G., 139
Gergen, K. J., 35, 112
Gergle, D., 107
gestalt, 94, 105, 157
Goldberg, P., 104–105
Goldin-Meadow, S., 94
Grohol, J., 166
Grotstein, J. S., 79, 135, 146–147
Grubaugh, A. L., 101

Hanly, C., 30, 45, 47–48, 56
Hannaford, C., 33
Hanselman, S., 87
Harrison, A. M., 80, 91–92, 98, 127
Healy, M., 89
Heeter, C., 149
Heidegger, M., 46, 93
Hen, L., 100
Hildreth, P., 103
Hill, D., 44, 54
Hilty, D., 101
Hirsch, I., 60
Hirsh, S., 124
Hoffman, J., 13
Holmes, J., 74, 157
Huang, P., 109

Iacoboni, M., 83
International Psychoanalytic
    Association, 45
International Society for Presence
    Research, 139
interpretation, 70, 76–77, 136 *see also*:
    transference
    implicit, 179
    verbal, 179–180
intervention, 48, 65, 76–77, 100–101,
    159
Isaacs, E. A., 102
Iverson, J. M., 94

Jackson, M., xiii
Jacobs, T., 51, 79
Jarrett, C., 85
Johnson, M., 80–81
Jordan, B., 127, 147

Katz, B., 44, 46, 48, 55
Kelly, M., 4
Kevin, R. C., 163
Kimble, C., 103
Kirk, D. S., 44, 103–104
Kliner, J. M., 85
Knoblauch, S., 6, 51, 84
Kojima, S., 96
Kuschel, S., 97

Lakoff, G., 19, 66, 80–81
Langs, R., 73
Lanier, J., xiv, 6
Leffert, M., 48
Leli, U., 44, 46, 48, 55
Lemon, R. N., 85
Liberman, N., 97
Loewald, H. W., 70–71, 75–76
Lombard, M., 137, 139
Lucci, G., 96–97
Lyons-Ruth, K., 80, 91–92, 97–98, 127

Maclaren, K., 24, 148
Maheu, M., 45, 164
Mantovani, F., 31, 81, 93, 128, 137,
    140, 142, 146

Mantovani, G., 114, 137–138
Mark, G., 116
Marks, S., 101
Marziali, C., 112
Masson, J. M., 51
Matsuoka, S., 96
Mayer, M., 33
Mazzatenta, A., 96–97
mediation, 31, 58, 139, 154, 159, 170,
    181
    computer, 12, 38, 124, 160
    Internet-based, 100
    non-, 139
    technological, xv, xviii, 4, 9, 12, 21,
        28–30, 39, 41, 45, 47, 49–50, 57,
        77–78, 112, 114–115, 128, 143,
        156–160, 165, 167, 182
Meissner, W. W., 31, 93, 135, 182
Meltzoff, A. N., 84, 144–146
memory, xii, 74–75, 85–90, 109,
    136–137, 159, 183 *see also*:
    conscious(ness)
    autobiographical, 90
    episodic, 86, 90
    explicit, 86, 90
    implicit, 86, 90, 156–157
    procedural, 86, 92
    processes, 90, 157
    semantic, 86
    social, 177
Merleau-Ponty, M., 81–82, 93
Migone, P., 83–85, 143
Milner, M., 73
Minagawa-Kawai, Y., 96
Minsky, M., 139
Misra, S., 111–112
Mitchell, J. P., 155
Modell, A. H., 73, 181
Moore, B., 77
Moore, M., 84
Morgan, A. C., 80, 91–92, 98, 127
Moser, E. I., 89
Moser, M. B., 89

Nahum, J. P., 80, 91–94, 99, 127, 157
Nakamura, K., 96

Naoi, N., 96
Nesbitt, T., 101
Netflix, 28
neurons, 83, 89–90
    mirror, 57, 82–85, 93, 143
    motor, 143
    premotor, 82
North American Society for
    Psychotherapy Research, 78

object, 23, 35–40, 51, 71, 75–76,
    103–105, 135–137, 141, 159, 164,
    179
    autistic sensation, 32
    external, 32, 76, 138, 141, 145,
        148–149
    inanimate, 148–149
    loved, 23, 75
    non-retaliating, 76
    part, 105
    physical, 54, 102
    primary, 135
    relations, 36, 71, 75–76, 83
    subjective, 36
    survival, 37
    transitional, 40
    -usage, 36
    viewable, 103
O'Conaill, B., 102
Ogden, T. H., xi, 22, 24, 75, 105
Olds, D., 80
Olson, G. M., 103, 105, 107, 113–117,
    126–127, 147
ooVoo, 7, 126
Osnos, E., 9, 55

Pacella, B., 63
Pally, R., 66, 80
Papousek, M., 96
Parsons, M., 149, 178–181
Prensky, M., 44

Richards, A. K., 47–48
Richardson, L., 101
risk, 38–39, 54, 58, 154, 163, 169, 173,
    179

Riva, G., 31–32, 66, 81, 93, 114, 128,
    136–138, 140–148
Rizzolatti, G., 83
Rocco, E., 106–107, 156
Rodriguez de la Sierra, L., 48
Rosen, C., 55
Roy, J., 82
Ruhleder, K., 127, 147
Rustin, J., 6, 51, 84
Rutter, D., 102
Rycroft, C., 76

Sachs, D. M., 48
Salwiczek, L. H., 90
Sand, S., 50
Sander, L. W., 80, 91–92, 98, 127
Saporta, J. A., 44
Saul, L. J., 43, 48
Scharff, J. S., 30, 44–48, 56–57, 115,
    164, 170
Schore, A. N., 66, 80, 95–99, 156
self, 24, 27–28, 32, 37, 40, 53, 71, 97,
    128, 135–148, 182 *see also*:
    conscious(ness)
    -analysis, 37, 40
    autobiographical, 136, 141–142
    -awareness, 59, 97
    basic, 145, 148
    core, xii, 136–137, 141–142
    damaged, 20
    -description, 116
    emergent, 135, 137, 146–148
    -experience, 144
    explicit, 95
    -exploration, 98, 129
    -exposure, 78
    extended, 136, 142
    false, 17
    finding of, 35
    -help, 100
    -hood, 32, 35, 134, 137, 146–148
    implicit, 95, 98
    infant, 17
    intentional, 145–146, 179
    layer of, 136
    narrative, 137

non-, 135, 141, 146
-perpetuating, 174
proto-, 136–137, 141
public, 125
real-life, 123
recognition of, 148
-regulating, 137
representations of, 129
-revealing, 14
sense of, 13, 31, 65–66, 85, 94, 96,
    98, 105, 129, 134, 136, 139, 146,
    148, 176
separate, 34, 134, 146
-soothing, 32
subjective, 137
true, 42
whole, 53
Sellen, A. J., 44, 102–104, 124, 147
Shapira, N., 100
Shapiro, S., 51
Shaw, G. B., 59
Sheets-Johnstone, M., 31, 80, 93
Shellenbarger, S., 123
Shockley, T., 40
Silver, C. B., 163
simulation, 6, 32, 42, 57, 60, 63–64, 108,
    121, 123–125, 131, 154–155, 159,
    166, 172–174, 176, 178, 180–181
    avoidance, 59, 169
    awareness of, 38
    computer, 173
    embodied, 82–85
    entrapment, 59–61, 64
Skalski, P. D., 114
Skype, xi–xii, 4–7, 13, 16–19, 22–23,
    25–29, 31–33, 38–40, 43–47, 54,
    60–61, 87, 104, 107–108, 121, 123,
    126, 153, 160, 164–165 see also:
    treatments
    analysis, 4
    connections, 34
    meeting, 16
    patient, 15
    session, 17, 32, 34, 45, 60–61, 88,
        132–133
    therapy, 13, 41

Slade, A., 128–129
Sletvold, J., 6
Small, G., 109
Smolen, A. G., 61
Snyder, E., 4, 44, 46, 48, 55–56, 61
Sorter, D., 6, 51, 84
Spezio, M. L., 109
Stephenson, G., 102
Stern, D. N., 80, 84, 91–92, 98, 127,
    135, 137, 145–146
Stewart, H., 77
Stone, L., 109–110
Strachey, J., 75
Suler, J., 40, 47, 53–54
Summersett, B., 127
symbol(-ism), 40, 49–50, 52–53, 82, 84,
    91–92, 111, 138, 180

Tabin, J., 4
Tang, J. C., 102
Target, M., 76, 139
TeleMental Health Institute, 45, 164
Todorov, A., 106
Tommasi, L., 96–97
transference, xi, xv, 5, 16, 20, 30, 41,
    47–48, 55–56, 71, 85–86, 92,
    96–97, 130, 153
    counter-, xi, xv, 19–20, 27, 41,
        47–48, 56, 60, 71, 85, 96–97,
        124, 130, 157, 175
    development of, xii
    interpretation, 70, 77, 179
    negative, 62
    positive, 62
transferential
    encounter, 50
    material, 77
    relationship, 61
treatments, xiv, 19, 55, 133, 175
    co-present, 8, 128
    didactic, 101
    in-person, xvi, 175
    mediated, xv, xviii, 5, 8, 59, 64, 149,
        161
    personal, 160
    psychopharmacological, 162

remote, xiv, 5
screen, 159, 172
short-term, 162
Skype, 60
technological, 8, 64, 161–162
Tronick, E. Z., 80, 91–92, 98, 127
Trope, Y., 106
Turkle, S., xiii, 6, 34–35, 42, 107, 112,
    154–156, 171–175, 180–181

UCLA Brain Mapping Center, 83
unconscious(ness), 6, 19, 22, 37, 60,
    70, 74–75, 77, 82, 86, 90, 97–98,
    107, 113, 148, 154–157, 181
    see also: affect(ive),
    communication, conscious(ness)
    anticipation, 21
    content, 70
    dialogue, 85, 99
    engagement, 23
    expectation, 111
    fantasy, 39
    human, 95
    induction, 85
    interplay, 22, 75
    material, 56, 70
    meanings, 71
    mechanisms, 95
    mental activity, 74
    mind, 99
    process, 52, 95–96, 157
    relational, 96
    repressed, 92
    separation, 144
    tendency, 60
Urness, D., 101

von Wahlde, L., 40
Vorgan, G., 109

Wallerstein, R. S., 70
Waterworth, E. L., 53, 66, 114,
    137–138, 140
Waterworth, J. A., 53, 66, 114,
    136–138, 140–143, 147
Weinblatt, M., 13, 16, 21, 111

Weitz, P., 164, 170, 174
Weizenbaum, J., 155–156
Westen, D., 71, 77–78, 80, 82, 86
Whittaker, S., 102–103, 107, 147
Wiederhold, B. K., 31, 81, 93, 128,
    137, 140, 142, 146
Wikipedia, 133
Wilbur, S., 102
William Alanson White Institute, 28
Wilson, R. A., 80
Winnicott, D. W., xi, 13, 16–17, 20–21,
    30, 34–37, 39–40, 71–74, 76, 79,
    84–85, 105, 124, 129–130,
    134–135, 146, 148, 174, 178–179
Woodall, G., 76
world
    being-in-the-, 93, 128
    external, 20, 24, 31–32, 40, 62, 95,
        105, 138, 140–147, 173–174
    floating, 35
    internal, 19, 24, 30, 40–41, 77, 95,
        135–136, 140, 146, 174
    mediated, 108
    new, 3
    of signification, 35
    perceptual, 136
    personal, 18
    physical, 89, 138, 140
    present-day, 9
    psychical, 19
    real, 108
    sharable, 53
    technologically evolving, 48
    virtual, 105
Wright, P., 103
Wright, Z., 107

Xerox Palo Alto Research Center, 127

Yamin Habib, L. E., 48
Yellowlees, P., 101
YouTube, 28, 133
Yuan, M., 111–112

Zalusky, S., 45, 48
Zeine, F., 164